Theoretical Foundations of Learning Environments

Theoretical Foundations
of Learning Environments

Edited by

David H. Jonassen
Susan M. Land
Pennsylvania State University

LAWRENCE ERLBAUM ASSOCIATES, PUBLISHERS

2000   Mahwah, New Jersey   London

Lawrence Erlbaum Associates, Inc., Publishers
10 Industrial Avenue
Mahwah, New Jersey 07430

Library of Congress Cataloging-in-Publication Data

Theoretical foundations of learning environments / edited by David H. Jonassen,
Susan M. Land.
    p. cm.
    Includes bibliographical references and index.
    ISBN 0-8058-3215-7 (cloth: alk. paper) – ISBN 0-8058-3216-5 (pkk.: alk.
paper) 1. Learning, Psychology of. 2. Cognition. 3. Learning. I. Jonassen,
David H., 1947- II. Land, Susan M.

    LB1060.T47 2000
    370.15'23–dc21

                   99-058073

Books published by Lawrence Erlbaum Associates are printed
on acid-free paper, and their bindings are chosen
for strength and durability.

Printed in the United States of America

10 9 8 7 6 5 4 3 2 1

Contents

Preface

This book is about the learning theories that provide the foundation for the design and development of open-ended learning environments (defined in Chap. 1). During the 1990s, we have witnessed a convergence of learning theories never before encountered. These contemporary learning theories are based on substantively different ontologies and epistemologies than were traditional objectivist foundations for instructional design. This book is intended to provide an introduction to the theoretical foundations for these new learning environments for instructional designers, curriculum specialists, mathematics and science educators, learning psychologists, and anyone else interested in the theoretical state of the art.

Instructional design, as an activity system (see Chap. 4, this volume), emerged during World War II as a mechanistic process for producing reliable training. Rooted in behavioral psychology and communications theory, instructional designers focused on developing instruction that emphasized the conveyance of ideas supported by operant practice and reinforcement. These approaches assumed that learning is a process of knowledge transmission and reception that result in changes in learner behavior. What are the assumptions of these beliefs?

Traditional instruction is regularly referred to as transmissive instruction, where knowledge is transmitted from teachers (or technologies) to learners. Transmissive instruction is based on a communications model of instruction (Figure i) that continues to dominated practice in many settings. Educators believe that improving learning is a matter of more effectively communicating ideas to learners by improving the clarity of the message. The assumption of most educational enterprises has always been that if teachers communicate (transmit) to students what they know, then students will know it like the transmitter. Teaching is a process of conveying ideas to students. Good teaching means more effective communication. The assumption has been that because teachers have studied ideas longer, they understand them better and are therefore better able to communicate (transmit) them. Epistemologically, it assumes knowledge is an object that can be conveyed and owned by individuals, which assumes that students can come to know the world as the teacher does. That assumption further assumes that students want to know the world as the teacher does. But do they, and if so, why?

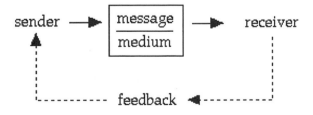

Figure i. Communications model.

In modern societies, being a student is a culturally accepted responsibility of the maturing process. It is a right and responsibility of passage into adulthood — a way of inculcating socially accepted beliefs. Merrill, Drake, Lacy, Pratt, and the ID2 Research Group (1996) claimed that "Students are persons who submit themselves to the acquisition of specific knowledge and skill from instruction; learners are persons who construct their own meaning from their experiences. All of us are learners, but only those who submit themselves to deliberate instructional situations are students." The transmissive model of education relies on the submission model of learning as well as the transmissive model of instruction. Although most students in most educational institutions have no desire, need, or personally mediated intention to learn what teachers transmit to them, they are required to submit themselves to "acquiring" what teachers tell them, because presumably, the teachers know better.

In instructional design processes, behavioral psychologists have focused their efforts on amplifying the communication (submission - transmission) process by adding practice and feedback to the basic communication processes. Behaviorists assumed that if learning were a change in behavior, that behavior had to be shaped through reinforced practice. And so, various practice strategies (drill, mnemonics, mathemagenics, algorithimization, and many others) have been appended to the communication process (Figure ii) to strengthen the students' abilities to simulate the knowledge of their teachers. Throughout the 1970s and 1980s, cognitive psychology provided internal, mentalistic explanations for these learning processes, but unfortunately those explanations were unable to systemically change the practices of education. Having more complex representations of the processes of learning did not provide enough impetus to change the processes of education. Perhaps the cognitive revolution was not revolutionary enough.

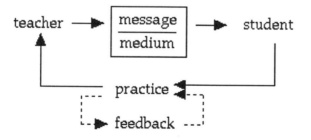

Figure ii. Behaviorally supported communication.

The past decade, we believe, has witnessed the most substantive and revolutionary changes in learning theory in history. What makes this revolution more substantive are the shifts in the underlying ontology, epistemology, and phenomenology of learning? Contemporary situated, sociocultural, and constructivist conceptions of learning are built on different ontological and epistemological foundations than communications theory, behaviorism, and cognitivism. We have entered a new age in learning theory. Never in the relatively short history of learning theories (one hundred plus years) have there been so many theoretical foundations that share so many assumptions and common foundations. Never have alternative theories of knowledge and learning been so consonant in their beliefs and methods they espouse.

In this book, we have aggregated descriptions of theories of learning and meaning making, including socially shared cognition, situated learning, everyday cognition and everyday reasoning, activity theory, ecological psychology, distributed cognitions, and case-based reasoning. These conceptions of learning share many beliefs and assumptions. They are based on a similar ontology, epistemology, and phenomenology. Their theoreticians believe that learning is neither a transmissive or a submissive process. Rather learning is willful, intentional, active, conscious, constructive practice that includes reciprocal intention—action—reflection activities (Figure iii). Humans are distinct from primates in their abilitites to articulate an intention and then to willfully plan to act on it. Actions are integrations of perceptions and conscious thinking. Activity theory (Chap. 4, this volume) claims that conscious learning and activity (performance) are completely interactive and interdependent (we cannot act without thinking or think without acting). Ecological psychology (Chap 6, this volume) claims that learning results from the reciprocal perception of affordances from the environment and actions on the environment. Learning is frequently conceived as an active process. These two theories provide a clear explanation of what active means. However, activity is generally regarded as necessary but not sufficient for learning. Reflection on these percepetual and conscious actions is necessary for constructing meaning. Therefore, learning, from the perspectives presented in this book, is conscious activity guided by intentions and reflections.

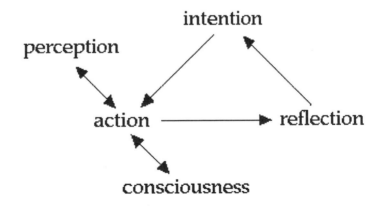

Figure iii. Learning as intention—action—reflection.

There are at least three fundamental shifts in thinking that are entailed by the theories described in this book. First, learning is a process of meaning making, not of knowledge transmission. Humans interact with the other humans and with artifacts in the world and naturally and continuously attempt to make sense of those interactions. Meaning making (resolving the dissonance between what we know for sure and what we perceive or what we believe that others know) results from a puzzlement, perturbation, expectation violations, curiosity, or cognitive dissonance. Making meaning from phenomena and experiences involves dissonance between what we know and what we want or need to know. This dissonance ensures some ownership of the knowledge by the learner. Knowledge that is personally or socially constructed is necessarily owned by and attributed to the meaning makers. So when encountering a puzzlement or problem, learners must articulate an intention to make sense of some phenomenon and then interact with it, consciously reflecting on the meaning of those interactions. The underlying epistemological revolution here is the rejection of dualistic beliefs that mind and behavior are separate phenomena. Rather mind and behavior and perception and action are wholly integrated. That is, we cannot separate our knowledge of a domain from our interactions in that domain. Nor can we consider the knowledge that is constructed from the activity outside the context in which we constructed.

Second, contemporary learning theorists focus increasingly on the social nature of the meaning making process. Behavioral and cognitive theories focused on the individual as the medium of learning. Information is processed, stored, retrieved, and applied by individuals who are able to compare their representation with others but not to share them. However, just as the physical world is shared by all of us, so is some of the meaning that we make from it. Humans are social creatures who rely on feedback from fellow humans to determine their own existence and the veridicality of their personal beliefs. Social constructivists (Chapters 7 and 8) have believed for many years that meaning making is a process of social negotiation among participants in any activity. Learning, from this perspective is dialogue, a process of internal as well as social negotiation. Learning is inherently a social-dialogical process.

The third fundamental shift in assumptions relates to the locus of meaning making. Many psychologists cling to the belief that knowledge resides only in the head. Humans are the only information processors that can make meaning from experience or anything else. However, as we engage in communities of practice, our knowledge and beliefs about the world are influenced by that community and their beliefs and values. Through legitimate peripheral participation (Lave & Wenger, 1991), we absorb part of the culture that is an integral part of the community, just as the culture is affected by each of its members. As we engage in communities of discourse and practice, our knowledge and beliefs are influenced by those communities. So is our identity formation, which is also a major outcome of learning. Not only does knowledge exist in individual and socially negotiating minds, but it also exists in the discourse among individuals, the social relationships that bind them, the physical artifacts that they use and produce, and the theories, models, and methods they use to produce them. Knowledge and cognitive activity is distributed among the culture and history of their existence and is mediated by the tools they use (see Chap. 5, this volume).

So, when we investigate learning phenomena, we are obligated to consider not only the performances of the learners, but also the sociocultural and sociohistorical setting in which the performance occurs and tools and mediation systems that learners use to make meaning (Figure iv).

COMMUNITY

Figure iv. Learning in context.

STUDENT-CENTERED LEARNING ENVIRONMENTS

These new theories of learning and thinking have influenced education in many ways. This book is focused on the effects of these theories on the design of student-centered learning environments. Throughout the 1990s, research has focused increasingly on problem-based, project-based, inquiry-oriented pedagogies in the forms of open-ended learning environments, cognitive apprenticeships, constructivist learning environments, microworlds, goal-based scenarios, anchored instruction, social-mediated communication, and so on. Land and Hannafin (Chapter 1) describe these generically as student-centered learning environments (SCLEs).

SCLEs are compared with those of direct instruction that preceded them in Table i. SCLEs are designed based on the beliefs of the theories described in this book. Rather than focusing on how information can more effectively be conveyed (transmitted) by teachers and understood by learners, these environments focus on the affordances they provide learners for effecting their environment and making meaning.

To us, researchers are currently enjoying a renaissance in the evolution of learning theory. It is remarkable to us how consonant the theories described in this book are. What they each believe and say about learning is similar, although in some cases using slightly different lexicons. The theoretical foundations described in this book are coherent, theoretically consistent, and mutually supportive. At no time in the history of learning psychology has there been so much fundamental agreement about the epistemology, ontology, and phenomenology of learning. To support our claim, we invite you to perform any kind of linguistic analysis on the American Educational Research Association (or similar) conference programs in 1989, and compare the results with a similar analysis of the 1999 program, and you will be struck by the depth and breadth of change in the fields of learning theories and educational research.

TABLE i. Traditional Instruction versus SCLEs

Instruction	Student-Centered Learning Environments
transmission, acquisition	interpretation, construction
mastery, performance	meaning making
external reality	internal reality
dualism, absolutism	cultural relativism, perspectival
abstract, symbolic	contextualized, authentic, experiential
individually interpreted	socially negotiated, co-constructed
mind-centered	community-based, culturally mediated
directed	intentional
reductionistic	complex, self-organizing
individual	collaborative
idealist, rational	pragmatist
encoding, retention, retrieval	articulation and reflection
internal, mental	social
receptive, reproductive	constructive
symbolic reasoning	situated learning
psychology	anthropology, sociology, ethnography
laboratory	in situ
theoretical	everyday
central processing architecture	distributed architecture
objective, modelable	experiential, interpretive
symbol processor	symbol builder
disembodied	experiential
conceptual, memorial	perceptual
atomistic, decomposable	gestalt
independent	emergent
possessed	distributed
objective, stable, fixed	subjective, contextualized, fluid
well-structured	ill-structured
decontextualized	embedded in experience
compliant	self-regulated

The purpose of this short book is to provide students, faculty, and designers with an introduction to these theories and how they have contributed to the conception of learning environments. Readers can compare and contrast these theoretical foundations, synthesizing from their own perspective what characteristics are most essential in different learning environments. The book also provides theoretical justifications for the many learning environments that are being developed and researched.

There is an important perspective missing in this book—that provided by John Dewey. Numerous times in the past few years, we have heard someone ask, "Isn't all of this innovation simply a replication of Dewey's ideas?" To some degree, that is true. We had contracted a chapter on Deweyian Pragmatism to complete the suite of learning theories that are used to describe and justify SCLEs; unfortunately, the intended author was unable to deliver for this volume as planned. So a learning activity that you may wish to engage your students in would be to look for instances of the ideas described in this book in the original works of Dewey in order to determine for yourselves to what degree contemporary learning theory is a replication of Dewey's ideas.

David Jonassen, Susan Land

References

Lave, J., & Wenger, E. (1991). *Situated learning: Legitimate peripheral participation*. Cambridge: Cambridge University Press.

Merrill, M.D., Drake, L., Lacy, M. J., Pratt, J., & the ID2 Research Group. (1996). Reclaiming instructional design. *Educational Technology, 36*(5), 5-7.

Authors

Sasha A. Barab is an assistant professor of instructional systems technology and cognitive science at Indiana University, Bloomington. He earned his doctorate in 1997 at the University of Connecticut, Storrs. His research has focused on establishing rich learning environments, frequently with the aid of technology, that are both engaging and complex, potentially assisting students in learning the whats in a manner that provides insights into the whys. Much of this work was built on current literature regarding situated cognition and focused on the use of multimedia as one practical means of connecting classroom knowledge to its functional and social context. In addition to this design focus, his research focused on developing research methods for capturing cognition in situ within the context of intentional learning environments. In capturing cognition in situ, he found that it became necessary to develop an account of the broader context through which knowing and doing has meaning. It is this latter realization that led Dr. Barab to his current research focus on communities of practice.

Philip Bell is an assistant professor of cognition and technology in the College of Education at the University of Washington. His research focuses on the design and use of innovative learning technologies and curricula in science classrooms. He has also organized and studied curriculum development partnerships involving classroom teachers, natural scientists, educational researchers, and technologists. Professor Bell received his doctorate in cognition and development from the University of California, Berkeley in 1998. He has a technical background in electrical engineering and computer science.

Katherine Brown is a visiting scholar at the Laboratory of Comparative Human Cognition at the University of California at San Diego (UCSD) and a lecturer in the Department of Communication at UCSD. Brown is coauthor with Cole of several papers and foundation reports about the Fifth Dimension project, including "Conceptual Change in a Community of Practice" (G. Wells, Ed.) and "A Utopian Methodology for Critical Communication and Psychology: Toward a Positive Critical Theory" (Martin Packer & M. Tappan, Eds.), both forthcoming in 1999. Her e-mail address is kbrown@weber.ucsd.edu.

David W. Carraher is a senior scientist at TERC in Cambridge, Massachusetts and co-principal investigator of the project Bridging Research and Practice, which has been investigating videopublishing as a means of promoting grounded discussions among researchers and teachers in mathematics education. He loves to focus on how people attempt to reconcile deeply ingrained ways of thinking with new mathematical ideas.

Michael Cole, professor of communication and psychology and director of the laboratory of comparative human cognition at the University of California at San Diego is a fellow of the American Association of Arts and Sciences and the National Academy of Education. Cole is coauthor, with S.R. Cole, of the *Development of Children* (3rd.ed) and with J. Gay, J.A. Glick and D.W. Sharp of the *Cultural Context of Learning and Thinking* and editor of the journals *Mind, Culture and*

Activity and the *Journal of Russian and East European Psychology*. His e-mail address is mcole@weber.ucsd.edu.

Thomas M. Duffy, professor of education and cognitive science, is the Barbara B. Jacobs chair of Education and Technology and the director of the Center for Research on Learning and Technology in the School of Education, Indiana University. He came to Indiana from Carnegie Mellon where he was director of the Communications Design Center and an associate professor of english and psychology. Duffy's work during the 1990s has focused on the use of technology to support the design of inquiry based learning environments as well as on the implications of constructivism and situated cognition for the design of instruction. He has published more than 100 articles as well as coauthoring, *Online Help: Design and Evaluation* and co-*editing Constructivism and the Technology of Instruction: A Conversation* and *Designing Environments for Constructivist Learning*. Duffy and his colleagues have also developed the Ready Program (adult literacy instruction), Strategic Teaching Frameworks (multimedia, teacher professional development), and ACT, an asynchronous collaboration tool for small group problem solving. He received his doctorate in cognitive psychology from the University of Illinois.

Steve Garrett is a doctoral student in psychology at the University of Connecticut. His area of concentration is cognition and instruction with a focus on ecological psychology and intentional dynamics. His research background is in perception and coordination. In particular, he is interested in interactive learning environments, music perception and production, and skill acquisition.

Mark Guzdial is an associate professor in the College of Computing at Georgia Institute of Technology. His research is in technological support for project-based learning. He builds a variety of kinds of tools (from case libraries to computer-supported collaborative learning environments) and evaluates them in real classrooms. He is one of the inventors of the learner-centered design approach to software design for students. He is on the editorial board *of Journal of the Learning Sciences, Interactive Learning Environments, Journal of Interactive Learning Research*, and *IEEE Multimedia*. His web page can be accessed at http://www.cc.gatech.edu/~mark.guzdial and e-mail address at guzdial@cc.gatech.edu.

Michael J. Hannafin earned his doctorate in educational technology from Arizona State University in 1981. He is the Wheatley-Georgia Research Alliance Eminent Scholar chair in technology-enhanced learning, professor of instructional technology, and director of the Learning and Performance Support Laboratory at the University of Georgia. Previously, he was a member of the instructional systems faculty at Florida State University, and served as a visiting professor at the United States Air Force Academy and in faculty positions at Pennsylvania State University (1984-89) and University of Colorado. His research focuses on developing and testing frameworks for the design of technology-enhanced, student-centered learning environments. His e-mail address is hannafin@coe.uga.edu and his web page is at http://lpsl.coe.uga.edu.

David H. Jonassen is professor of instructional systems at Penn State University. He previously taught at the University of Colorado, the University of Twente, the University of North Carolina at Greensboro, Syracuse University, and Temple University and has consulted with businesses, universities, and other institutions around the world. He is working on his twentieth book and has written numerous articles, papers, and technical reports. His current research focuses on designing constructivist learning environments, cognitive tools for learning, knowledge representation formalisms, problem solving, computer-supported collaborative argumentation, and individual differences and learning. His web page is located at http://www.ed.psu.edu/~jonassen/ and his email address is jonassen@psu.edu.

Janet L. Kolodner is professor of computing and cognitive science in Georgia Institute of Technology's College of Computing. Her research addresses issues in learning, memory, and problem solving, both in computers and in people. She pioneered the computer reasoning methods called case-based reasoning, a way of solving problems based on analogies to past experiences, and her lab has emphasized case-based reasoning for situations of real-world complexity. Her book, *Case-Based Reasoning*, synthesizes work across the field of case-based reasoning from its inception to 1993. Kolodner currently focuses most of her research on learning by design (LBD), an approach to curriculum development and pedagogy based on case-based reasoning's implied cognitive model and several approaches to pedagogy coming from the cognitive science community. Her focus, in LBD, is on design and development of curriculum for middle school science and software in support of project-based, problem-based, and collaborative learning. Kolodner was founding director of Georgia Tech's EduTech Institute, whose mission is to use what is known about cognition to inform the design of educational technology and learning environments. She served as coordinator of Georgia Tech's cognitive science program for many years. Professor Kolodner is founding editor in chief of *The Journal of the Learning Sciences*, an interdisciplinary journal that focuses on learning and education.

Susan M. Land is an assistant professor of instructional systems at Penn State University. She earned her doctorate in instructional systems from Florida State University in 1995. Previously, she worked as a postdoctoral fellow at the University of Georgia's Learning and Performance Support Laboratory and held a faculty position at the University of Oklahoma, Department of Educational Psychology. Her research emphasizes how learners build and evolve understanding while learning with open-ended, technology-rich environments. Her e-mail address is sland@psu.edu and her web page is at http://www.personal.psu.edu/sml11.

Karen Madsen Myers is director, Clinical Laboratory Science Division, HealthOne Health Sciences Education. She is a doctoral student at the University of Colorado at Denver, with a focus on adult learning and development, professional communities of practice, and systems and system change. Her e-mail address is karen_myers@ceo.cudenver.edu.

Analucia D. Schliemann is professor of education at Tufts University. She did her studies in education in Brazil and in psychology in France and received her doctorate in developmental psychology from the University of London. In 1986, she was a Fulbright Visiting Scholar at the Learning Research and Development Center at the University of Pittsburgh. Before moving to the United States, she worked for more than 20 years at the Federal University of Pernambuco in Recife, Brazil, where she developed research on mathematical reasoning among Brazilian street sellers, carpenters, lottery bookies, and cooks. Part of these studies are published in the book *Street Mathematics and School Mathematics* written with Terezinha Nunes and David Carraher and published in 1993 by Cambridge University Press. Her current research interests are children's early algebraic reasoning and the role of notations and other cultural tools in the development logicomathematical reasoning.

Brent G. Wilson is professor of information and learning technologies at the University of Colorado at Denver. Research interests include the adoption and use of learning technologies and instructional design as a human activity. His e-mail address is brent.wilson@cudenver.edu and his web page can be accessed at http://www.cudenver.edu/~bwilson.

William Winn is a professor in curriculum and instruction at University of Washington. He earned his doctorate from Indiana University in 1972. His research and teaching specializes in instructional theory, design of computer-based instruction, instructional effects of illustrations, theories of visual perception applied to instructional materials design, computer interfaces, virtual environments in education and training, and the roles and effectiveness of virtual environments in education and training.

Michael F. Young has been at the University of Connecticut since Fall 1990 and prior to that was associated with Vanderbilt's Learning Technology Center (LTC) for 3 years. He received his degree in 1989 in the areas of cognitive and educational psychology, perception and spatial cognition. His background includes 5 years as a high school mathematics and computer teacher with K-12 responsibility for the use of computers at the University School of Nashville. His research concerns situated cognition as a theory for understanding how people think and learn and focuses primarily on how educational technology can enhance thinking and learning. Research on assessment using log files (dribble files) from multimedia hypertext is currently funded by Spencer Foundation. Dr. Young's work and research combine an emphasis of theory from cognitive science and educational psychology with development activities with the latest instructional technologies. He contributed to Uconn's successful Internet II proposal and in cooperation with his graduate students has ongoing research concerning Jasper videodiscs, motivation from a situated cognition perspective, mindful engagement in the Jason Project, and preconception of technology by preservice teachers.

1

Student-Centered Learning Environments

Susan M. Land
Pennsylvania State University

Michael J. Hannafin
University of Georgia

CONCEPTIONS AND MISCONCEPTIONS OF STUDENT-CENTERED LEARNING ENVIRONMENTS

Technological advances have stimulated researchers and educators to expand their conceptions of learning as well as the design of learning environments. This renaissance has Balkanized factions of the educational and research communities in their separate pursuits of an epistemological "silver bullet," fueling a lively debate as to the wisdom and appropriateness of competing approaches. For example, traditional instructional approaches have been criticized widely for failing to support higher order thinking and problem solving while cultivating compliant (McCaslin & Good, 1992) and superficial understanding (Spiro, Feltovich, Jacobson, & Coulson, 1991). Constructivists have likewise been criticized for allegedly propagating approaches that are unproven, atheoretical, and impractical (Dick, 1991; Merrill, 1991).

We do not intend to fuel what is often a rancorous ongoing debate, but to advance a more principled approach to linking teaching, learning, and technology. In this chapter, we introduce the tenets of grounded learning environments that align the foundations, assumptions, and methods associated with constructivist epistemology and identify several principles underlying their design. We emphasize similarities as well as differences among learning environments of diverse underlying foundations and assumptions, focusing specifically on those that are consistent with constructivist epistemology.

Epistemology, Technology, and the Shifting Landscape of Student-Centered Learning

Epistemological shifts in the 1990s have engendered a variety of innovative and provocative learning environments. For example, renewed interest in student-centered teaching and learning has yielded a myriad of approaches purported to provide flexible and powerful alternatives to the design of instruction (Jonassen, 1991). Such environments, tacitly or explicitly, are purported to reflect constructivist epistemology (Hannafin & Land, 1997; Jonassen, 1999). They are designed to support individual efforts to negotiate meaning while engaging in authentic activities. Student-centered, learner-centered environments provide interactive, complimentary activities that enable individuals to address unique learning interests and needs, study multiple levels of complexity, and deepen understanding" (Hannafin & Land, 1997, p. 168). Technology is frequently employed as a tool to support experimentation, manipulation, and idea generation (Jonassen, 2000).

A myriad of student-centered epistemologies has emerged in recent years, including problem-based learning (Hmelo, 1999; Koschmann, Kelson, Feltovich, & Barrows, 1996; Savery & Duffy, 1996), anchored instruction (Cognition & Technology Group at Vanderbilt, 1992), cognitive apprenticeships (Collins, Brown, & Newman, 1989), reciprocal teaching (Palincsar & Brown, 1984), goal-based scenarios (Schank, 1992), project-based learning (Blumenfeld et al., 1991), constructivist learning environments (Jonassen, 1999), and open learning environments (Hannafin, Land, & Oliver, 1999). Though somewhat varied in their scope, technology, and methods, student-centered approaches embody similar assumptions about the nature of understanding and the methods best suited to facilitate learning.

To illustrate, many open learning environments, such as simulations and microworlds, rely heavily on technology to support student experimentation. Problems and contexts are often externally generated, and learners manipulate variables to solve problems such as determining the conditions under which insulation materials retain or lose heat (Lewis, Stern, & Linn, 1993). Other approaches, such as anchored instruction and problem-based learning, define broad organizing contexts wherein knowledge and skills are applied across content areas, and diverse problems are pursued. Others, such as reciprocal teaching and cognitive apprenticeships, capitalize on social interactions to scaffold and negotiate problem-solving and self-regulatory procedures. Hence, although diverse approaches may differ in function, they nonetheless share common assumptions and values about the importance of student-centered learning.

With the increase in alternatives, however, several issues have surfaced. Fundamental questions have arisen related to the kinds of learning such environments support, how best to design them, and whether or not designs can be generalized across varied domains and contexts (Dick, 1991; Merrill, 1991). Questions have surfaced surrounding the feasibility of implementing emerging learning environments within traditional classroom environments given their conventional assessment priorities (Salomon, 1997). Numerous "how to" guidelines have been offered, but they typically lack adequate theoretical or empirical framing (Hannafin & Land, 1997). Unlike for traditional instruction, no unifying theory seems to guide the design of student-centered learning environments (Hill & Land, 1998). Given the unique student-centered learning goals and requirements, it may be impossible to derive an inclusive design model. Rather, researchers need to identify frameworks for analyzing, designing, and implementing learning environments that embody and align particular foundations, assumptions, and practices.

A GROUNDED DESIGN PRIMER

Grounded design is "the systematic implementation of processes and procedures that are rooted in established theory and research in human learning" (Hannafin, Hannafin, Land, & Oliver, 1997, p.102). Grounded approaches emphasize the deliberate alignment of core foundations and assumptions, and the linking of methods and approaches in ways that are consistent with their corresponding epistemological perspectives. It does not advocate or presume the inherent superiority of a specific epistemology or methodology for design. Rather, grounded design provides a framework for reconciling diverse design practices with the basic tenets of the associated belief systems.

To illustrate, consider the belief systems and approaches associated with instruction and instructional design. Dick (1991) defined *instruction* as "...an educational intervention that is driven by specific outcome objectives... and assessments that determine if the desired changes in behavior [learning] have occurred" (p. 44). Associated instructional design processes emphasize the careful a priori engineering of the teaching-learning process: articulation of explicit learning objectives paired with systematic and empirically verifiable approaches to analyzing, designing, developing, implementing, and evaluating instruction. Instruction in such cases is grounded in objectivist epistemology; the foundations, assumptions, and methods are presumably aligned accordingly.

Foundations and Assumptions

Learning environments, directed as well as constructivist, are rooted in five core foundations: psychological, pedagogical, technological, cultural, and pragmatic (Hannafin et al., 1997; Hannafin & Land, 1997). Psychological foundations emphasize theory and research related to how individuals think and learn. For instance, behavioral psychology and cognitive psychology form the cornerstone psychological foundations of traditional direct instruction. Behaviorists view S->R->S->R associationism as their prime precept; learning is a relatively permanent change in behavior associated with the contiguous linking of stimuli, responses, and reinforcers (Skinner, 1957). For cognitive psychologists, constructs such as schema, depth of processing, mental models, and cognitive load are central to learning (see, for example, Chap. 3, this volume), Gagné & Glaser, 1987). Individuals have presumably limited processing capacity, respond to external stimuli based on the selective perception, transfer and decode selected stimuli to working memory, and so forth (Hannafin & Rieber, 1989).

Pedagogical foundations form the affordances and activities of the environment and should be inextricably linked to corresponding psychological foundations. For instance, grounded pedagogical strategies consistent with bevaviorists' assumptions should reflect objective-based, hierarchically organized, and tightly engineered response-feedback instructional activities. Cognitively based pedagogical foundations may reflect external strategies (e.g., heighten alertness to forthcoming information, amplify key terms and concepts, and so forth) associated with Gagne's (1985) internal instructional events.

Technological foundations influence how media can support, constrain, or enhance the learning environment. A variety of media can be exploited to support learning in a variety of ways, but grounded deployment of technology is linked to the particular epistemological frame in particular ways. Technology can control the pacing and chunking of information where cognitive load limitations are assumed; in contrast, it can support user-directed access to World-Wide Web (WWW) resources and support the manipulation of ideas when the importance of individual negotiation is assumed. Technology foundations determine what is technologically possible, but grounded practice requires determination of how capabilities should be exploited. In grounded design, the manner in which technology is utilized depends on its appropriateness to the particular epistemological assumptions of a given learning environment.

Cultural foundations reflect the prevailing values of a learning community. For instance, cultural foundations may reflect particular values such as "back to basics," "interdisciplinary learning," or "global society." Some higher education institutions, for instance, value production of student-credit hours; large classes and group lectures might be commonplace. Learning environments that are application-oriented, such as engineering, business, and medical schools, might emphasize case-based, laboratory-intensive, or project-based methods for solving complex, realistic problems. Grounded learning environments both mirror and operationalize their corresponding cultural context (see also Chap. 8, this volume).

Finally, pragmatic foundations emphasize the reconciling of available resources and constraints with the actual design of any given learning environment. Many schools, for instance, perceive the benefits of connecting teachers, students, and administrators to others across the world. Limitations in connectivity, bandwidth, and hardware, however, often limit what *can be* accomplished pedagogically and technologically. Pragmatic foundations represent the reality check of learning environment design and implementation, frequently causing a reassessment of alignment among one or more foundation.

Grounded design, therefore, involves the simultaneous alignment of each foundation in order to optimize coincidence across all foundations; as the intersection across foundations increases, the better grounded the design. A wide array of psychological perspectives can be drawn on, for which a multitude of pedagogical alternatives is available. All perspectives and methods, however, are not interchangeable; in grounded design they are interdependent.

The Principles of Grounded Design. We consider four conditions as basic to grounded design practice (see Hannafin et al., 1997). First, designs must be rooted in a defensible and publicly acknowledged theoretical framework. Learning environments are grounded to the extent that core foundations are identified and aligned; they link corresponding foundations, associated assumptions, and methods. Next, methods must be consistent with the outcomes of research conducted to test, validate, or extend the theories upon which they are based. The sources of grounded methods exist in instances, cases, and research in which strategies have been evaluated; grounded design practice builds on tested and proven approaches. In addition, grounded designs are generalizable, that is, they transcend the individual instances in which isolated success may be evident and can be adapted or adopted by other designers. This does not suggest a literal, algorithmic mapping of methods according to strictly defined conditions but rather the heuristics-based application of design processes appropriate in comparable circumstances. Finally, grounded designs and their frameworks are validated iteratively through successive implementation. Methods are proven effective in ways that support the theoretical framework on which they are based and extend the framework itself as successive implementations clarify the approach. The design processes and methods continuously inform, test, validate, or contradict the theoretical framework and assumptions upon which they were based, and vice-versa.

Clearly, many learning systems are not grounded instructional systems. By default or design, many learning environments simply do not adhere to the definition, foundations, assumptions, and methods of grounded instruction. This is the case both for learning systems that purport to be instruction but fail to reflect the requisite alignment as well as for learning environments that are rooted in fundamentally different perspectives. Compared with instructivist methodologies, for example, constructivist approaches support different learning goals, utilize different methods, and adopt different assumptions about the nature of knowing and understanding. However, as with instruction, not all alleged constructivist learning environments are well grounded. Many are rooted in appropriate foundations, yet the methods seem incompatible with the associated assumptions. Gaps frequently exist between the presumed underlying constructivist epistemology and the associated affordances and activities (Perkins, 1985; Salomon, 1986).

Constructivism and Grounded Design Principles

Although operationalized somewhat differently, constructivist learning environments share key epistemological foundations and assumptions. Constructivists view reality and meaning as personally rather than universally defined. Such environments draw heavily from psychological research and theory related to areas such as situated cognition (Brown, Collins & Duguid, 1989; see also Chap. 3) with attendant assumptions emphasizing the interlacing of content, context and understanding, the individual negotiation of meaning, and the construction of knowledge (Jonassen, 1991; see also Chap. 2, this volume). Pedagogically, constructivists favor rich, authentic learning contexts over isolated, decontextualized knowledge and skill, student-centered, goal-directed inquiry over externally directed instruction, and supporting personal perspectives over canonical perspectives. Technology tools support the individual's identification and manipulation of resources and ideas (Jonassen & Reeves, 1996).

Grounded constructivist learning environments, therefore, support individuals or groups as they attempt to negotiate multiple rather than singular points of view, reconcile competing and conflicting perspectives and beliefs, and construct personally relevant meaning accordingly (Hannafin & Land, 1997). Key overarching assumptions and values are reflected in seemingly diverse environments. For instance, one environment might support collaboration activities to facilitate shared meaning of scientific events; others might rely on individually mediated use of technology tools to generate, test, and refine personal theories. Both environments emphasize learning as a goal-directed activity, yet each provides a somewhat different context to support learner-constructed meaning (e.g., rich technological support, rich social support).

As noted previously, not all learning environments, constructivist or other, meet the criteria of grounded design. Some, however, appear to do so in especially noteworthy ways. In the following section, examples from one or more exemplary constructivist learning environments are used to illustrate grounded design practice.

Linking Key Foundations, Assumptions, and Methods. The *Blueprint for success/ASK Jasper* component of *The adventures of Jasper Woodbury*, represents strong articulation and alignment among underlying foundations and assumptions. Like other applications in the *Jasper* series, *Blueprint* presents open-ended dilemmas with key ideas anchored in rich, video vignettes. Learners are then asked to design a playground that satisfies the requirements and constraints depicted in the vignette (Williams, Bareiss, & Reiser, 1996). Students create designs for the playground that reflect their own personal goals and experiences, yet require the application of precise geometry skills such as measurement, proportion, and creating or reading scale drawings. Rather than requiring the use of secondary sources to solve the problem, required information is embedded into the storyline itself. A technology enhancement, *ASK Jasper*, is used in conjunction with *Blueprint for Success* to scaffold problem-solving processes as learners engage complex problems presented in the *Jasper* vignettes. Finally, multimedia databases of previously-produced designs are available as additional sources of performance support.

The *Blueprint* components are rooted in situated cognition theory (Brown, Collins, & Duguid, 1989; see also Chap. 3, this volume) which emphasizes the importance of situating thinking within complex contexts.

Blueprint anchors key concepts and information authentically within problem vignettes. Learners generate problems to be solved then learn and apply relevant geometry knowledge and skills through progressive problem generation, framing, and solving. Technological features and methods are aligned in ways that augment the pedagogical and psychological links. Scaffolding for solving the problem is supported with the *ASK Jasper* software, which models the design task and assists learners in generating questions, subgoals, and subproblems. A task model is provided that scaffolds key problem-solving processes—understand the problem, design and combine components, and reflect on the success of the design. *ASK Jasper* incorporates annotation structures such as *"why?"* and *"how to?"* to encourage learners to explain their rationales and procedures underlying their designs. Whereas other technology features support the incorporation of text, drawings, and videos, the task model provides a means for students to organize their designs in ways that reinforce and guide the complexity of problem-solving approach.

Model It (Jackson, Stratford, Krajcik, & Soloway, in press) also aligns its underlying foundations, assumptions, and methods. *Model It* is a dynamic modeling tool developed by the Highly Interactive Computing Group (Hi-C) at the University of Michigan. *Model It* allows learners to create qualitative models of everyday scientific phenomena. They define connections between related factors and analyze the model for its validity in representing those relationships. *Model It* supports learners in the process of generating, testing, and revising qualitative models of scientific events. Psychologically, it builds upon considerable research on the influence of tacit, informal models in understanding scientific phenomena (Carey, 1986; Driver & Scanlon, 1988; Twigger et al., 1991). *Model It* supports relationship modeling and causal reasoning processes in ways that are conceptually and procedurally accessible for novice learners. Their causal accounts of scientific phenomena are expressed qualitatively using common sense reasoning that serves as a benchmark for eventual accommodation of more formal, quantitative reasoning.

Technology both enables and extends underlying psychological assumptions and pedagogical approaches. For instance, direct manipulation interfaces enable learners to graphically represent models of systems and the objects that act on them. Learners can take digital photographs or create graphical images to illustrate the system they are investigating. Factors can be connected to one another using portable relationship representations that resemble concept maps. Learners define how various factors affect each other in terms of qualitative units such as greater than, increases, decreases, and so forth. For instance, learners investigating the factors affecting stream contamination can use pull-down menus to describe relationships such as "As fecal coliforms increase, stream quality decreases/increases by about the same/a lot/a little/more and more/less and less" (Jonassen, Peck, & Wilson, 1999, p. 215). Once factors and relationships are defined qualitatively, learners can test working models by running simulations of their designs. Models and hypotheses can then be refined by adjusting the numeric relationships between and among them. Technology enables learners to visualize the consequences of their reasoning and to provide a means for reflection.

CSILE, which stands for Computer Supported Intentional Learning Environment, is a networked learning environment that enables learners to enter information into a common database to be browsed, retrieved, linked, and commented on by others (Scardamalia, Bereiter, McLean, Swallow, & Woodruff, 1989). The primary goal of CSILE is to support learners in intentional and purposeful processing of information. Through networked collaboration with peers and teachers, learners both provide and receive process-related feedback that guides the continual revision and restructuring of knowledge. CSILE builds on psychological foundations rooted in active learning, self-regulation, metacognition, and scaffolding. Learners, especially weaker students, tend to be characterized by passive learning strategies that are remarkably persistent and enduring (McCaslin & Good, 1992). Successful learners, on the other hand, use a variety of cognitive strategies and self-regulation procedures to plan and pursue goals, integrate new knowledge with existing, formulate questions and inferences, and continually review and reorganize their thinking (Bereiter & Scardamalia, 1989; Scardamalia et al., 1989). Rather than assume that such strategic processes will become manifest as a natural consequence of instruction, CSILE scaffolds and facilitates learner sense-making and self-regulatory processes as explicit learning goals (Bereiter & Scardamalia, 1989).

Pedagogically, CSILE provides metacognitive and procedural facilitation to help learners identify learning goals and make thinking (typically covert processes) overt. The facilitation serves as a temporary scaffold for learners to engage in more complex self-management strategies, until they learn to adopt them independently. Scaffolding is provided through both social and technological support mechanisms. Consistent with cognitive apprenticeship theory (Collins et al., 1989) and reciprocal teaching (Brown & Palincsar, 1989), learners and teachers share in the responsibility for providing feedback, modeling their own thinking, and evaluating the thinking of others. Technology features are also aligned in ways that support psychological and pedagogical influences. Networking and database capabilities provide a means for students to conveniently store and retrieve information and to share, access, and revise ongoing ideas (see also Chap. 5, this volume). Through menu structures and icons developed by students, learners select and annotate the type of mental activity in which they plan to engage (e.g., confusion, new learning, questions, hypotheses, etc.). Labeling entries helps learners recognize the underlying management processes of learning, and retrieve, link, comment on and rate one another's entries. Database indexing supports learners in accessing cross- or within-subject searches to identify common themes.

Empirically-verified Methods. The second requirement is that the strategies and methods used are empirically based and validated. Science educators have long valued and successfully used analogs, such as balls and sticks to represent molecules or solar systems, to concretize abstract scientific concepts (e.g., Black, 1962). Similarly, *Model It* utilizes technology to enable virtual construction. It incorporates methods and provides tools through which students can dynamically model and test their thinking. Similar dynamic modeling methods have been used elsewhere to help learners formalize and clarify their understanding of complex systems (Lewis, Stern, & Linn, 1993; Mandinach, 1989; White & Horwitz, 1987). Finally, *Model It* methods are rooted in the scientific method and the development of science process skills (Roth & Roychoudury, 1993). Such methods require learners to identify research questions and variables, set hypotheses, test results, analyze observations, and refine hypotheses and causal variables accordingly (Lewis et al., 1993).

The video narratives used to orient students to the *Jasper* problems are akin to similarly successful methods used in other programs (see, for example,*Voyage of the Mimi* and *Science Vision*, Tobin & Dawson, 1992). Using familiar structures for problem presentation is considered important to help learners frame the problem context and recognize realistic applications (Bransford & Johnson, 1973; Brown, Collins, & Duguid, 1989). Methods that anchor concepts within broad, complex, and realistic scenarios are also consistent with problem-based or case-based approaches typically found in both medical and business school contexts (Hmelo, 1999).

Both CSILE and *ASK Jasper* use procedural and metacognitive prompts to scaffold the problem-solving process, methods used in studies investigating the role of scaffolding and procedural facilitation in complex learning activities. Palincsar and Brown (1984), for instance, reported that procedural and metacognitive scaffolding of self-regulatory procedures assisted learners in successfully engaging higher level thinking strategies. Both teacher and peer models were successful in helping learners to bridge the gap between current abilities and desired abilities. Modeling the thought processes of others can assist learners in identifying and using these processes in their own thinking. The deployment of methods, therefore, is informed by both others' and the developer's published research and theory.

Generalizability of Design. The third criterion for groundedness is that a design can be generalized, that is, it can be extended to or applied across comparable contexts, problems, content areas, and learners. This test is particularly significant for constructivist environments, given their emerging and formative nature. The *Jasper* series, for instance, successfully generalized the anchored instruction construct to encompass varied problem sets and contexts. One problem, for instance, requires learners to determine whether Jasper can drive his new boat home before sunset. A different problem, represented in the *Blueprint for Success* episode, requires learners to use geometry concepts to design a virtual playground. Another problem asks learners to consider whether Jasper will be able to transport a wounded eagle to safety using his ultralight airplane, and still another problem asks learners to plan a school fair and determine how to design and fill a dunking booth for teachers.

In addition, *Jasper* addresses issues related to transfer through a series of analog and extension problems. By presenting pairs of related adventures (e.g., trip planning), students are assisted in analyzing which concepts are generalizable across contexts and which are specific to the given context. All problems are anchored, yet the methodology has been applied successfully across multiple problem contexts.

CSILE and *Model-It* have also been applied across contexts and problems. CSILE, for instance, has been used by learners to address problems in science, history, writing, and biology. Although the content investigations vary, the interface, design, and functions scaffold a variety of teaching-learning activities. Similarly, *Model-It* has been used to model phenomena across a variety of contexts. Students have constructed and tested models using structured topics such as biodiversity (impact of pollution on stream macroinvertibrates), cultural eutophication (excess of phosphates leading to algal blooms), and land uses (impact of man-made structures on stream quality; Jackson et al., in press). These topics were identified a priori for learners to investigate. Yet, the design has also been extended to support learner definition of unique objects and systems to model across a variety of contexts. For instance, some students generated their own objects and models to investigate the impact of different drugs (e.g., marijuana, caffeine, etc.) on the human body, climate systems, air pollution systems, and predatory-prey systems (Soloway et al., 1997).

Jasper strategies have also proven generalizable across students of varied age, expertise, and demographics. *Jasper* problems, for instance, are designed for fifth and sixth graders, yet they have been used with students ranging from first graders to college freshmen (Cognition and Technology Group at Vanderbilt, 1991). Similarly, although CSILE was initially designed for university and graduate level students (Scardamalia et al., 1989), subsequent applications have emphasized encouraging reflection on and revision of understanding among fifth and sixth graders

Designs and Frameworks Successively Tested and Refined. The final criterion for groundedness is that designs have been iteratively implemented, tested, and revised to inform both the framework and the design itself. Essentially, designers and their environments become "smarter" through use and refinement. CSILE, for instance, has been tested, implemented, and refined with both children and adults for more than a 10-year period. *Jasper* design features were revised to address practical implementation issues. Initially, videotapes were used to depict the Jasper adventures; subsequently, videodiscs were used to enable learners to rapidly access specific segments of the vignettes quickly and accurately. *ASK Jasper* was created to address learner needs for process-related scaffolding (Williams et al., 1996). Alternative implementation options were developed to address pragmatic situational constraints; a variety of alternative methods and materials were created to support implementation, ranging from "basics first" to fully complex open-ended approaches.

Similarly, *Model-It* has been progressively implemented, tested, and refined. It has been redesigned over a 3-year period based on student and teacher feedback, results of empirical studies, and usability considerations (Soloway et al., 1997). For instance, the features were extended to support the modeling and testing of uniquely user-defined phenomena rather than only of predefined problems. Additionally, classroom testing indicated that although student prediction was critical for model refinement, many students failed to either establish a model or test their predictions. Therefore, a new tool for scaffolding and eliciting student predictions about the system is planned for future development (Jackson et al., in press). Finally, in order to assist learners in better validating models, simulations of real-world data may also be incorporated.

Assumptions and Values of Student-Centered Learning Environments

From a grounded design perspective, constructivist epistemologies are widely espoused but rarely practiced in schools and classrooms in the late 1990s. It is difficult to determine the theory-based principles that underlie many supposed constructivist practices. The problem is often exacerbated in technology-rich environments. Technology can be deployed to promote individual sense making, but misalignment has often yielded trendy activities rather than grounded practice. Isolated constructivist terms and strategies are tendered without clear links to or alignment with underlying foundations and assumptions. For example, learner controlled directed practice is mischaracterized as a constructivist methodology despite the concurrent focus on explicit instruction; conversely, a lack of external support is mistaken for student-centered learning despite the absence of needed scaffolding. For constructivist as well as other learning environments, grounded educational practices align foundations, assumptions, and methods as a matter of design.

Consider a scenario that typifies the blurring between epistemological roots and corresponding practices. Increased interest in technology, such as the Internet, has prompted the development of numerous web-based learning environments. Such environments often feature a series of hypertext links to sites that presumably contain classroom-related topics (e.g., geography, physics, Civil War, weather). The open nature of such learning environments has led some educators to deem them constructivist because the outcomes, boundaries, and methods are driven by the unique choices of learners. Yet, although student-centered and open in nature, grounding in other key aspects of constructivist epistemology is not evident. Designs often emphasize the technological capabilities of the web without reference to key elements such as context, tools to extend or augment thinking, and pedagogical scaffolding.

Despite differences manifested in various constructivist designs, several core values and assumptions can be identified (see Chap. 2 and Chap. 3, this volume). The purpose of this section is to identify key values shared among constructivist designers: (a) centrality of the learner in defining meaning, (b) importance of situated, authentic contexts, and (c) negotiation and interpretation of personal beliefs and multiple perspectives, (d) importance of prior learner experiences in meaning construction, and (e) use of technology to scaffold higher mental processes.

The Centrality of the Learner in Defining Meaning. In learner-centered environments, the learner actively constructs meaning. External learning goals may be established, but the learner determines how to proceed based on individual needs and questions that arise while generating and testing beliefs (Hannafin, Land, & Oliver, 1999; Land & Hannafin, 1996). *Astronomy Village*, a multimedia environment developed by the National Atmospheric and Space Administration (NASA), provides a virtual observatory for learners to inquire, experiment, and evaluate astronomy concepts (cited in Jonassen, Peck, & Wilson, 1999). Rather than simply read about astronomy concepts such as nebula, constellations, and asteroids, learners collect data and conduct virtual scientific investigations within the observatory context. As they conduct an investigation, such as a search for asteroids that cross Earth's path, they draw on observatory resources and tools to progressively develop, test, and refine explanations of their findings.

Presumably, given opportunities to make choices and pursue individual interests, learners evolve greater responsibility for their own learning. In traditional environments, learners are often denied opportunities to develop the decision-making, self-monitoring, and attention-checking skills necessary to optimize learning experiences (Perkins, 1993). Learners become increasingly compliant in their learning, viewing the task as one of matching their meanings to those expected by external agents (McCaslin & Good, 1992).

In contrast, successful learners evolve a variety of cognitive strategies and self-regulation procedures to plan and pursue goals, integrate new knowledge with existing, formulate questions and inferences, and continually review and reorganize their thinking. Consequently, constructivist environments often scaffold student thinking and actions to facilitate self-regulation (Bereiter & Scardamalia, 1989). As introduced previously, CSILE is a networked learning environment designed in large part to model and scaffold reflection and performance (Scardamalia et al., 1989). CSILE encourages learners to reflect on and take active control over learning processes such as problem solving, planning, goal setting, and self-regulation. It provides metacognitive and procedural facilitation to help learners identify learning goals and make thinking overt. The mediating role of the individual in both uniquely defining and monitoring understanding is essential to promote autonomy and ownership of the learning process.

Importance of Situated Thinking and Authentic Contexts

Knowledge, thinking, and the contexts for learning are inextricably tied (Brown, et al., 1989). Although all learning is contextually based, not all contexts support the application of knowledge equally. Knowledge acquired in decontextualized situations, for example, tends to be inert and of little practical utility (Whitehead, 1929). For instance, learning to solve classical textbook mathematical equations independently of their authentic context tends to promote isolated, naive, and oversimplified understanding (Spiro et al., 1991). Learners may successfully solve near transfer problems (e.g., other textbook problems) where the algorithm can be equivalently matched but fail to flexibly apply or critically reason through a problem on far-transfer or novel tasks (Perkins & Simmons, 1988).

Rather than isolating information, some constructivist environments provide macrocontexts that situate and embed relevant information (Choi & Hannafin, 1995). Again, *The Jasper Woodbury Series* (Cognition and Technology Group at Vanderbilt, 1992) anchors mathematics within realistic contexts. Video vignettes present stories about everyday problems faced by the story's lead character, Jasper. The information needed to solve the problems is embedded within the story itself rather than presented and practiced in isolation. One of Jasper's dilemmas, for instance, is determining whether or not sufficient time is available to drive his newly purchased boat home before sunset. Information relevant to solving the dilemma is embedded naturally within the story, and students must themselves generate the appropriate problems and subproblems. For instance, mile markers, periodic fuel readings, amount of fuel purchased, time of day and so on are set within the story. Once the macro-context is introduced, students generate subproblems because the dilemma is multifaceted and complex, and many alternative solution paths are possible.

Rather than applying standard equations to problems involving only a single correct solution, students create unique approaches to addressing complex problems involving multiple perspectives and solution paths. Pedagogical strategies associated with problem-based learning (Savery & Duffy, 1996) and anchored instruction (Cognition and Technology Group at Vanderbilt, 1992) are commonly referenced foundations that are well-aligned with psychological foundations of situated cognition. In situated contexts, learning occurs naturally as a consequence of the learner recognizing knowledge's practical utility as well as the need to use it in an attempt to interpret, analyze, and solve real-world problems (see Chap. 3, this volume).

Negotiation and Interpretation Involving Multiple Perspectives

Many constructivists emphasize the socially mediated aspects of learning. Through exploration, interpretation, and negotiation, understanding is deepened as multiple perspectives are considered. Such approaches may use teacher-student or student-student interactions to model or scaffold reflection and performance (see for example, Bereiter & Scardamalia, 1989; Palincsar & Brown, 1984). Accordingly, varied perspectives from teachers, experts, or peers can be coordinated to form a knowledge base from which learners evaluate and negotiate varied sources of meaning (Hill & Land, 1998).

For instance, the *Knowledge Integration Environment* (KIE) (Bell & Davis, 1996; see also Chap. 5, this volume) uses web technology to support sharing of learner-constructed evidence to evaluate scientific phenomena. Students are initially provided open-ended questions such as "how far does light travel?" Rather than define and present the information needed to answer the question, *KIE* requires that learners induce personal, everyday experiences as a foundation for interpretation and explanation. Once learners generate explanations and examples, they can browse databases of evidence constructed by themselves, other students, and teachers. Learners review the varied and often conflicting evidence to determine whether it supports or contradicts their position. As divergent views are deliberated, learners inquire further to reconcile differences and refine explanations. *KIE* scaffolds the learning process by providing guidance, prompts, and opportunities to integrate and share personal experiences with formal concepts. Varied methods and perspectives are viewed as critical to developing deeper, divergent, and more flexible thinking processes.

Importance of Prior or Everyday Experiences

Another value underlying constructivist learning environments is that individual beliefs and experiences provide the uniquely personal framework for new understanding. Background knowledge and experience form the conceptual referent from which new knowledge is organized and assimilated (Piaget, 1976). Integrating new knowledge with existing conceptions is assumed to result in more meaningful learning (Mayer, 1984).

Understanding is viewed as a process that continuously and dynamically evolves, as ideas are generated, expanded, tested, and revised (Land & Hannafin, 1996). Learners hold powerful, often naïve and incomplete, beliefs and models that are deeply rooted in their everyday experience (see also Chap. 7, this volume). Although the models tend to be tacit and sometimes at odds with accepted scientific theories (Carey, 1986; Driver & Scanlon, 1988), they provide the basis through which learners interpret and explain everyday as well as formal scientific events. Such beliefs and models tend to persist even in the face of contradictory evidence; typically, they fail to evolve through conventional teaching practices (Land & Hannafin, 1997). Yet, in constructivist design practices, erstwhile tacit beliefs are frequently externalized and formalized so they can be tested. Microworlds and simulations, for instance, allow learners to generate and test working models of their understanding (Edwards, 1995). By varying parameters and hypothesizing outcomes, learners test assumptions and revise thinking based on resultant observations. Through technology-facilitated manipulations, new experiences are enabled that offer counter evidence, and models of understanding change accordingly (Land & Hannafin, 1997).

Frequently, constructivists utilize familiar problems (Cognition and Technology Group at Vanderbilt, 1992), driving questions (Wallace & Kupperman, 1997), and enabling contexts (Hannafin et al., 1999) to induce access to and deployment of personal theories and experiences during learning. For instance, *ErgoMotion* is designed to support middle schoolers' exploration of force and motion concepts through the development a virtual roller coaster (Tobin & Dawson, 1992). The context employs a familiar referent (riding roller coasters) to assist learners in relating to-be-investigated concepts to familiar experiences. They are induced to use these experiences to interpret, explain, and subsequently formalize their scientific knowledge. Personal theories based on prior knowledge and experience are considered theories-in-action that can be accessed, elaborated, and revised through interaction with the environment.

Technology Scaffolding and Deep Understanding

Constructivist environments scaffold thinking and actions in order to deepen understanding. They provide opportunities for learners to amplify and extend cognitive capabilities, as well as to reorganize thinking processes by altering the tasks available to them (Pea, 1985). Technology tools "provide models, opportunities for higher level thinking, and metacognitive guidance ... in a learner's zone of proximal development" (Salomon, Globerson, & Guterman, 1989, p. 620). That is, technology is used to facilitate understanding that would be difficult, if not impossible, to otherwise support. For instance, visualization tools used in microworlds such as *Geometer's Sketchpad*™ and *Interactive Physics*™ allow learners to construct models or objects, then manipulate them in order to test their parameters. Technology enables learners to represent their thinking in concrete ways and to visualize and test the consequences of their reasoning. Similarly, three-dimensional and virtual reality environments, such as the *Virtual human*, provide opportunities for learners to examine, rotate, test, and otherwise focus on anatomical concepts and structures not normally accessible or visible to the human eye. Thus, tools and resources are used to extend and augment thinking capabilities, rather than supplant integral cognitive processes and operations (Hannafin & Land, 1997; Salomon, Perkins, & Globerson, 1991).

Model It (Jackson, et al., in press) allows learners to create and test their largely intuitive and informal understanding of everyday scientific phenomena. The programs support the process of learning science in ways that mirror the practices of scientists. Using an object-oriented interface, learners build models of real-world phenomena without requiring mastery of advanced mathematics, lab equipment, or computer programming. *Model It* enables learners to conduct virtual scientific investigations that might be otherwise precluded due to time, laboratory, or equipment constraints. It supports learners in the process of initially generating, testing, and revising qualitative models of events, without the often-confounding computational or technical task requirements (Salomon et al., 1991). When technology is used to eliminate low-level or non-essential requirements, the cognitive load associated with such tasks is minimized. Cognitive resources can then be reallocated to support higher-order thinking and learning activities (Gavora & Hannafin, 1995).

Closing Thoughts

During the 1990s, considerable interest has been generated in the design of constructivist learning environments. The promise of these systems to leverage capabilities of technology, empower learners to pursue unique goals and needs, and reconceptualize teaching-learning practices has sparked both provocative ideas as well as heated debate. Yet, problems in grounding designs within established theory and research are commonplace, as designers grapple with questions regarding epistemology, assumptions, and methods. Problems in implementation and practice are also commonplace, as pragmatic constraints surface and conflicting values emerge. We suggest three key issues that are likely to dominate the constructivist learning environment landscape.

Inertia and the Tyranny of Tradition: Old Dogs, New Tricks? Although as educators we espouse support for constructivist approaches to teaching and learning, we continue to rely on familiar pedagogical approaches such as lectures, worksheets, and rote learning practices. At the moment, educators perceive such approaches as more compatible with traditional expectations and methods of student assessment and better supported by existing infrastructures. Stated differently, it is easier and more efficient to maintain current practices than to promulgate approaches for which significant shifts--epistemological, technological, cultural—are required. In truth, few designers have acknowledged, much less successfully negotiated, the hurdles associated with transforming a highly traditional community of educational practice.

Yet, as constructivist learning environments are repurposed to fit traditional classroom practices, mismatched theoretical foundations, assumptions, or methods may result. Instructional methods or assessment practices are often added to (or taken away from) original designs to make them more compatible with classroom pragmatics and constraints. In essence, constructivist pedagogy is applied to attain traditional goals, and the environment becomes an instance of what Petraglia (1998) refers to as "domesticated constructivism" (cited in Salomon, 1997).

For instance, a teacher may intend to use a constructivist environment within a climatology unit to support hypothesis generation, prediction, data collection, and analysis. The environment may also employ powerful visualization tools and complex sets of meteorology databases and resources (perhaps from the WWW) in ways that are consistent with the environment's constructivist foundations. Yet, as pedagogical methods are considered, they may be tempered by the prevailing cultural values of high standardized test scores and mastery learning of basic skills. Consequently, rather than engage in prediction, interpretation, and data analysis, learners instead search databases to find specific answers to questions established in advance (e.g., find the temperature in San Diego; define the greenhouse effect; what is the coldest day on record in Los Angeles). Pragmatic influences may also intervene. Activity may be limited to the traditional two 50-minute class meetings per week and conventional tests and assessments of the unit's meteorology content. Perhaps only a single computer is available, and consequently the teacher chooses to project and demonstrate the tools and resources rather than allow students to define, solve, and collaborate on weather prediction problems.

Learned Helplessness and Learner Compliance: "Will This Be on the Test?" In typical constructivist learning environments, students establish (or adopt) learning goals and needs, navigate through and evaluate a variety of potentially relevant resources, generate and test hypotheses, and so forth (Holland, Holyoak, Nisbeth, & Thargard, 1986). Teachers clarify rather than tell, guide rather than direct, and facilitate student effort rather than impose their own approaches. For both teachers and learners, these represent radical departures from conventional school-based learning activities. Teachers have traditionally possessed the required knowledge, determined what is correct and what is incorrect, and set and enforced grading standards. Students are told what knowledge is required, which answers are correct and which are incorrect, and the standards that separate good from bad students, average from substandard performance, and robins from bluebirds. A pact between teacher and student is tacitly struck and enforced: Good teachers make the preceding explicit and direct student effort accordingly, while good students learn quickly to detect and comply with the standards.

Research in the late 1990s on student engagement in constructivist learning environments has underscored several disturbing patterns. Land and Hannafin (1997), for instance, examined how seventh graders used the *ErgoMotion* (Tobin & Dawson, 1992) roller coaster microworld to learn about force and motion concepts. Despite numerous and varied features and opportunities for learners to hypothesize, manipulate, and test predictions, many learners failed to either connect key concepts well or internalize their understanding. In lieu of the teacher, and perhaps in an attempt to identify what the system required of them, most relied exclusively on the explicit proxy structure provided by the system. They frequently queried the researchers as to whether or not responses were correct or whether they had "done enough yet." Students were dependent on, and sought compliance with, external agents to tell them what, when, and in what order to respond, as well as to judge the quality, accuracy, and completion of their efforts—skills essential to constructivist learning environments.

Similarly, numerous compliant strategies in web-based, hypermedia environments were reported among middle school (Oliver, 1999) and adult (Hill & Hannafin, 1997) students. Learners tended to use externally provided questions almost exclusively to navigate the system and find "answers" to open-ended problems (Oliver, 1999). Similarly, Wallace and Kupperman (1997) reported that children attempted to apply traditional strategies to presumably web-based inquiry-oriented learning tasks. They tended to view the activity as finding the correct answer to their research question and "thus reduced the task to finding a single page, the perfect source, on which the answer could be found" (p. 13).

In these instances, learners invoked methods that do not typically support or promote open or inquiry-based learning—ironically the strategies required for successful performance in formal education. In the late 1990s, constructivists have emphasized the importance of scaffolding learner self-regulation and strategic processes to help learners manage the complexity of the environment (Scardamalia et al., 1989). It is important to determine how learners use available scaffolds and to adapt accordingly. Without strategies appropriate to student-centered learning tasks, learners may fail to either invoke the affordances of the environment or to develop the strategies engendered by them.

The Situated Learning Paradox: "I Know What I Know." Although prior knowledge and situated contexts enhance transfer potential (Brown, Collins, & Duguid, 1989), they also engender incomplete, naïve, and often inaccurate theories that interfere with rather than support learning. Paradoxically, these are precisely the types of thinking constructivist learning environments build upon. Most learners, for instance, believe that heavier objects sink and lighter objects float; their personal experiences confirm this intuitive theory. The resulting misconceptions, rooted in and strengthened by personal experience, are highly resilient and resistant to change. Although personal theories are considered critical to progressive understanding, they can become especially problematic when learners become entrenched in faulty theories to explain events that cannot be tested within the boundaries of a system or fail to recognize important contradictory evidence.

Previously, we reported that learners referenced prior knowledge and experiences that either contradicted or interfered with the environment's treatment of the concepts of force and motion (Land & Hannafin, 1997). In one case, theory preservation seriously limited the ability to learn from the system. One student failed to either detect system-provided information or seek confirmatory data due to the intractability of his beliefs; he was so entrenched in his beliefs that he failed to seek and repeatedly overlooked counterevidence (see Chinn & Brewer, 1993 and Wilson & Brekke, 1994 for similar findings on the influence of beliefs on the ability to detect and reconcile contradictory data). In another case, a learner recalled an operator remarking that roller coaster brakes and clamps would terminate a problem run immediately. Consequently, she mistakenly perceived the coaster to be slowing down around curves, falsely confirming her belief that brakes were applied when they were not. Because they were strongly rooted in personal experience and could not be tested using the available tools, faulty conceptions endured. Thus, the completeness of a system's representation of simulated phenomena is critical because learners access related prior knowledge and experiences that may contradict the environment's treatment of those concepts.

In sum, several perspectives regarding design of learning environments have emerged in response to interest in alternative epistemologies. Although considerable progress has been made to advance researchers' understanding, many questions and issues remain. Whereas some studies have identified problems and issues related to the design and implementation of constructivist learning environments, others have reported noteworthy benefits. It is imperative that efforts continue not only to ground design practices more completely but also to better understand the promise and limitations of constructivist learning environments.

REFERENCES

Bell, P., & Davis, E. (1996, April). *Designing an activity in the knowledge integration environment*. Paper presented at the annual meeting of the American Educational Research Association, New York.

Bereiter, C., & Scardamalia, M. (1989). Intentional learning as a goal of instruction. In L. B. Resnick's (Ed.), *Knowing, learning, and instruction* (pp. 361-391). Hillsdale, NJ: Lawrence Erlbaum Associates.

Black, M. (1962). *Models and metaphors: Studies in language and philosophy.* New York: Cornell University Press.

Blumenfeld, P., Soloway, E., Marx, R., Krajcik, J., Guzdial, M., & Palincsar, A. (1991). Motivating project-based learning: Sustaining the doing, supporting the learning. *Educational Psychologist, 26*, 369-398.

Bransford, J., & Johnson, M. K. (1973). Contextual prerequisites for understanding: Some investigations of context and recall. *Journal of Verbal Learning and Verbal Behavior, 11*, 717-726.

Brown, A., & Palincsar, A. (1989). Guided, cooperative learning and individual knowledge acquisition. In L. B. Resnick (Ed.), *Knowing and learning: Essays in honor of Robert Glaser* (pp. 393-451). Hillsdale, NJ: Lawrence Erlbaum Associates.

Brown, J. S., Collins, A., & Duguid, P. (1989). Situated cognition and the culture of learning. *Educational Researcher, 18*(1), 32-41.

Carey, S. (1986). Cognitive science and science education. *American Psychologist, 41*(10), 1123-1130.

Chinn, C., & Brewer, W. (1993). The role of anomolous data in data acquisition: A theoretical framework and implications for science instruction. *Review of Educational Research, 63*(1), 1-49.

Choi, J. I. & Hannafin, M. J. (1995). Situated cognition and learning environments: Roles, structures, and implications for design. *Educational Technology Research and Development, 43* (2), 53-69.

Cognition and Technology Group at Vanderbilt. (1991). Technology and the design of generative learning environments. *Educational Technology, 31*(5), 34-40.

Cognition and Technology Group at Vanderbilt. (1992). The Jasper experiment: An exploration of issues in learning and instructional design. *Educational Technology Research & Development, 40(1),* 65-80.

Collins, A., Brown, J. S., & Newman, S. (1989). Cognitive apprenticeship: Teaching the crafts of reading, writing, and mathematics. In L. Resnick (Ed.), *Knowing, learning, and instruction* (pp. 453-494). Englewood Cliffs, NJ: Lawrence Erlbaum Associates.

Dick, W. (1991). An instructional designer's view of constructivism. *Educational Technology, 31(5),* 41-44.

Driver, R., & Scanlon, E. (1988). Conceptual change in science. *Journal of Computer-Assisted Learning, 5,* 25-36.

Edwards, L. D. (1995). The design and analysis of a mathematical microworld. *Journal of Educational Computing Research, 12(1),* 77-94.

Gagné, R. (1985). *The conditions of learning* (4th ed.). New York: Holt, Rinehart, & Winston.

Gagné, R., & Glaser, R. (1987). Foundations in learning research. In R. Gagné (Ed.), *Instructional technology: Foundations* (pp. 49-84). Hillsdale, NJ: Lawrence Erlbaum Associates.

Gavora, M., & Hannafin, M. J. (1995). Perspectives on the design of human-computer interactions: Issues and implications. *Instructional Science, 22,* 445-477.

Hannafin, M. J., Hannafin, K. M., Land, S., & Oliver, K. (1997). Grounded practice in the design of learning systems. *Educational Technology Research and Development, 45(3),* 101-117.

Hannafin, M. J., & Land, S. (1997). The foundations and assumptions of technology-enhanced, student-centered learning environments. *Instructional Science, 25,* 167-202.

Hannafin, M.J., Land, S.M., & Oliver, K. (1999). Open learning environments: Foundations, Methods, and Models. In C. Reigeluth (Ed.), *Instructional Design Theories and Models (Vol. 2).* Mahwah, NJ: Lawrence Erlbaum Associates.

Hannafin, M. J., & Rieber, L. P. (1989). Psychological foundations of instructional design for emerging computer-based instructional technologies: Parts 1 & 2. *Educational Technology Research and Development, 37,* 91-114.

Hill, J., & Hannafin, M. J. (1997). Cognitive strategies and learning from the World-Wide Web. *Educational Technology Research and Development, 45(4),* 37-64.

Hill, J. R., & Land, S. M. (1998). Open-ended learning environments: A theoretical framework and model for design. In N. Maushak & C. Scholosser (Eds.), *Proceedings of the 1998 International Conference of the Association of Educational Communications and Technology* (pp. 167-178). Ames, IA: Iowa State University.

Hmelo, C. E. (1999). Problem-based learning: Effects on the early acquisition of cognitive skill in medicine. *Journal of the Learning Sciences, 7*(2), p173-208

Holland, J., Holyoak, K., Nisbett, R., & Thagard, G. (1986). *Induction: Processes of inference, learning, and discovery*. Cambridge, MA: MIT Press.

Jackson, S., Stratford, S., Krajcik, J., & Soloway, E. (in press). Making dynamic modeling accessible to pre-college science students. *Interactive Learning Environments*.

Jonassen, D. (1991). Objectivism versus constructivism: Do we need a new philosophical paradigm? *Educational Technology Research and Development, 39*, 5-14.

Jonassen, D. (1999). Constructivist learning environments. In C. Reigeluth (Ed.), *Instructional Design Theories and Models* (Vol. 2) (pp.215-239). Mahwah, NJ: Lawrence Erlbaum Associates.

Jonassen, D.H. (2000). Mindtools for Schools: Engaging Critical Thinking WITH Technology, (2nd Ed.).Columbus, OH: Merrill/Prentice-Hall

Jonassen, D.H., Peck, K.L., & Wilson, B.G. (1999). *Learning with technology: A constructivist perspective*. Upper Saddle River, NJ: Merrill.

Jonassen, D. H., & Reeves, T. C. (1996). Learning with technology: Using computers as cognitive tools. In D. H. Jonassen (Ed.), *Handbook of Research on Educational Communication and Technology* (pp. 693-719). New York: Scholastic Press.

Koschmann, T., Kelson, A., Feltovich, P., & Barrows, H. (1996). Computer-supported problem-based learning: A principled approach to the use of computers in collaborative learning. In T. Koschmann (Ed.), *CSCL: Theory and Practice of an Emerging Paradigm*. Mahwah, NJ: Lawrence Erlbaum Associates.

Land, S. M., & Hannafin, M. J. (1996). A conceptual framework for the development of theories-in-action with open-ended learning environments. *Educational Technology Research & Development, 44*(3), 37-53.

Land, S. M., & Hannafin, M. J. (1997). Patterns of understanding with open-ended learning environments: A qualitative study. *Educational Technology Research & Development, 45*(2), 47-73.

Lewis, E., Stern, J., & Linn, M. (1993). The effect of computer simulations on introductory thermodynamics understanding. *Educational Technology, 33*(1), 45-58.

Mandinach, E. (1989). Model-building and the use of computer simulation of dynamic systems. *Journal of Educational Computing Research, 5*(2), 221-243.

Mayer, R. E. (1984). Aids to text comprehension. *Educational Psychologist, 19*, 30-42.

McCaslin, M., & Good, T. (1992). Compliant cognition: The misalliance of management and instructional goals in current school reform. *Educational Researcher, 21*(3), 4-17.

Merrill, M. D. (1991). Constructivism and instructional design. *Educational Technology, 31*(5), 45-53.

Oliver, K. (1999). *A case study of student use of computer tools in support of open-ended problem solving with hypermedia resources.* Unpublished doctoral dissertation, University of Georgia, Athens, GA.

Palincsar, A., & Brown, A. (1984). Reciprocal teaching of comprehension-fostering and monitoring activities. *Cognition and Instruction, 1* (2), 117-175.

Pea, R. (1985). Beyond amplification: Using the computer to reorganize mental functioning. *Educational Psychologist, 20*(4), 167-182.

Perkins, D.N. (1985). The fingertip effect: How information processing technology shapes thinking. *Educational Researcher, 14,* 11-17.

Perkins, D.N. (1993). Person-plus: A distributed view of thinking and learning. In G. Salomon's (Ed.), *Distributed intelligence* (pp. 89-109). New York: Cambridge University Press.

Perkins, D., & Simmons, R. (1988). Patterns of misunderstanding: An integrative model for science, math, and programming. *Review of Educational Research, 58,* 303-326.

Petraglia, J. (1998). *Reality by design: Rhetoric, technology, and the creation of authentic learning environments.* Mahwah, NJ: Lawrence Erlbaum Associates

Piaget, J. (1976). *The grasp of consciousness.* Cambridge, MA: Harvard University Press.

Roth, W.M., & Roychoudhury, A. (1993). The development of science process skills in authentic contexts. *Journal in Research in Science Teaching, 30*(2), 127-152.

Salomon, G. (1986). Information technologies: What you see is not (always) what you get. *Educational Psychologist, 20,* 207-216.

Salomon, G. (1997, August). *Novel constructivist learning environments and novel technologies: Some issues to be concerned with.* Paper presented at the annual meeting of the European Association for Research in Learning and Instruction, Athens, Greece.

Salomon, G., Globerson, T., & Guterman, E. (1989). The computer as a zone of proximal development: Internalizing reading-related metacognitions from a reading partner. *Journal of Educational Psychology, 81*(4), 620-627.

Salomon, G., Perkins, D., & Globerson, T. (1991). Partners in cognition: Extending human intelligence with intelligent technologies. *Educational Researcher, 4,* 2-8.

Savery, J. R., & Duffy, T.M. (1996). Problem-based learning: An instructional model and its constructivist framework. In B. G. Wilson (Ed.), *Constructivist learning environments: Case studies in instructional design* (pp. 135-150). Englewood Cliffs, NJ: Educational Technology Publications.

Scardamalia, M., Bereiter, C., McLean, R., Swallow, J., & Woodruff, E. (1989). Computer-supported intentional learning environments. *Journal of Educational Computing Research, 5,* 51-68.

Schank, R. (1992). *Goal-based scenarios* (Tech. Rep. No. 36). Evanston, IL: Northwestern University, Institute for the Learning Sciences.

Schoenfeld, A. (1985.)*Mathematical problem-solving.* Orlando, FL: Academic Press.

Skinner, B.F. (1957). *Verbal behavior.* Englewood Cliffs, NJ: Prentice Hall.

Soloway, E., Pryor, A., Krajcik, J., Jackson, S., Stratford, S., Wisnudel, M., & Klein, J. (1997). *ScienceWare's Model-It: Technology to support authentic science inquiry.* [On-line]. Available:http://hice.eecs.umich.edu/papers/Revised%20Final%20Version/Model-It%20Paper.html.

Spiro, R., Feltovich, P., Jacobson, M., & Coulson, R. (1991). Cognitive flexibility, constructivism, and hypertext: Random access instruction for advanced knowledge acquisition in ill-structured domains. *Educational Technology, 5,* 24-33.

Twigger, D., Byard, M., Draper, S., Driver, R., Hartley, R., Hennessy, S., Mallen, C., Mohamed, R., O'Malley, C., O'Shea, T., Scanlon, E. (1991). The 'Conceptual Change in Science' project. *Journal of Computer-Assisted Learning, 7,* 144-155.

Tobin, K., & Dawson, G. (1992). Constraints to curriculum reform: Teachers and the myths of schooling. *Educational Technology Research and Development, 40*(1), 81-92.

Voyage of the Mimi. (1984). [video]. Available from Sunburst Communications, Pleasantville, NY.

Wallace, R., & Kupperman, J. (1997, April). *On-line search in the science classroom: Benefits and possibilities.* Paper presented at the annual meeting of the American Educational Research Association, Chicago, IL.

White, B., & Horwitz, P. (1987). *ThinkerTools: Enabling children to understand physical laws.* Cambridge, MA: BBN Laboratories.

Whitehead, A. N (1929). *The aims of education.* New York: MacMillan.

Williams, S., Bareiss, R., & Reiser, B. (1996). An environment for supporting independent, individualized learning and problem-solving. In D. C. Edelson & E. A. Domeshek (Eds.), *Proceedings of the International Conference of the Learning Sciences* (pp. 332-338). Charlottesville, VA: Association for the Advancement of Computers in Education.

Wilson, T., & Brekke, N. (1994). Mental contamination and mental correction: Unwanted influences on judgments and evaluations. *Psychological Bulletin, 116*(1), 117-142.

2

From Practice Fields to Communities of Practice

Sasha A. Barab
Indiana University at Bloomington

Thomas M. Duffy
Indiana University at Bloomington

PREFACE

*In writing this chapter, we (a constructivist and a situativity theorist) strug-
gled with the distinction between situativity and constructivism and the implications in terms of the design of learning contexts. In clarifying (and
justifying) our two sides, we created straw man and pointed fingers with
respect to the limitations of each other's perspectives. We found that
although discussions of situativity and of constructivism draw on different
references and clearly have specialized languages, actual interpretations of
situativity and of constructivism share many underlying similarities. Further, when it came to the design of learning contexts predicated on our respective theories, we found ourselves continuously forwarding similar principles
and advocating for similar learning contexts.*

    *We are dealing with evolving concepts—and people use new terms to
include and extend old ones. Constructivism was the label used for the de-
parture from objectivism; however, even among those who call themselves
constructivists there are different perspectives and different sets of assumptions (see Cobb, 1994, 1995; Phillips, 1995). Now the term more commonly
used is situated, reflecting the key proposal from both the constructivist and
situativity perspective that knowledge is situated through experience. In the
context of this chapter, we found it trivial to distinguish among those learning theories and principles related to constructivism and those related to situativity theory. Rather, we discuss the various learning theories that have
informed our understanding all under the heading of situativity learning
theories. This term, and its associated assumptions and current interpretations, seemed to better capture the essence of the learning contexts we are
forwarding as useful. However, even within the context of situativity theories we found it necessary to make distinctions, and it was these distinctions
(not the distinction between constructivist and situativity views) that best
captured the essence of this chapter.*

INTRODUCTION

The late 1990s are a period in which theories of learning and cognition seem to be in a state of perturbation, with numerous books and scholarly articles being published that forward radically new theories of what it means to know and learn. As learning theorists, we have been moving from cognitive theories that emphasize individual thinkers and their isolated minds to theories that emphasize the social nature of cognition and meaning (Resnick, 1987). More recently, we have been moving to situative theories that emphasize the reciprocal character of the interaction in which individuals, as well as cognition and meaning, are considered socially and culturally constructed (Lave, 1988, 1993; Michael, 1996). In these latter situative theories (of anthropological origin), interactions with the world are viewed as not only producing meanings about the social world but also as producing identities; that is, individuals are fundamentally constituted through their relations with the world (Lave, 1993; Lemke, 1997; Walkerdine, 1997; Wenger, 1998).

In general, situative perspectives suggest a reformulation of learning in which practice is not conceived of as independent of learning and in which meaning is not conceived of as separate from the practices and contexts in which it was negotiated (see Chapter 3, this volume). Although the dominant movement during the 1990s has been to a situated perspective of cognition, there has been considerable variation in the understanding just what is meant by situated cognition or, the term we prefer, *situativity theory* (Greeno, 1998; Lave & Wenger, 1991; Resnick, 1987; Young, 1993). In this chapter, we examine two dominant themes. First, there is an approach arising from work in psychology and education that is focused on learning (or the failure to learn) in school contexts. Because of the schooling context, this work has focused on meeting specific learning objectives or content. For example, the question that arises is how to design learning environments to support students in learning mathematics (or learning algebra) or science (or Newtonian principles). Here, the focus has been on situating content in authentic learner activities. In Senge's (1994) terms, the focus has been on creating practice fields[1] in which students in schools engage in the kinds of problems and practices that they will encounter outside of school.

Second, parallel to the development of the psychological perspective of situativity, there is an "anthropological" approach[2], reflected most heavily in the work of Lave and her colleagues. Rather than focus on the situatedness of meaning or content, the anthropological perspective focuses on communities and what it means to learn as a function of being a part of a community. This shift in the unit of analysis from the individual's context to the community context leads to a shift in focus from the learning of skills or developing understandings to one in which "developing an identity as a member of a community and becoming knowledgeably skillful are part of the same process, with the former motivating, shaping, and giving meaning to the latter, which it subsumes" (Lave, 1993, p. 65).

The goal of this chapter is to explore the implications of these two views of situativity for architecting learning environments. We begin with an examination of the movement from a representational view of learning to a situated perspective. We then examine the psychological perspective of situativity theories in some detail, considering the theoretical underpinnings, distinctions between this perspective and the anthropological perspective, the learning environments associated with this framework, and finally, the key principles for the design of learning environments (practice fields) associated with this group of situativity theories. We then turn to the anthropological perspective and consider how this perspective, in our view, encompasses and enriches the psychological perspective and significantly complicates the design of learning environments (from practice fields to communities of practice). We propose three characteristics of communities of practice that extend beyond those features typically found in psychologically based designs for learning. Finally, we examine in greater detail several examples of learning environments that purport to reflect the anthropological perspective on situativity, that is, to focus on the development of self in the context of an individual's participation in a community.

Before beginning this discussion, let us emphasize two points that guide the design of this chapter. First, our focus is on schooling—we seek to understand the principles for the design of learning environments that can be utilized in schools. Although the designs may require systemic change in the schools, the learning context and the motivation for learning are nonetheless framed within a school environment. Second, it is our belief that the epistemological assumptions people make and their practices are reciprocally determined. Most clearly, an individual's assumptions about learning and knowledge will reciprocally interact with the design of learning environments and how one participates in those environments (Bednar, Cunningham, Duffy, & Perry, 1992; see also Chapter 1, this volume). It is inconceivable that a teacher or instructional designer would advocate a particular lesson or activity without at least a tacit theory of how students think and learn. In turn, however, dissatisfaction with teaching practices is likely to lead to a questioning of the epistemological assumptions on which that instruction is based. Indeed, dissatisfaction with schooling practices, along with the need for theories that account for learning that occurs outside of schools, is a major factor in the development of situativity theories.

FROM AN ACQUISITION TO A PARTICIPATION METAPHOR

Since the cognitive revolution of the 1960s, representation has served as the central concept of cognitive theory and the representational theory of mind has served as the most common view in cognitive science (Fodor, 1975; Gardner, 1985; Vera & Simon, 1993). The central tenet of the representational position is that "knowledge is constituted of symbolic mental representations, and cognitive activity consists of the manipulation of the symbols in these representations, that is, of computations" (Shanon, 1988, p. 70). Conse-quently, learning is "acquiring" these symbols, and instruction involves find-ing the most efficient means of facilitating this acquisition.

Since the late 1980s, Sfard (1998) argued, learning theorists have been witnessing a move away from the predominant acquisition metaphor that has guided much of the practice in K-12 schools towards a participation meta-phor in which knowledge is considered fundamentally situated in practice. In large measure, this epistemological shift was stimulated by a growing dissatis-faction with schooling. Learning in school was seen as resulting in inert knowledge; that is, knowledge that was known but simply not used outside of schools (Whitehead, 1929). Resnick (1987), in her presidential address to the American Educational Research Association, examined the practices in schools, which are predicated most strongly on the acquisition metaphor, comparing them to how individuals learn and use knowledge outside of schools. Her analysis focused attention on the collaborative, contextualized, and concrete character of learning outside of school, as opposed to the indi-vidual and abstract character of learning that occurs inside of school. Argua-bly, it was this analysis that served as one of the principal stimuli for the development of the participatory perspective with its emphasis on situated activity.

Shortly after Resnick's (1987) seminal work, Brown, Collins, and Duguid (1989) argued that knowing and doing are reciprocal—knowledge is situated and progressively developed through activity. Central to this theory is the contention that participation in practice constitutes learning and under-standing. They further suggested that the notion that concepts are self-con-tained entities should be abandoned, instead conceiving them as tools, which can only be fully understood through use. Reinforcing this view, Greeno and Moore (1993) argued that "situativity is fundamental in all cognitive activity" (p. 50). It is the contention from this perspective that learning involves more than acquiring understanding; instead, it involves building an "increasingly rich implicit understanding of the world in which they use the tools and of the tools themselves" (Brown et al., 1989, p. 33). This understanding is framed by those situations in which it is learned and used.

The central tenets of this perspective regarding how individuals con-ceive of knowledge or of "knowing about" are the following: Knowing about refers to an activity—not a thing; knowing about is always contextual-ized—not abstract; knowing about is reciprocally constructed within the indi-vidual-environment interaction—not objectively defined or subjectively cre-ated; and knowing about is a functional stance on the interaction—not a "truth" (see Barab, Hay, & Duffy, 1998, or Bereiter, 1994, for further elabora-tion on these points). This position, we feel, is consistent with the views of Clancey (1993), the Cognition and Technology Group at Vanderbilt (1990, 1993), Greeno (1997, 1998), Roschelle and Clancey (1992), Tripp (1993), Young (1993), Resnick (1987), and Brown et al. (1989). However, there is another set of discussions related to situativity theory that emphasizes the situatedness of identities as well as cognitions. It is through these discussions, with their roots in anthropological circles, that we explore theories of situativity that focus on the construction of whole persons within communities of practice, not simply "knowing about" (Lave, 1997).

Discussions of situativity that have their genesis in anthropological research, including those being made by some educational psychologists (See Kirshner & Whitson, 1997, 1998), focus on learning in relation to communities of practice and provide a different perspective with respect to what is situated and what is constituted within an interaction. In this broadened view, what Lave (1997) referred to as *situated social practice*, there are no boundaries between the individual and the world; instead, "learning, thinking, and knowing are relations among people engaged in activity *in, with, and arising from the socially and culturally structured world*" (p. 67, italics in the original). From this anthropological perspective[3] it is not only meanings that are produced but entire identities that are shaped by and shape the experience. In other words, the interaction constitutes and is constituted

TABLE 2.1
Focus of Psychological and Anthropological Views of Situativity Theory

	Psychological Views	Anthropological Views
Focus	Cognition	Individuals' Relations to Community
Learners	Students	Members of Communities of Practice
Unit of analysis	Situated activity	Individual in community
What is produced from Interactions	Meaning	Meanings, identities, and communities
Learning arena	Schools	Everyday world
Goal of learning	Prepare for future tasks	Meet immediate community/societal needs
Pedagogical implications	Practice fields	Communities of practice

by all of the components—individual, content, and context. There are no clear boundaries between the development of knowledgeable skills and the development of identities; both arise as individuals participate and both become central to the community of practice. We believe that the collection of psychological perspectives of situativity that were fashioned out of an interest in cognition, and the work of Resnick (1987) and Brown et al. (1989) in particular, constituted a decisive move away from representational theories of mind and away from didactic models of instruction. The anthropological framework further helps to enrich our conceptualization of this framework for what is meant by situated. These two perspectives of situativity theories are described in Table 2.1. It is with this initial analysis of situativity theory that we now seek to develop principles, derived from the psychological framework, for the design of learning environments.   Later in this chapter we will take a similar tack with respect to the anthropological framework

ARCHITECTING LEARNING ENVIRONMENTS: PRACTICE FIELDS

Within this theoretical perspective on situativity, the unit of analysis is the situated activity of the learner—the interaction of the learner, the practices being carried out, the reasons the learner is carrying out particular practices, the resources being used, and the constraints of the particular task at hand. From an instructional perspective, the goal shifts from the teaching of concepts to engaging the learner in authentic tasks that are likely to require the use of those concepts or skills. As Brown et al. (1989) argued, concepts are seen as tools that can only be understood through use.

Designing a learning environment begins with identifying what is to be learned and, reciprocally, the real world situations in which the activity occurs (Barab, 1999). One of those situations is then selected as the goal of the learning activity. Thus, the emphasis is on creating circumscribed activities or experiences for the learner. Consistent with Resnick (1987), these activities must be authentic; they must present most of the cognitive demands the learner would encounter in the real world. Hence, authentic problem-solving and critical thinking in the domain is required. Learning activities must be anchored in real uses, or it is likely that the result will be knowledge that remains inert.

Senge (1994), in his discussion of the development of learning organizations, referred to designs like this as the creation of *practice fields* and advocates their use as a primary approach to corporate training. Practice fields are separate from the real field, but they are contexts in which learners, as opposed to *legitimate participants*, can practice the kinds of activities they will encounter outside of schools. Furthermore, every attempt is made to situate these authentic activities within environmental circumstances and surroundings that are present while engaged in these activities outside of schools. However, these contexts are practice fields, and, as such, there is clearly a separation in time, setting, and activity from them and from the life for which the activity is preparation.

Problem-based learning (PBL) is an example of one approach to creating practice fields. In the medical profession, where PBL began and is still most pervasive, the students are presented with real, historical patient cases to diagnose (Hmelo & Evenson, in press; Koschmann, Kelson, Feltovich, & Barrows, 1996). Problem-based learning has extended well beyond the medical profession to elementary and secondary schools, business schools (Milter & Stinson, 1995), higher education (Savery & Duffy, 1996), and a host of other instructional areas. In all of these instances, the goal is to present the students with real societal, business, or educational problems. The PBL approach differs from studying cases in that the students are responsible for developing their own position on the issue (their solution to the problem), rather than studying someone else's solution. Thus, they are engaged as if they were in the real world working on this problem.

Anchored instruction, as represented in the work of the Cognition Technology Group at Vanderbilt (CTGV, 1990, 1993), is another approach to creating practice fields. As with PBL, the goal is to capture a real problem and the context for that problem from the real world. However, in anchored instruction, there is no pretense that this is an existing problem for the students. Rather, learners are invited to engage in a fictitious problem. In the *Jasper Woodbury* Series, rich and realistic video contexts are used to present information relevant to working on the problem. For example, in "Escape from Boone's Meadow," the students must buy into the fact that they are helping to save the eagle in the video, and in "A Capital Idea," they must adopt the idea that they are helping the students at the school develop a fall festival booth[4]. It is only when students own these problems that they will be engaged in the same form of problem solving in which people in the video would engage. Of course, the method of gathering evidence and the range of distractions are considerably different from these practices in the real world. But indeed, in terms of solving the specific problems—developing the most efficient strategy for retrieving the eagle or maximizing profits from the booth at the fair—the students are engaged in solving ill-structured problems.

Cognitive apprenticeship is another approach to conceptualizing and designing practice fields (Collins, Brown, & Newman, 1989). The cognitive apprenticeship framework emphasizes learning at the elbows of experts; that is, experts are present to coach and model the cognitive activity. In reciprocal teaching (Palincsar & Brown, 1984), for example, the teacher and learner take turns in the roles of student and teacher as they seek to understand a text. Or, in the work of Schoenfeld (1996), the expert thinks aloud as he or she works through a novel problem and then reflects with the students on the strategies used and the paths followed.

Design of Practice Fields

The design of practice fields has received extensive attention during the 1990s (Barab, Hay, et al., in press; Barab & Landa, 1997; Cognition and Technology Group at Vanderbilt, 1990, 1993; Duffy & Jonassen, 1992; Duffy, Lowyck, & Jonassen, 1992; Edwards, 1995; Hannafin, Hall, Land, & Hill, 1994; Hmelo & Emerson, in press; Kommers, Grabinger, & Dunlap, 1996; Koschmann, 1996; Roth, 1996, 1998; Roth & Bowen, 1995; Savery & Duffy, 1996; Wilson, 1996; Young & Barab, 1999). There also have been numerous lists of principles for design since Resnick's (1987) contribution. In the following sections, we summarize the design principles.

Doing Domain-Related Practices. Learners must be actively doing domain-related practices, not listening to the experiences or findings of others as summarized in texts or by teachers. The notion of an active learner has its roots in the work of Dewey (1938) who advocated for learning by doing.

Schoenfeld (1996) prompted learning theorists to think further about the nature of this doing by considering whether students are engaged in performance dilemmas (such as getting a good grade) or domain-related dilemmas (such as finding a cure for cancer). The latter situations give rise to a more authentic appreciation for, and understanding of, the content being learned.

Ownership of the Inquiry. The students must be given and must assume ownership for the dilemma and the development of a resolution. That is, they must see it as a real dilemma worth investing their efforts in, and they must see their efforts as geared toward a solution that makes a difference (not a school solution). Furthermore, students must feel they are responsible for the solution. If they seek a solution from the teacher or a solution the teacher wants, they will not be engaged in the sorts of thinking in the domain that they would be engaged in outside of schools (Savery & Duffy, 1996; Schoenfeld, 1996).

Coaching and Modeling of Thinking Skills. The teacher's role is not solely that of a content expert but rather a learning and problem-solving expert. Hence, the teacher's job is to coach and model learning and problem solving by asking questions that students should be asking themselves. This is not directive but rather participatory; it is based not on moving to the right answer but rather on the questions an expert problem-solver would be asking him or herself (Savery & Duffy, 1996; Schoenfeld, 1996). In part, it is the availability of coaching and modeling as well as other scaffolding (see Duffy and Cunningham, 1996), including support for reflective activities, that distinguishes practice fields from those situations in which individuals are simply doing the job[5].

Opportunity for Reflection. Too often when individuals are engaged in work they simply do not have the opportunity to reflect on what they are doing, going to do, or what they have done. The time demands are such that they must move forward, understanding just enough to permit progress in resolving the dilemma. However, in a practice field, opportunity for reflection must be central; indeed, it should be central in the work environment as well. It provides individuals the opportunity to think about why they are doing what they are doing and even to gather evidence to evaluate the efficacy of their moves. Reflecting on the experience afterward (debriefing in the terminology of business) provides the opportunity to correct misconceptions and fill in where understanding was inadequate. The reflective process—an active, rigorous, and analytic process—is essential to the quality of learning (Clift, Houston, & Pugach, 1990; Schön, 1987).

Dilemmas are Ill-Structured. The dilemmas in which learners are engaged must either be ill-defined or defined loosely enough so that students can impose their own problem frames (Roth, 1996; Savery & Duffy, 1996). It is only with ill-defined dilemmas that students can own the problems and the process. When working with an ill-defined problem, the quality of the solution depends on the quality of the effort in the domain. It is always possible to work a little longer in an attempt to develop a different rationale for a solution, or a more detailed solution, or to consider better alternatives. It is in this inquiry into ill-structured dilemmas that ownership and learning occurs.

Support the Learner Rather than Simplify the Dilemma. The dilemma students encounter should reflect the complexity of the thinking and work they are expected to be able to do outside of the school context when this learning is completed. That is, the problem presented must be a real problem. Students should not start with simplified, unrealistic problems because this would not be reflective of a practice field but rather would reflect the more traditional building-blocks approach to instruction characteristic of the representational perspective. Scaffolding is meant to support the learner in working in the practice field by providing the learner with the necessary support to undertake complex problems that, otherwise, would be beyond his or her current zone or proximal development (Duffy & Cunningham, 1996; Vygotsky, 1978).

Work is Collaborative and Social. Meaning is a process of continual negotiation. The quality and depth of this negotiation and understanding can only be determined in a social environment. That is, individuals can see if their understanding can accommodate the issues and views of others and see if there are points of view that they can usefully incorporate into their understanding (Bereiter, 1994; see also Chap. 5 and Chap. 8, this volume). The importance of a learning community where ideas are discussed and understandings are enriched is critical to the design of effective practice fields (Scardamalia & Bereiter, 1993).

The Learning Context is Motivating. In the educational environment, students cannot be allowed to only pursue problems that arise in their lives naturally; that is, learning issues cannot be solely self-determined. Rather, there is some need to introduce students to communities and issues or problems that engage that community. In doing so, researchers are faced with the problem of bringing the issue home to the learner (Barrows & Myers, 1993). That is, dilemmas brought to the attention of the learner are seldom engaging in and of themselves. The students must be introduced to the context of the problem and its relevance, and this must be done in a way that challenges and engages the student. The importance of being challenged and engaged has a long history in education (Cordova & Lepper, 1996; Dweck & Leggett, 1988) and psychology (Csikszentmihalyi, 1990).

EXTENDING THE PARTICIPATION METAPHOR: PRACTICE COMMUNITIES

Clearly, the design of practice fields, as defined previously, addresses the differences between in-school learning and out-of-school learning presented

by Resnick (1987). In these contexts, learners are working in teams with concrete artifacts and examples as they address contextualized problems. The
design of practice fields is consistent with the implications of situativity
theory forwarded by many psychologists and is consistent with much of the
work being carried out by us. More generally, this view has certainly pushed
many educators' understanding of learning and cognition beyond representational views in suggesting to them a new contextualized emphasis to education. However, the practices that the learner engages in are still school tasks
abstracted from the community, and this has important implications for the
meaning and type of practices being learned, as well as for the individual's
relations to those meanings and practices.

With respect to the practices themselves, the cultural context of schools
all too often emphasizes learning and grades, not participation and use, and
the identity being developed is one of student in school, not contributing
member of the community who uses and values the content being taught.
Lave and Wenger (1991) argued that:

> there are vast differences between the ways high school physics stu-
> dents participate in and give meaning to their activity and the way pro-
> fessional physicists do. The actual reproducing community of practice,
> within which schoolchildren learn about physics, is not the commu-
> nity of physicists but the community of schooled adults... [As such]
> problems of schooling are not, at their most fundamental level, peda-
> gogical. Above all, they have to do with the ways in which the com-
> munity of adults reproduces itself, with the places that newcomers can
> or cannot find in such communities, and with relations that can or
> cannot be established between these newcomers and the cultural and
> political life of the community. (pp. 99-100)

From this perspective, the main problem of practice fields is that they
occur in schools rather than in the community through schools. This creates
a bracketing off of the learning context from the social world through which
the practices being learned are of value and of use. If interactions with the
world produce meaning and identity, then educators need to place more
emphasis on the types of interactions and, hence, the identities are being created within the context of schools. Instead of a culture emphasizing the contribution of the activity to the community, all too frequently school culture
accords knowledgeable skill a reified existence, commodifying it, and turning
knowledge into something to be acquired.

To clarify, when official channels only offer possibilities to participate
in institutionally mandated forms of commoditized activity, children
develop identities in relation to their ability to engage in these commoditized
activities directed toward the production of grades (Walkerdine, 1997). For
some students, good students, this helps enculturate them into the identity of
a successful student (all too frequently associated with being a nerd), but for
many others this context results in the "widespread generation of negative
identities [under achievers, failures]," as well as the emergence of "institu-

tionally disapproved interstitial communities of practice [burnouts, trouble makers]" (Lave, 1993, pp. 78-79). Indeed, despite the school emphasis on curriculum and discipline, it is frequently the relations to these noncurricular communities of practice that are the most personally transformative (Wenger, 1998).

Although practice fields do not fully decontextualize the learning activities or the outcomes (i.e., there is a focus on more than simply the achievement of a grade), the activities are nonetheless divorced from their contribution to society — they are practice, not contributions. Hence, even here there is a decomposition of the activity, with the societal contribution (from which societal identity and the meaning of the activity develop) separated from the activity itself. Although this does not necessarily result in the production of negative identities, it also does not create an opportunity for membership in the community of practitioners. It is in response to these concerns that many educators are looking toward communities as an arena for learning. However, as researchers, we are still in our infancy with respect to understanding the potential of, and what constitutes, a community. Although Lave (1993, 1997; Lave & Wenger, 1991) has brought the most focused attention to the concept of communities of practice, this has been done through an anthropological perspective, with an examination of practices in everyday society and not environments intentionally designed to support learning (see Chapter 7, this volume).

There have been numerous efforts to introduce the concept of community into educational practice. For example, Brown and Campione (1990) proposed the design of communities of learners and thinkers, Lipman (1988) offered communities of inquiry, Scardamalia and Bereiter (1993) advanced knowledge building communities, the Cognition and Technology Group at Vanderbilt (see Barron et al., 1995) proposed learning communities, and Roth (1998) suggested communities of practice. However, examining these "community" efforts, we are not convinced that they do in fact capture the essence of *development of self through participation in a community*. Indeed, most appear to be in the realm of practice fields. It is for this reason that we want to reemphasize the importance of the development of the self, and the importance of legitimate participation as part of a community in the development of that self. We seek to promote an appreciation for the limitations of the practice field approach and to establish the strategic direction of making legitimate participation in the community an integral part of meeting our educational goals.

To summarize thus far, being a participant in a community is an essential component of the educational process, and the community that is most clearly evident in schools is that of schooled adults, not professional practitioners who use the practices being learned. If educators move toward a learning-as-participating-in-community approach, what communities are included? Is this a trade school or professional school approach? How can the breadth of learning experiences be provided that our children need if they must be members of all of the communities in order to have the necessary experiences? It sounds beyond what can be managed in even a dramatic and systemic restructuring. It is with these questions in mind that we turn to a more in-depth discussion of communities of practice and their characteristics.

Characteristics of Communities of Practice

Lave and Wenger (1991) coined the term communities of practice, to capture the importance of activity in binding individuals to communities and of communities to legitimizing individual practices. Roughly, a community of practice involves a collection of individuals sharing mutually defined practices, beliefs, and understandings over an extended time frame in the pursuit of a shared enterprise (Wenger, 1998). Roth (1998) suggested that these communities "are identified by the common tasks members engage in and the associated practices and resources, unquestioned background assumptions, common sense, and mundane reason they share" (p. 10). Lave and Wenger defined a community of practice in the following manner:

> [Community does not] imply necessarily co-presence, a well-defined identifiable group, or socially visible boundaries. It does imply participation in an activity system about which participants share understandings concerning what they are doing and what that means in their lives and for their communities. (p. 98)

Just what is a community and what characteristics of the community—of an individual's participation in a community—are relevant to the educational process? Predicated on research in fields such as anthropology, education, and sociology, we found the following features to be consistently present and, we would argue, requisite of communities (see Table 2.2): a common cultural and historical heritage, including shared goals, negotiated meanings, and practices; an interdependent system, in that individuals are becoming a part of something larger than themselves; and a reproduction cycle, through which newcomers can become old timers and through which the community can maintain itself.

Common Cultural and Historical Heritage. A community has a significant history, a common cultural and historical heritage. This heritage includes the shared goals, belief systems, and collective stories that capture canonical practice. These shared experiences come to constitute a collective knowledge base that is continually negotiated anew through each interaction.

The negotiation of meaning is a productive process, but negotiating meaning is not constructing it from scratch. Meaning is not pre-existing, but neither is it simply made up. Negotiated meaning is at once both historical and dynamic, contextual and unique. Wenger (1998, p. 54).

When learning as part of a community of practice, the learner has access to this history of previous negotiations as well as responsiveness from the current context on the functional value of a particular meaning.

TABLE 2.2. Characteristics of a Community.

Common Cultural and Historical Heritage	Communities go beyond the simple coming together for a particular moment in response to a specific need. Successful communities have a common cultural and historical heritage that partially captures the socially negotiated meanings. This includes shared goals, meanings, and practices. However, unlike the social negotiation of practice fields that primarily occurs on the fly, in communities of practice new members inherit much of these goals, meanings, and practices from previous community members' experiences in which they were hypothesized, tested, and socially agreed on.
Interdependent System	Individuals are a part of something larger as they work within the context and become interconnected to the community, which is also a part of something larger (the society through which it has meaning or value). This helps provide a sense of shared purpose, as well as an identity, for the individual and the larger community.
Reproduction Cycle	It is important that communities have the ability to reproduce as new members engage in mature practice with near peers and exemplars of mature practice. Over time, these newcomers come to embody the communal practice (and rituals) and may even replace old timers.

Of course, practice fields are designed to support the development of shared goals, understandings, and practices among those collaborators working on a particular problem or issue. The contrast, however, is in the embeddedness of the experiences in the community and the impact of that larger experiential context on the development of self. For example, it is through stories (narratives) that community members pass on casual accounts of their experiences to replace the impoverished descriptions frequently codified in manuals and texts. Through this telling and retelling, individuals do more than pass on knowledge. They contribute to the construction of their own identity in relationship to the community of practice and, reciprocally, to the construction and development of the community of which they are a part (Brown & Duguid, 1991).

It is also through this heritage that communities find legitimacy. When individuals become legitimate members of the community, they inherit this common heritage, which becomes intertwined with the their identities as community members. This is a central component in the development of self. Individuals develop a sense of self in relation to a community of practice, and this can only arise by enculturation into the history of the community. They do not develop a sense of self as scientist simply by engaging in scientific problems but rather through engagement in the discourse of the scientific community and in the context of the values of that community as they become members of the community (Bereiter, 1994; 1997). Through participation in a practice field or even as a peripheral participant to a community of practice, rules and behavior expectations may feel arbitrary, artificial, and even unnecessary. However, through participation in the community over time, an individual comes to accept the historical context and the importance of socially negotiated norms for defining community and his or her own identity. It is only through extended participation in a community that this history and, hence, a sense of self, can develop.

Interdependent System. Most community members view themselves as part of something larger. It is this part of something larger that allows the various members to form a collective whole as they work towards the joint goals of the community and its members. A community is an interdependent system in terms of the collaborative efforts of its members, as well as in terms of the greater societal systems in which it is nested. Being a member entails being involved in a fundamental way within this dynamic system (the community), which is continually redefined by the actions of its members (Barab, Cherkes-Julkowski, Swenson, Garrett, & Shaw, 1999). In other words, the individual and the community constitute nested interactive networks, with individuals transforming and maintaining the community as they appropriate its practices (Lemke, 1997; Rogoff, 1990), and the community transforms and maintains the individual by making available opportunities for appropriation and, eventually, enculturation (Reed, 1991). "Education and learning, from this perspective, involve taking part and being a part, and both of these expressions signalize that learning should be viewed as a process of becoming a part of a greater whole" (Sfard, 1998, p. 6).

It is through this legitimate participation in the greater community, and the community's legitimate participation in society, that communities and identities are formed. These practices, including the adoption of particular goals, belief systems, and cognitions, are ordinarily framed and valued by this greater community, and it is through the carrying out of these practices that an individual binds himself to this community. It is also in this way that learning comes to involve the building of relationships with other community members, with tools and practices, with those outcomes valued by society, and with oneself.

> Our activity, our participation, our "cognition" is always bound up with, codependent with, the participation and the activity of Others, be they persons, tools, symbols, processes, or things. How we participate, what practices we come to engage in, is a function of the whole community ecology... As we participate, we change. Our identity-in-practice develops, for we are no longer autonomous Persons in this model, but Persons-in-Activity. Lemke (1997, p. 38)

However, it is not just the community members who are a part of something larger. The community itself functions within a broader societal role that gives it, and the practices of the community members, meaning and purpose. If the community isolates itself from the societal systems of which it is a part, then both the individuals and the community become weaker—this relationship to other communities and the products they offer society have proven to be a central challenge for Amish and Mennonite communities, for example. "This interdependent perspective prevents communities, from small families to nations, from becoming worlds unto themselves" (Shaffer & Anundsen, 1993, p. 12). This interdependent perspective also prevents individuals from becoming worlds unto themselves. With each newly appropriated practice, individuals become more central to (constitutive of) the community and, in a fundamental way, develop self—a self that is partly constituted by their participation and membership in the community of practice.

Reproduction Cycle. Lastly, a community is constantly reproducing itself such that new members contribute, support and eventually lead the community into the future (see also Chapter 8, this volume). Communities are continually replicating themselves, with new members moving from peripheral participant to core member through a process of enculturation (Lave & Wenger, 1991). It is this line of thinking that led to Lave and Wenger's (1991) discussion of legitimate peripheral participation in which the primary motivation for learning involves participating in authentic activities and creating an identity that moves an individual toward becoming more centripetal to a community of practice. In this line of thinking, developing an identity as a member of the community and becoming able to engage in the practices of the community are one and the same (Lave, 1993; Wenger, 1998)[6].

Reproducibility, in which newcomers are able to become central to and expand the community, is essential if the community is to have a common cultural heritage. It is a process that is continually occurring in all communities of practice. Simply consider the experiences of academics: Students apprentice with teachers, working closely at their elbows. However, students tend to remain apprentices, seeing the world through the teachers' eyes and remaining as peripheral participants. Eventually, when they must teach others, when they must fill the role of old timers, they enter a new level of learning and begin to expand the thinking of the community of which they are a part. They come to mentor junior faculty in the research process and in teaching. They continue to learn this process and, perhaps more importantly, grow more confident in their contributions to the community and in their sense of self in the community. During this process, they appropriate and contribute to the negotiation and reification of meanings. It is through this cycle that a community of practice and the individuals that constitute the community reproduce and define themselves.

It is also these reproduction cycles that define learning. In other words, the social and physical structure that defines and is defined by this cycle defines the possibilities, and what is considered legitimate participation, for learning. In fact, for Lave and Wenger (1991), legitimate peripheral participation is learning. Any discussions of learning, therefore, must begin within a community of practice and must consider the individual's position with respect to the hierarchical trajectory of the social and power structures of that community. Assumedly, and ignoring other social and political obstacles, it is this position in relation to the community trajectory from novice to expert that defines a particular member's ability with respect to community practices. And, "because the place of knowledge is within a community of practice, questions of learning must be addressed within the developmental cycles of that community" (Lave & Wenger, 1991, p. 100). It is in understanding how educators have supported the emergence of community trajectories and have developed scaffolds to support learners in participating in movement along these trajectories that we now move from practice fields to communities of practice.

MOVING FROM PRACTICE FIELDS TO COMMUNITIES OF PRACTICE

Our notion of practice fields and our notion of communities of practice have much in common, and their creation can be guided by some similar learning principles. For example, both of these contexts move away from the criticisms leveled at in-school learning by Resnick (1987). Specifically, her criticism that in schools there is frequently an isolated learner engaged in unaided thought using symbols that frequently have no direct connection to any real-world particulars. In contrast, while working in practice fields and in communities of practice, students are usually working collaboratively and with concrete referentials (signifieds) so that they may address contextualized problems. Further, central to both these learning contexts is the opportunity for students to actively engage in negotiating meanings through practice.

Despite of these similarities, there are also some important differences (see Table 2.1). For example, learning through participation in practice fields frequently involves students working collaboratively in a temporary (as opposed to a sustained and continuously reproducing) coming together of people (as opposed to a community of practitioners with a substantial history) around a particular task (as opposed to a shared enterprise that cuts across multiple tasks considered to be the workings of the community). Of prime importance in distinguishing practice fields from community learning contexts are whether there exists a sustainable community with a significant history to become enculturated into, including shared goals, beliefs, practices and a collection of experiences; whether individuals and the community into which they are becoming enculturated are a part of something larger; and whether there is an opportunity to move along a trajectory in the presence of, and become a member alongside, near peers and exemplars of mature practice—moving from peripheral participant to core member.

It is these three characteristics, which we suggest are central to communities of practice, that determine whether there is an opportunity for learning and building identities through legitimate peripheral participation. These differences intimate the importance of supporting the emergence of communities with meaningful trajectories of participation or, at the very least, that connect learners into existing communities. Previously, we mentioned the work of the CTGV and medical fields as examples of practice fields. In this section, we continue to examine examples to illuminate characteristics of, and differences between, practice fields and communities of practice.

The SMART Project. The work of the CTGV illustrates the movement from the design of practice fields to the attempt to develop a community of practice. The early work (CTGV, 1990; 1993) focused on video-based macrocontexts intended to overcome inert knowledge by anchoring learning within the context of meaningful problem-solving activities. In contrast to the disconnected sets of application problems located at the end of textbook chapters, macrocontexts refer to stories that take place in semantically rich, open-ended environments. In these anchored macrocontexts, students begin with a higher-order problem and then use top-down strategies to generate the necessary subgoals to reach the final state. This top-down processing helps students learn the lower level skills (i.e., mathematical algorithms and facts) in a manner that also gives them insights into the relationships between the skills being learned and the reciprocal opportunities for using them. Anchors "allow students who are relative novices in an area to experience some of the advantages available to experts when they are trying to learn new information about their area" (CTGV, 1992, p. 294).

These learn`g environments nicely illustrate the design of practice fields. However, hrough the Special Multimedia Arenas for Refining Thinking (SMART) project, the CTGV extended engagement with the problems and broke the isolation of the classroom with a learning community of 100 students (Barron et al., 1995). This project, using the *Jasper* videodisc problems and a series of video programs, linked classrooms to each other and to the Vanderbilt community. The CTGV developed four Challenge programs composed of four segments called Smart Lab, Roving Reporter, Toolbox, and the Challenge. These segments were designed to link up the participating classrooms, grounding discussions with actual student data and video clips collected by the roving reporter as he went out to the various classrooms. At the end of the show, as a culminating event, students attempted the Big Challenge in which a problem was shown live on the local Public Broadcasting System (PBS) television station. Students in the learning community were expected to call in answers to the problems, and then their answers were summarized and shown at the end of the program for students to see.

The SMART program clearly moves closer to our notion of community than the isolated *Jasper* videos. Students are, to some degree, developing a socially negotiated knowledge and practice base. Through the Roving Reporter, they are able to share stories about their experiences. Individuals are, to some degree, becoming a part of something larger as they see themselves and their peers as well as an expert problem solver engaged in solving the

Jasper series episodes. However, the problems are contrived and not neces-sarily addressing a real-world need, undermining the legitimacy of the com-munity in terms of its interdependence with society. Further, the community itself has little common heritage. This, again, potentially limits the legiti-macy of the students' experience in terms of being a part of something larger. Additionally, the community is formed only for the duration of the project and will not continue to reproduce. As a consequence, there is little move-ment over time in terms of becoming more central to the core.

In sum, although the SMART project moves toward a community concept, the key elements for the development of self in a community are absent. The project is still a school project—it does not link to or contribute to the needs of society or the ongoing needs of the community itself. The stu-dents are not playing a role in society and hence do not develop a sense of their identity in society. They are not making a lasting contribution and are not developing a sense of the history of the community and all that implies. Rather, their community is a temporary one, beginning and ending with the task (or set of tasks), much as with practice fields. The SMART project does, however, provide a richer set of perspectives and a greater motivational con-text for the students to assume ownership of the task. Again, these are charac-teristics of practice fields.

Community of Learners. During the 1990s, Brown and Campione (Brown & Campione, 1990; Brown et al., 1994) have been engineering communities of learners. Central to this work has been the use of reciprocal teaching and jig-saw methods to engage students in collaborative work. The reciprocal teach-ing approach begins with the teacher modeling and coaching students in the various skills they will be expected to teach. It involves students adopting the role of a teacher as they appropriate their practices by watching more experi-enced peers and teachers model the learning process. The approach is termed reciprocal teaching because the teacher and students alternate playing the role of the teacher and student.

The jigsaw method, in contrast, involves students working collabora-tively and developing expertise on one component of a larger task. Then, once they have mastered their component, they use the reciprocal teaching method to share what they have learned with other group members. Using these techniques, they are able to develop repetitive structures in the class-room so that students can gain mastery over the approaches as they perceive themselves developing mastery over time. Students participate in a research cycle lasting approximately 10 weeks. These cycles begin with a teacher or vis-iting expert who introduces a unit and a benchmark lesson, stressing the big picture and how the various topics can be interrelated to form a jigsaw. Stu-dents then spend the majority of the time in the research-and-teach part of the cycle. Over time, the distributed expertise begins to emerge as students be-come more competent in their sections. In addition to face-to-face interac-tions, students can use e-mail to communicate with the wider community as well as with each other. The teacher models this practice over the course of the research cycle. At the completion of the unit, students conduct full recip-rocal teaching sessions in groups where each child is an expert on one fifth of the topic material. Two features central to communities of learners are dis-tributed expertise (integral to the jigsaw method) and mutual appropria-tion—mutual in the sense that experts appropriate student understandings in addition to students appropriating the practices and thinking of experts.

Brown et al. (1994) discussed a classroom ethos in which there is an atmosphere of individual responsibility coupled with communal sharing. There is an atmosphere of respect in which students' questions are taken seri-ously and students listen to one another. They also develop a community of discourse, in which "meaning is negotiated and renegotiated as members of the community develop and share expertise. The group comes to construct new understandings, developing a common mind and common voice" (p. 200). The final aspect is that of ritual, in which participation frameworks are few and practiced repeatedly so that students develop expertise. "The repeti-tive, indeed ritualistic, nature of these activities is an essential aspect of the classroom, for it enables children to make the transition from one participant structure ... to another quickly and effortlessly (pp. 200-201).

In our mind, although the community of learners classrooms and the principles for community they present are exemplary, they more completely reflect the design of practice fields rather than the concept of communities that we are forwarding. There is little difference between this communities of learners project and problem-based learning (Barrows & Myers, 1993; Savery & Duffy, 1996) or any project-based environment where students are expected to learn collaboratively. Again, we see great value in the design of practice fields, and Brown et al. (1994) provided an excellent example of strategies for creating practice fields in the lower grades.

However, our goal in this section is to examine communities of prac-tice occurring in schools in order to explore the implications of community for the design of learning environments. That is, how can instructional designers facilitate the emergence of learning environments that engage stu-dents as legitimate peripheral participants in a community, so that they develop their self in relation to society? The students that Brown et al. (1994) discussed were not engaged in tasks that contribute to a community that has a heritage or that guides practice, nor is there a community that is larger than the classroom and task. Of course, the student is developing a sense of self as a learner in school and as a collaborator in school tasks and as a teacher of text information. However, we question the advantages (beyond other practice fields) of having students teach other kids or of bringing in experts to set up a particular context when the learning occurs within the classroom context in relation to a classroom-defined task. The goal of participation in community is to develop a sense of self in relation to society—a society outside of the classroom. We are not convinced that this occurs in the communities of learners project.

NGS Kids Network and Teleapprenticeships.   The National Geographic Kids Network, a collaborative effort between TERC and the National Geographic Society, is one example of a growing number of telecommunications projects that involve students in real world projects and link them to experts and other students around the world in scientific or social research. The focus in Kids Network is on socially relevant scientific issues like acid rain and solar energy.

The projects have the following design principles: students can explore real and engaging scientific problems that have an important social context; students do the work and engage in the discourse of scientists; and the science is done collaboratively using telecommunications to link the students with others outside of their school (Tinker, 1996). Additionally, students have contact with scientists who help to interpret student-collected data and to present findings to the community. These presentations have the potential to become more than parents' night displays of student work, because students are talking about issues relevant to the community, and they have a rich scientific database from which to draw their conclusions.

Bradsher and Hogan (1995), two National Geographic Society (NGS) project personnel, describe the Kids Network curriculum as follows: "Students pose and research questions about their local community, form hypotheses, collect data through experiments, and analyze results. The answers are largely unknown in advance, and the findings are of interest beyond the classroom." (p. 39). Although the curriculum is considerably more structured than these descriptions suggest and the findings more prescriptive (Hunter, 1990; Karlan, Huberman, & Middlebrooks, 1997), the approach nonetheless holds potential for engaging students in real scientific problems and real scientific discourse with other students and scientists.

The Kids Network curriculum, begun in 1989, consists of 8 week curriculum units designed for fourth through sixth graders. Ten geographically dispersed classrooms (including classrooms in other countries) are linked by the Kids Network personnel to form a research team. The students begin by reading about the curriculum area (e.g., acid rain) and discussing the issue in relation to their community. The 10 classes work as a team, negotiating the approach to the research issues based on the local interests (relevance to their community) of each group. This allows for ownership and legitimacy, as well as support for the process of interdependency and social negotiation whereby groups make global comparisons. The students develop data collection tools and collect samples from their community, with experts from Kids Network available to discuss issues or offer guidance. The data is collected and submitted to Kids Network staff where it is integrated across sites. Data summaries are prepared, along with the interpretation of the data by a scientist, the latter serving to model the way scientists think (Bradsher & Hogan, 1995). The data is then sent to the classrooms. The students complete the lesson by making their own interpretation of the data, drawing conclusions relevant to the community, and preparing a presentation of the findings to a community audience.

There is considerable potential for extending the curriculum unit.   As one teacher noted, "learning extends into other lessons.   For language arts, students write letters to their teammates; for science they may look at ecosystems; for science and geography they use a dynamic mapping tool" (Bradsher & Hogan, 1995, p. 40).   Student teams can also conduct additional experiments, collecting data on related issues and extending the web of inference. Thus, Kids Network provides a framework, and the communication technology provides the opportunity for collaboration with peers and experts on socially relevant issues. The Kids Network curriculum has been widely adopted, with more than a 250,000 children from 49 different countries involved (Tinker, 1996). But, as we noted, it is only representative of a growing number of teleapprentice projects (Hunter, 1990). Two additional efforts, briefly described, follow.

INSITE.   This project was a joint effort among eight school districts, two universities, the Indianapolis Children's Museum, and local industry. Buchanan, Rush, and Bloede (as cited in Hunter, 1990) described the goal as not creating textbook science lessons, but creating lessons that reflect current areas of concern and real world issues. Students pose questions to the scientists (via the network) and develop cooperative experiments that require students to contact other students in the various schools.   As described, this project involves students working and thinking at the elbows of experts in real world contexts.

I*EARN.   Copen (1995) described the I*EARN telecommunications environment as establishing a global network, allowing "K-12 students to work on joint social and environmental projects concerning issues of international importance"(p. 44).   The focus is on international linkages.   Hence, classes from around the world are paired in environmental, community development, and service projects linked to their curricular goals. Clearly, the students in these projects are making significant contributions to society through their work. The practices in schools have become practices of consulting,, where children can find support for their work in society. They are part of something larger—the larger community of scientists studying environmental issues and the other newcomers (other classes) to the community. And there is a heritage—the databases from their project as well as other projects.

Community of Teachers.   The community of teachers (CoT) is a professional development program at Indiana University, Bloomington for preservice teachers working toward teacher certification. It is highly field-based in that each participant is expected to commit to one school where he or she will do all of her fieldwork. Preservice teachers are not assigned to a teacher but rather spend time visiting the classes of and talking with teachers who are a part of the program. An apprentice relationship is formed with one of the teachers based on a social negotiation and a mutual determination that the relationship will be beneficial. Hence, each student is paired with a mentor teacher in their first year in the program and continues to work with that teacher for the duration.

Similarly, each student negotiates membership in a community of students who are studying to be teachers. They join an ongoing community and remain a part of that community for the duration of their study. Students in the community attend seminars together, and, as with any community, there are wizened veterans (seniors or students with teaching experience), new comers (sophomores), and levels between, mixed together in a common endeavor.

The CoT program was designed to allow students to fulfill their individual requirements for certification by becoming a part of a community. The emphasis is not on grades but on participation: "Students achieve a teaching license, not by accumulating credits and grades, but by collecting evidence that they, indeed, possess 30 qualities of good teachers that are described in CoT's Program Expectations" (Gregory, 1993, p. 1).

The CoT is founded on six principles. First is the notion of community and its goal is to bring a heterogeneous collection of individuals together around a shared goal. The second principle, personalization, has to do with students being able to own their part in becoming good teachers. Students are also participating in apprenticeships, working alongside an in-service teacher and other more competent peers. The program involves intensive fieldwork, with students spending approximately one full day each week with their mentor teacher. Students are engaged in authentic performance with the certificate predicated on their ability to accumulate a body of evidence that indicates their capacity to teach in a school. Lastly, there is a democratic governance with each member having the opportunity to propose a change in the program's operation that will be put to a vote.

The program involves a core seminar run by the students at all stages of preparation (from newcomer to student teacher) and supported by a university professor. The community has about 15 members who meet once a week for 3 hours to discuss readings, expectations, and work in the schools. Students take turns leading various seminars, planning presentations, bringing information to the group, and leading discussions related to teaching and learning. Over the course of the semester, various issues du jour that students are facing in the classroom are discussed. In addition to the weekly seminars, students communicate through electronic mail and the telephone. Over time, students graduate and move on, and beginning teachers enter the community. Further, many former students, now teachers working nearby, return to share their experiences with the current community of teachers.

In the CoT program, students are continually negotiating goals and meanings of the community as well as the profession. Further, there is a growing collection of personal narratives that come to embody the canonical practices of the community, and students have developed a shared language to describe particular group practices (e.g., issue du jour) and group members (e.g., grizzled veterans, T. Gregory, personal communication, July 7, 1998).

The community has a tradition and heritage (7 years going) at Indiana University that captures much of the community's understandings. This heritage is continually developed and inherited by members as they become a part of the CoT program. The community also has a trajectory that extends across multiple classrooms and multiple occasions. Individuals view themas becoming a part of the CoT as well as the communities (those formed by in-service teachers) in which the project is nested. Lastly, the community continually reproduces itself as rolling cohorts cycle from newcomers to grizzled veterans to graduated students (working teachers).

Both KidsNet and CoT characterize the sorts of communities that schools can foster and support. There is an historical context for the activity, a history of experience to be used[7], and the results of the activity (and hence the learner or doer) contribute to the community. It is this context that keeps not only the learning but also the overall activity from being an end in and of itself, that is, a commodity. As such, participants develop a sense of self in their work in society — not simply in the work of being a student. Practices are not just performances but meaningful actions, "actions that have relations of meaning to one another in terms of some cultural system" (Lemke, 1997, p. 43). In this sense, students learn not just what and how to carry out a set of practices but the meaning of the performance. This understanding is central to becoming a full member of the community. The fact that students have full access to the practices and outcomes, as well as a legitimate role in the functioning of the community, helps to overcome the alienation of students from the full experiences, or what Lave (1997) refers to as the "widespread generation of negative identities." It is for the aforementioned reasons that we view these as exemplary models of building communities of practice in schools.

CONCLUSIONS AND IMPLICATIONS

In this chapter, we have adopted a perspective of situativity theory in which meaning as well as identities are constructed within interactions. The construction of these meanings and identities is greatly influenced by the broader context in which they reside. This perspective expands previous notions of constructivism in which it was the subjective world, not the individual constructor, that was bracketed off and treated as that which was being constructed. It also expands notions of situativity theory in which, again, it was the meaning of that which was learned, and not the individual doing the learning, that was described as constituted in the situation. Instead, the perspective forwarded in this chapter is intended to couple individual and environment, and thereby move beyond dualistic treatments, treating both as constituted by and constituting the other—that is, to establish an ecology of learning (Barab, 1999; Barab, Cherkes-Julkowski, et al., 1999). Predicated on this assumption, we explored the notion of the communities of practice as an arena for learning that can be integrated into the practices of schools.

One difficulty with schools is that they frequently do not practice what they preach. They teach about practices of other communities but provide students with only limited access to these external communities. As such, experience is commoditized, and learners are alienated from full experiences, resulting in the bracketing off of academic performance and identity formation in relation to this performance (Lave, 1997; Lemke, 1997; Walkerdine, 1997). One attempt to address these limitations of school learning, as well as the abstract, decontextualized, and individualistic nature of school learning, is to design practice fields. In practice fields, students work as part of activity groups as they investigate and engage in practices that are consistent with the methods of real world practitioners. Although practice fields address some of the criticisms leveled at school learning (see Resnick, 1987), they still treat knowledge as a commodity and fail to connect learners to a greater identity (i.e., a member of a community).

Lave and Wenger (1991) described a community focus as a focus on "the development of knowledgeable skill and identity—the production of persons...[resulting from]... long-term, living relations between persons and their place and participation in the communities of practice"[8] (pp. 52-53). As such, there is not a separation between the development of identity and the development of knowledgeable skill. Both reciprocally interact through a process of legitimate peripheral participation within the context of a community of practice.

This is a considerable shift in focus from the design of practice fields—a shift from a focus on the activity of an individual in a collaborative environment to a focus on the connections an individual has with the community and the patterns of participation in the community. It is not that a sense of self does not or cannot develop in practice fields. If successfully designed (especially in terms of developing learner ownership), the practice field not only supports the development of specific skills but offers the individual the opportunity to assess his or her competencies and motivation for that kind of work. Similarly, it contributes to a sense of self, as all experiences do. However, there is something more to membership in a community; something beyond the temporary collaborative environment of a practice field. Lave (1993) described how formal learning environments (i.e., schools) tend to commodify knowledge and learning:

> The products of human labor are turned into commodities when they cease to be made for the value of their use in the lives of their maker and are produced in order to exchange them, to serve the interests and purposes of others without direct reference to the lives of their maker. (p. 75)

In essence, through commodification, human activity becomes a means rather than an end in itself.

This is indeed true of practice fields. The problems, although authentic in the complexity they bring to the learner, are not authentic in the sense that they are an integral part of the ongoing activity of the society. This has implications both in terms of how individuals come to participate and assign meaning to the activity, as well as in terms of the identities that emerge. With the practice field, education is viewed as preparation for some later sets of activities, not as a meaningful activity in its own right. In fact, it is with this reference to something and someplace else that parents, teachers, and even students use to ascribe value to that which is taught. It is also this situation that led Dewey (1897) to criticize the educational system. Dewey (1897) argued that this is the wrong model: "I believe that education, therefore, is a process of living and not a preparation for future living" (p. 78). Further, while participating in communities of practice, the constraints on practices are present in the everyday workings of the community (e.g., more expert member practices, the demands of the clientele, contained in community generated documents and artifacts). In classrooms, these constraints are frequently presented by one instructor (or an occasional visiting expert) who must serve as a stand-in for the greater community (Barab, Cherkes-Julkowski et al., 1999).

In other words, a community is not simply bringing a lot of people together to work on a task. Extending the length of the task and enlarging the group are not the key variables for moving to the community concept; rather, the key is linking into society—giving the students a legitimate role (task) in society through community participation and membership. We described communities as having three components: a common cultural and historical heritage, including shared goals, understandings, and practices; individuals becoming a part of an interdependent system; and the ability to reproduce as new members work alongside more competent others.

Within schools, we see the emergence of many communities of practice can be seen (jocks, burnouts, musicians, etc.). In fact,

> Communities of practice sprout everywhere—in the classroom as well as on the playground, officially or in the cracks. And in spite of curriculum, discipline, and exhortation, the learning that is most personally transformative turns out to be the learning that involves membership in these communities of practice. Wenger (1998, p. 6)

We have already seen some exciting projects in schools that develop and link students to communities with consonant practices. The goals of this chapter are to further thinking on the characteristics of communities of practice, the advantages of learning from them, and the approaches used by educators to develop them in schools. We hope that this discussion stimulates continued thinking around these questions, and we look forward to educators continuing to share their work that is contextualized in learning environments that are predicated on notions of communities of practice and, just as importantly, the individual learner.

NOTES

[1] Senge introduced the term practice field as a metaphor in relation to the practice field of sports.

[2] We caution the reader to not interpret our labels psychological and anthropological as referring to disciplines or, more specifically, to individuals within disciplines; rather, we chose these labels to denote foci or the unit of analysis typically associated with the work of practitioners of these disciplines.

[3] Although we describe these contrasting alternatives as opposing views and have associate one approach more with the psychological lens and the other with the anthropological lens, it is important to note that much discussion in practice cuts across these two perspectives. For example, many psychologists rely heavily on the anthropological findings in explaining their views of situativity theory and view whole persons (including cognitions and identities) as being created when learning. In fact, we find few explanations of situativity theory that do not reference the work of the anthropologist Jean Lave, whether these explanations are being forwarded by psychologists or anthropologists. However, many discussions of situated cognition within educational circles are still focused on contextual influences with respect to cognition and not with respect to identity creation or the reciprocal influence of negotiated meanings, identities, and the communities through which it all emerges. Therefore, we do find the distinctions outlined in Table 2.1 to be useful in capturing some of the different interpretations of situativity theory (see Kirshner & Whitson, 1997) and in drawing out the implications for designing learning environments. We urge the reader to view these labels as denoting foci or the unit of analysis typically associated with these disciplines and not the work of individual practitioners within these disciplines.

[4] Two fictitious problems established in Jasper episodes (see CTGV, 1990, 1993).

[5] But of course, decontextualizing the problem from the full community context is the overriding characteristic distinguishing a practice field from doing the job.

[6] It is this opportunity to become a member of and extend the community that motivates, shapes, and gives meaning to learning the practices and negotiated meanings. This is in sharp contrast to schools in which students pass through practice fields that maintain motivation only through the exchange value (i.e., grades), not through any contribution to the community or any real-world application.

[7] Let us emphasize that experientially-based does not mean that all learning comes from experts telling their stories. Those experts can in fact be noting what references and resources they found most useful for their own learning. It is also not that the experts have the correct answers, but rather they have had related experiences and this is what they did (and it failed or succeeded to

some degree). The main issue is that the learning is embedded not just in a task but in the history of the community.

[8] Of course there is a reciprocal relation, in that through participation there is continued productions and reproduction of the community. However, the present focus is on learning—the development of self—through participation in the practices of the community.

REFERENCES

Barab, S. A. (1999). Ecologizing instruction through integrated Units. *Middle School Journal, 30,* 21-28.

Barab, S. A., & Landa, A. (1997). Designing effective interdisciplinary anchors. *Educational Leadership, 54,* 52-55.

Barab, S. A., Cherkes-Julkowski, M., Swenson, R., Garrett, S., Shaw, R. E., & Young, M. (1999). Principles of self-organization: Ecologizing the learner-facilitator system. *The Journal of The Learning Sciences, 8*(3&4), 349-390.

Barab, S. A., Hay, K. & Duffy, T. (1998). Grounded constructions and how technology can help. *Technology Trends,43*(2), 15-23.

Barab, S., A., Hay, K. E., Squire, K., Barnett, M., Schmidt, R. Karrigan, K., & Johnson, C. (in press). Virtual solar system project: Developing scientific understanding through model building. *Journal of Science Education and Technology.*

Barron, B., Vye, N. J., Zech, L., Schwartz, D., Bransford, J. D., Goldman, S. R., Pellegrino, J., Morris, J., Garrison, S., & Kantor, R. (1995). Creating contexts for community-based problem solving: The Jasper challenge series. In C. Hedley, P. Antonacci, & M. Rabinowitz (Eds.), *Thinking and literacy: The mind at work* (pp. 47-72). Hillsdale, NJ: Lawrence Erlbaum Associates.

Barrows, H. S., & Myers, A. C. (1993). *Problem based learning in secondary schools.* (Unpublished monograph). Springfield, IL: Problem Based Learning Institute, Lanphier High School, and Southern Illinois Medical school.

Bednar, A. K., Cunningham, D., Duffy, T. M., & Perry, D. J. (1992). Theory into practice: How do we link? In T. Duffy & D. Jonassen (Eds.), *Constructivism and the technology of instruction* (pp. 17-34). Hillsdale, NJ: Lawrence Erlbaum Associates.

Bereiter, C. (1994). Implications of postmodernism for science, or, science as progressive discourse. *Educational Psychologist, 29,* 3-12.

Bereiter, C. (1997). Situated cognition and how to overcome it. In D. Kirshner & J. A. Whitson (Eds.), *Situated Cognition: Social, semiotic, and psychological perspectives* (pp. 281-300). NJ: Lawrence Erlbaum Associates.

Bradsher, M. & Hogan, L. (1995). The Kids Network: Student scientists pool resources. *Educational Leadership, 53* (Oct.), 38-43.

Brown, A., Ash, D., Rutherford, M., Nakagawa, K., Gordon, A., & Campione, J. (1994). Distributed expertise in the classroom. In M. D. Cohen & L. S. Sproull (Eds.), *Organizational learning* (pp. 188-228). London: SAGE.

Brown, A. L., & Campione, J. C. (1990). Communities of learning and thinking, or a context by any other name. *Contributions to Human Development, 21*, 108-126.

Brown, J. S., Collins, A., & Duguid, P. (1989). Situated cognition and the culture of learning. *Educational Researcher, 18*, 32-42.

Brown, J. S., & Duguid, P. (1991). Organizational learning and communities of practice: Toward a unifying view of working, learning, and innovation. In M. D. Cohen & L. S. Sproull (Eds.), *Organizational Learning* (pp. 59-82). London: SAGE.

Clancey, W. J. (1993). Situated action: A neuropsychological interpretation response to Vera and Simon. *Cognitive Science, 17*, 87-116.

Clift, R., Houston, W., & Pugach, M. (Eds.). (1990). *Encouraging reflective practice in education.* New York: Teachers College Press.

Cobb, P. (1994). Where is the mind? Constructivist and sociocultural perspectives on mathematical development. *Educational Researcher, 23*, 13-20.

Cobb, P. (1995). Continuing the conversation: A response to Smith. *Educational Researcher, 24*, 25-27.

Cognition and Technology Group at Vanderbilt. (1990). Anchored instruction and its relationship to situated cognition. *Educational Researcher, 19*, 2-10.

Cognition and Technology Group at Vanderbilt. (1992). The Jasper Experiment: An exploration of issues in learning and instructional design. *Educational Technology Research and Development, 40*(1), 65-80.

Cognition and Technology Group at Vanderbilt. (1993). Anchored instruction and situated cognition revisited. *Educational Technology, 33*, 52-70.

Collins, A., Brown, J. S., & Newman, S. E. (1989). Cognitive apprenticeship: Teaching the crafts of reading, writing, and mathematics. In L. B. Resnick (Ed.), *Knowing, learning and instruction: Essays in honor of Robert Glaser* (pp. 453-494). Hillsdale, NJ: Lawrence Erlbaum Associates.

Copen, P. (1995). Connecting classrooms through telecommunications. *Educational Leadership, 53*(2), 44-47

Cordova, D. I., & Lepper, M. R. (1996). Intrinsic motivation and the process of learning: Beneficial effects of contextualization, personalization, and choice. *Journal of Educational Psychology, 88*, 715-730.

Csikszentmihalyi, M. (1990). *Flow: The psychology of optimal experience.* New York: Harper & Row.

Dewey, J. (1897). *My pedagogical creed. The School Journal, 543*, 77-80.

Dewey, J. (1938). *Experience and education.* New York: Collier MacMillan.

Duffy, T. M., & Cunningham, D. J. (1996). Constructivism: Implications for the design and delivery of instruction. In D. Jonassen (Ed.), *Handbook of research for educational communications and technology* (pp. 170-198). New York: Macmillan.

Duffy, T. M., & Jonassen, D. H. (1992). Constructivism: New implications for instructional technology. In T. Duffy & D. Jonassen (Eds.), *Constructivism and the technology of instruction* (pp. 1-16). Hillsdale, NJ: Lawrence Erlbaum Associates.

Duffy, T. M., Lowyck, J., & Jonassen, D. H. (Eds.). (1992). *Designing environments for constructivist learning.* Heidelberg, Germany: Springer.

Dweck, C. S., & Leggett, E. L. (1988). A social-cognitive approach to motivation and personality. *Psychological Review, 95,* 256-273.

Edwards, L. D. (1995). The design and analysis of a mathematical microworld. *Journal of Educational Computing Research, 12,* 77-94.

Fodor, J. (1975). *Language of thought.* Cambridge, MA: Harvard University Press.

Gardner, H. (1985). *The mind's new science.* New York: Basic Books.

Greeno, J. G. (1997). Response: On claims that answer the wrong questions. *Educational Researcher, 26,* 5-17.

Greeno, J. G. (1998). The situativity of knowing, learning, and research. *American Psychologist, 53,* 5-17.

Greeno, J. G., & Moore, J. L. (1993). Situativity and symbols: Response to Vera and Simon. *Cognitive Science, 17,* 49-61.

Gregory, T. (1993). *Community of teachers.* Unpublished manuscript, Indiana University at Bloomington.

Hannafin, M. J., Hall, C., Land, S. M., & Hill, J. R. (1994). Learning in open-ended environments: Assumptions, methods, and implications. *Educational Technology, 34,* 48-55.

Hmelo, C. E., & Evenson, D. H., (Eds.). (in press). *Problem-based learning: A research perspective on learning interactions.* Mahway, NJ: Erlbaum.

Hunter, B. (1990, April). *Computer-mediated communications support for teacher collaborations: Researching new contexts for teaching and learning.* Paper presented at the annual meeting of the American Educational Research Association, Boston, MA.

Karlan, J., Huberman, M., & Middlebrooks, S. (1997). The challenges of bringing the Kids Network to the classroom. In S. Raizen & E. Britton (Eds.), *Bold ventures: Case studies of U.S. innovations in science education* (Vol. 2). Boston: Kluwer Academic Publishers.

Kirshner, D., & Whitson, J. A. (1997). Editors' introduction. In D. Kirshner & J. A. Whitson (Eds.), *Situated cognition: Social, semiotic, and psychological perspectives* (pp. 1-16). Mahwah, NJ: Lawrence Erlbaum Associates.

Kirshner, D., & Whitson, J. A. (1998). Obstacles to understanding cognition as situated. *Educational Researcher, 27*(8), 22-28.

Kommers, P. A. M., Grabinger, R. S., & Dunlap, J. C. (Eds.). (1996). *Hypermedia learning environments: Instructional design and integration.* Mahwah, NJ: Lawrence Erlbaum Associates.

Koschmann, T.(Ed.). (1996). *CSCL: Theory and practice of an emerging paradigm.* Malwah, NJ: Lawrence Erlbaum Associates.

Koschmann, T., Kelson, A. C., Feltovich, P. J., & Barrows, H. S. (1996). In T. Koschmann (Ed.), *CSCL: Theory and practice of an emerging paradigm* (pp. 83-124). Mahwah, NJ: Lawrence Erlbaum Associates.

Lave, J. (1988). *Cognition in practice: Mind, mathematics, and culture in everyday life.* Cambridge, England: Cambridge University Press.

Lave, J. (1993). Situating learning in communities of practice. In L. B. Resnick, J. M. Levine, & S. D. Teasley (Eds.), *Perspectives on socially shared cognition* (pp. 17-36). Washington, DC: American Psychological Association.

Lave, J. (1997). The culture of acquisition and the practice of understanding. In D. Kirshner & J. A. Whitson (Eds.), *Situated cognition: Social, semiotic, and psychological perspectives* (pp. 63-82). Mahwah, NJ: Lawrence Erlbaum Associates.

Lave, J., & Wenger, E. (1991). *Situated learning: Legitimate peripheral participation.* New York: Cambridge University Press.

Lemke, J. (1997). Cognition, context, and learning: A social semiotic perspective. In D. Kirshner & J. A. Whitson (Eds.), *Situated cognition: Social, semiotic, and psychological perspectives* (pp. 37-56). Mahwah, NJ: Lawrence Erlbaum Associates.

Lipman, M. (1988). *Philosophy goes to school.* Philadelphia: Temple University Press.

Michael, M. (1996). *Constructing identities.* Thousand Oaks, CA: Sage.

Milter, R. G., & Stinson, J. E. (1995). Educating leaders for the new competitive environment. In G. Gijselaers, S. Tempelaar, & S. Keizer (Eds.), *Educational innovation in economics and business administration: The case of problem-based learning.* London: Kluwer Academic Publishers.

Palincsar, A. S., & Brown, A. L. (1984). Reciprocal teaching of comprehension-fostering and monitoring activities. *Cognition and Instruction, 1*(2), 117-175.

Phillips, D. C. (1995). The good, the bad, and the ugly: The many faces of constructivism. *Educational Researcher, 24*(7), 5-12.

Reed, E. S. (1991). Cognition as the cooperative appropriation of affordances. *Ecological Psychology, 3*(2), 135-158.

Resnick, L. B. (1987). Learning in school and out. *Educational Researcher, 16,* 13-20.

Rogoff, B. (1990). *Apprenticeship in thinking: Cognitive development in social context.* New York: Oxford University Press.

Roschelle, J., & Clancey, W. J. (1992). Learning as social and neural. *Educational Psychologist, 27,* 435-453.

Roth, W. M. (1996). Knowledge diffusion in a grade 4-5 classroom during a unit of civil engineering: An analysis of a classroom community in terms of its changing resources and practices. *Cognition and Instruction, 14,* 170-220.

Roth, W.-M. (1998). *Designing communities.* Dordrecht, Germany: Kluwer Academic Publishers.

Savery, J., & Duffy, T. (1996). Problem based learning: An instructional model and its constructivist framework. In B. Wilson (Ed.), *Constructivist learning environments: Case studies in instructional design* (pp. 135-148). Englewood Cliffs, NJ: Educational Technology Publications.

Scardamalia, M., & Bereiter, C. (1993). Technologies for knowledge-building discourse. *Communications of the ACM, 36*, 37-41.

Schoenfeld, A. (1996). In fostering communities of inquiry, must it matter that the teacher knows the "answer"? *For the Learning of Mathematics, 16*(3), 11-16.

Schön, D. A. (1987). *Educating the reflective practitioner.* San Francisco: Jossey-Bass.

Senge, P. (1994). *The Fifth Discipline fieldbook: Strategies and tools for building a learning organization.* New York: Doubleday.

Sfard, A. (1998). On two metaphors for learning and the dangers of choosing just one. *Educational Researcher, 27*, 4-13.

Shanon, B. (1988). Semantic representation of meaning: A critique. *Psychological Bulletin, 104* (1), 70-83.

Tinker, R. F. (1996) *Telecomputing as a progressive force in education.* Unpublished manuscript, The Concord Consortium, Concord, MA.

Tripp, S. D. (1993).Theories, traditions, and situated learning. *Educational Technology, 33*, 71-77.

Vera, A. H., & Simon, H. A. (1993). Situated action: A symbolic interpretation. *Cognitive Science, 17*, 7-49.

Vygotsky, L. (1978). *Mind in society: The development of higher psychological processes.* Cambridge, MA: Harvard University Press.

Walkerdine, V. (1997). Redefining the subject in situated cognition theory. In D. Kirshner & J. A. Whitson (Eds.), *Situated cognition: Social, semiotic, and psychological perspectives* (pp. 57-70). Mahwah, NJ: Lawrence Erlbaum Associates.

Wenger, E. (1998). *Communities of practice: Learning, meaning, and identity.* Cambridge, MA: Cambridge University Press.

Whitehead, A. N. (1929). *The aims of education and other essays.* New York: MacMillan.

Wilson, B. (Ed.). (1996). *Constructivist learning environments: Case studies in instructional design.* Englewood Cliffs, NJ: Educational Technology Publications.

Young, M. (1993). Instructional design for situated learning. *Educational Technology Research and Development, 41*, 43-58.

Young, M. F., & Barab, S. (1999). Perception of the raison d'etre in anchored instruction: An ecological psychology perspective. *Journal of Educational Computing Research, 20*(2), 113-135.

ACKNOWLEDGEMENTS

The authors would like to thank members of the Center for Research on Learning and Technology, specifically Thomas Keating and Donald Cunningham, for the valuable feedback on this chapter.

3

Situated Cognition in Theoretical and Practical Context

Brent G. Wilson
University of Colorado at Denver

Karen Madsen Myers
University of Colorado at Denver

INTRODUCTION

The discipline of instructional design (ID) has always depended heavily on psychology for its theoretical grounding, often to the neglect of other important theory bases. Educational psychologists and cognitive scientists periodically turn their attention to instructional design, engaging the field in conversation and leading toward exciting new conceptions of learning and instruction. For some time, the brand of psychology discussed in ID circles has been fairly progressive. Thus, although many of the systematic procedures for instructional development remain rooted in efficiency notions of curriculum, the newer instructional theories themselves tend to rest on constructivist and situated foundations. Consistent with this progressive shift, attention has been given to more open instructional metaphors such as learning environments and learning communities.

The situativity movement in particular exhibits a rigor and broad disciplinary base that is promising as a foundation for thinking about learning environments (Young, 1993). How does situated cognition (termed SitCog in this chapter for convenience) differ from other learning theories that have influenced ID practice over the years? What new design implications does the theory hold for learning environments? More fundamentally, what role should any psychological theory play in the design of learning environments? These are the questions we address in this chapter. Our focus is on situated cognition, presented within a broader historical context that includes behaviorism and symbolic cognition, two other learning theories that have significantly shaped ID practice. At the outset, we should share some recommendations for designers and participants in learning environments:

1. Look beyond psychology-based learning theories and seek out perspectives from anthropology, critical theory, political science, and so forth. Because of its broader foundation, the situativity movement can be seen as an attempt to do just that.

2. In designing or participating within learning environments, take care not to apply any particular theory too dogmatically or uniformly. Toward the latter sections of the chapter, we outline a way of reading SitCog theories to encourage more ad hoc, situated use of theories toward the design and creation of learning environments.

In writing the chapter, we faced a tension between conveying ideas in a technically adequate way and suggesting implications for practitioner audiences. To preserve a sense of the SitCog literature, we quote at length from the writing of various theorists. Although we value both goals of accuracy and utility, we feel a greater obligation to show how SitCog ideas might be useful as an organizing metaphor to guide the design and creation of learning environments. Thus some theoretical details are omitted, and other ideas are conveyed in language geared more for practitioners.

SitCog at a Glance

SitCog is a research approach, spanning many disciplines and objectives, that relates social, behavioral/psychological, and neural perspectives of knowledge and action (Clancey, 1997). Lave (1991) clarifies:

> 'Situated'...does not imply that something is concrete and particular, or that it is not generalizable, or not imaginary. It implies that a given social practice is multiply interconnected with other aspects of ongoing social processes in activity systems at many levels of particularity and generality (p. 84).

Thus SitCog should not be characterized as only allowing for concrete learning in localized situations. Instead, it emphasizes the web of social and activity systems within which authentic practice takes shape.

SitCog comes into clearer focus when contrasted against traditional information-processing views of cognition. Norman (1993) did a good job conveying the essential difference between these two views. In Norman's intentional caricature, traditional symbolic processing focuses on neural mechanisms and symbolic representations of mind:

> All the action is inside the head, yielding a natural distinction between the stuff out there and the processes taking place inside here. What could be more natural than to study the human by recognizing that the brain is the computational engine of thought, and thereby concentrating one's efforts upon understanding brain mechanisms and mental representations? Seems pretty obvious. Sure, there is a lot of action in the world at large and within sociocultural groups, but cognitive processing occurs within the heads of individuals. So, all we have to do is understand the internal mental processes and the nature of the input/output transformations of individuals, and we will have covered everything that matters. (pp. 3-4)

In contrast, SitCog focuses on "the structures of the world and how they constrain and guide behavior" (p. 4):

> Human knowledge and interaction cannot be divorced from the world.
> To do so is to study a disembodied intelligence, one that is artificial,
> unreal, and uncharacteristic of actual behavior. What really matters is
> the situation and the parts that people play. One cannot look at just the
> situation, or just the environment, or just the person: To do so is to
> destroy the very phenomenon of interest. After all, it is the mutual
> accommodation of people and the environment that matters, so to
> focus upon only aspects in isolation is to destroy the interaction, to
> eliminate the role of the situation upon cognition and action. (p. 4)

Table 3.1 offers an advance look at our views toward behaviorism,
information-processing theory (or more broadly, symbolic cognition), and
situated cognition. SitCog can be approached from a perspective that remains
committed to understanding individual cognitive mechanisms. This is the
approach taken by some artificial intelligence (AI) researchers and cognitive
scientists, whose root interest lies in the nature of mind. Alternatively, Sit-
Cog may be seen from an almost entirely social or cultural vantage point.

TABLE 3.1. Comparison of two traditions of situated cognition

What is Being Studied	**Locus of Knowing**	
	External or Group	*Internal or Individual*
Discrete events and information (meaning derived from the outside in)	Behaviorism	Information-processing theory, or cognition with a focus on symbolic computation
Culturally and physically embedded activities and meanings (meaning derived from the inside out)	Situativity with a focus on community participation and cultural construction, studied by anthropologists and ethnographers	Situativity with a focus on mind, neural, and physical embodiment, studied by cognitive scientists and AI researchers

Lave, for example, is loathe to acknowledge mental constructs and events.
Knowledge is not an object and memory is not a location. Instead, knowing,
learning, and cognition are social constructions, expressed in actions of people
interacting within communities. Through these actions, cognition is enacted
or unfolded or constructed; without the action, there is no knowing, no cognition. SitCog in this sense stands at the fringes of psychology much like

behaviorism, with both approaches seeking to avoid mental constructs, focusing instead on the context or environment of actions and behaviors.

Despite these two discernible strands, SitCog is positioned to bring the individual and the social together in a coherent theoretical perspective. This potential integration of individual and social or cultural levels of scale is a primary strength that we discuss at length in the chapter (see also Chap. 2, this volume).

OVERVIEW OF FOUNDATIONAL LEARNING THEORIES

We review in this section the main psychological foundations underlying the practice of instructional design and, by extension, the design of learning environments. Differences between these views can be understood in historical terms as part of evolving and competing paradigms for learning (Bruner, 1990; Cole, 1996; Mayer, 1992, 1996; Salomon & Perkins, 1998; Sfard, 1998).

Behaviorism

As Mayer (1992, 1996) has noted, behavioral psychologists such as Watson and Thorndike saw learning primarily as the acquisition and strengthening of responses. This view came to dominate U.S. psychology throughout the first half of the 20th century. Because instructional design evolved out of educational psychology, this also was the view of most founders of the movement (e.g., Baker & Schutz, 1971; Gagne, 1965; Glaser, 1965; Mager, 1962; Markle, 1965).

In the late 1990s, behaviorism is often dismissed as a serious theoretical stance for learning and instructional design, or given token attention. Even overview chapters such as ours apportion much less space to behavioral principles (cf. Mayer, 1992). Indeed, behaviorism is often shouldered with responsibility for status quo methods and conditions such as teacher-centered classrooms, lectures, and passive reception of material.

This is not entirely fair. Recall that behaviorism was once a reform movement with a core commitment to active learning. To fully appreciate the contribution of behaviorism, an individual's need to understand what the behaviorists were trying to reform, and what they brought to the table? Proponents of programmed instruction were dedicated to making instruction more individually tailored and effective in accomplishing its objectives. A full range of media and technologies were organized into new designs for instruction. Traditional methods such as teacher-centered classrooms and lectures were precisely what behaviorists were trying to reform.

We also find it provocative to realize that the core assumptions of behaviorism bring the individual in close association with the environment. In fact, environment and behavior mutually define one another with action as the principal unit of analysis. The connection to SitCog is evident.

A full treatment of the influence of behaviorism on instruction and learning is beyond our scope (see Cook, 1997; Dick, 1987; Gagné, 1987; Hilgard, 1987; and Kliebard, 1987, for historical perspectives). For comparison purposes and to suggest some concrete ways theory has indeed guided the design of learning environments, we have highlighted some key contributions of behaviorism to instructional design thinking (see Table 3.2). Although these principles were developed before the current notions of learning environment gained prominence, they are useful for designing a particular form of learning environment that is common in many classrooms today (see Perkins, 1991, on different kinds of learning environments).

We expect readers to respond differently to the enumerated principles. You may find some that you agree with, others that you feel strongly are outdated or damaging. Overall, their impact on education and training has been substantial, and many practitioners continue to rely on behavioral principles for designing learning environments in school and training settings.

For reasons of economy and objectivity, behaviorism sought to explain learning in terms of observable behavior, generally avoiding reference to mental events and entities. This avoidance of mind and meaning was challenged, of course, but generally withstood challenges until the advent of cognitive science in the 1950s and 1960s.

Information Processing Theory

At the threshold of what would become known as cognitive science, the founders intended to bring mind to the center of psychology. Bruner (1990), a key participant, observed:

> [The] aim of [the cognitive revolution] was to discover and to describe formally the meanings that human beings created out of their encounters with the world, and then to propose hypotheses about what meaning-making processes were implicated. It focused upon the symbolic activities that human beings employed in constructing and in making sense not only of the world, but of themselves. Its aim was to prompt psychology to join forces with its sister interpretive disciplines in the humanities and in the social sciences. (p. 2)

Concurrent with psychology's emerging focus on mind, computer technology was developing. With the overlap of the computer and cognitive revolutions in both time and place, it was natural that of the potential driving metaphors "one of the most compelling was that of computing" (Bruner, 1983, p. 274). Cognitive sciences ended up drifting away from the construction of meaning toward the processing of information, and the shift was metaphor driven (Bruner, 1990). Of course, there remained pockets of psychologists who continued to focus on mind and the construction of

TABLE 3.2. A Sampling of Behaviorist Insights for Designing Learning Environments.

Learn by doing. People learn best by actively engaging in tasks. This is commonly called practice or learning by doing.

Taxonomies. Learning outcomes can be differentiated in their type and complexity—for example, simple S-R bonds, concept classification, and rule-following. Such learning outcomes are compiled into classification schemes called learning taxonomies, which in turn guide selection of learning objectives and instructional strategies.

Conditions of learning. For each type of learning, conditions can be identified that lead to effective learning. Identifying optimal conditions of learning forms the basis of prescriptive instructional theory using the formula: To accomplish X learning outcome, apply or arrange for Y conditions.

Behavioral objectives. Instruction should be based on clear, behaviorally specified learning objectives. Explicit formulation of objectives helps link instructional goals with evaluation and assessment, leading to increased accountability.

Focus on results. Teachers and schools should be accountable for their students' learning. Measurable behaviors are the best index of true learning outcomes and should be used to gauge instructional effectiveness.

Alignment. Good instruction exhibits an alignment or consistency between learning objectives, instructional strategies, and strategies used to assess student learning. Misalignment of these components results in inadequate or unfair instruction.

Task decomposition. People learn best when complex tasks are broken down into smaller, more manageable tasks and mastered separately.

Prerequisites. Subtasks often become prerequisites to larger tasks. That is, students learn the larger task more easily when they have first mastered the subtasks. This leads to a parts-to-whole instructional sequence.

Small successes. Subtasks have another advantage: They allow students to succeed. Succeeding at tasks is reinforcing, resulting in greater motivation to continue.

Response-sensitive feedback. People learn best when they know the correctness of their efforts. When performance is not correct, specific information should be conveyed concerning what was wrong and how to improve the next time.

Science of instruction. Educators need to be precise and systematic in their thinking, their teaching, and their evaluation of students. Education can be treated as an applied science or technology, where through empirical inquiry, principles are discovered and applied.

Performance support. People need support as they perform their jobs, through the use of job aids, help systems, and feedback and incentive systems. On-the-job, just-in-time training and support works best. In general, the closer the training is to job conditions, the more effective learning will be.

Direct instruction. Giving clear directions, well prepared presentations, suitable examples, and opportunities for practice and transfer—are proven methods that result in substantial student learning.

Pretesting, diagnostics, and placement. Students should not all be forced to endure the same instructional program. Instead, instruction should branch into alternative treatments according to prior skills, motivation, and other critical variables.

Transfer. In order to be able to transfer a skill from one task to another, students need practice doing it. If students never have opportunities to practice transferring their skills, they should not be expected to be able to perform on demand in test situations.

meaning; this less visible thread has always been there and can be traced back to Wundt's work at the turn of the century.

Information processing theory (or symbolic cognition), although speaking a mechanistic language like that of behaviorism, held a number of advantages. Principally, the bottleneck caused by avoidance of mind was broken, resulting in a flood of new and productive research. Using methods such as reaction-time experiments, eye-movement studies, and think-aloud protocol, researchers were able to posit computational models of mind that filled many of the gaps left by behaviorism. There now was a dualistic framework: The world out there was represented by various memory structures inside the head. Human behavior within that outside world was thought to be accounted for by internal processes and mechanisms. Instructional designers could now think of learning in terms of taking experts' cognitive structures and mapping that knowledge into the heads of learners. The degree of similarity in cognitive structure between expert and novice was a good measure of whether learning objectives were being met.

Table 3.3 presents key concepts from information-processing research that have a bearing on the design of learning environments.

Like the previous table, Table 3.3 will strike readers in different ways. Most teachers and designers suffer an aversion to the computer metaphor. They do not like to think of themselves as machines or as belonging to the same species as symbol-processing machines. On the other hand, from our teaching experience, practitioners find in these concepts some concrete hooks for improving practice, for example, managing memory load or prompting schema-based conceptual change.

Over the years, it became increasingly clear that the information-processing metaphor provides a window into the mind, but a particular model of mind. According to this view, people (and computers) process information sequentially in a number of steps or stages. Humans selectively input information from the environment, then allow some of that information to be reflected on and acted on:

> [W]e think before we act.... [T]hinking goes on subconsciously, mediating every behavior. By this maneuver, we sought to distinguish human problem solving from uncontrolled, animal processes" (Clancey, 1993, p. 110)

The meditation of thought is useful for understanding many cognitive tasks but ultimately proves limiting as a complete framework. Do people really think about all their actions? How are humans like other animals in our cognition? Are people following rules, or are the rules applied after the fact in explanations of our behavior? The reliance on rule-based models and explicit memory structures seems constraining and stridently dualistic. Further, symbolic cognition focuses on individual processing, independent of cultural or physical context, as though information were a neutral construct. How does individual's cognition fit in with other people, tools,

TABLE 3.3.   Information-Processing Principles Relating to the Design
of Learning Environments.

Stages of information processing. Humans process information in stable, sequential stages, inputting sensory information into perceptual memory, then to working and long-term memory, and finally to response generation. In many ways, people are information-processing machines whose thinking and behavior can be modeled and simulated.

Task modeling. Tasks can be modeled using flowcharts and other sequential representations. These models—called cognitive task analysis—can be used to pinpoint likely errors and make instruction more specifically targeted to the skill.

Attention. Attention is often directed toward novelty or changes in an individual's environment. Attention can suffer when instruction offers too much—or not enough—novelty, leading to anxiety or boredom respectively.

Selective perception. Our goals, expectations, and current understandings color our perceptions. They serve as filters to the world and shape our cognitive structures and responses. This selective nature of perception has implications for instructional sequencing, motivation, and metacognitive training.

Memory load. Humans are only able to hold in mind about five to seven chunks of information at a time. Problems arise when instruction taxes the limits of working memory. Major improvements can be made by careful analysis and revision of instruction to reduce memory demands. Memory-sensitive strategies include sequencing instruction from simple to complex, allowing access to reference aids, and progressing in small steps with frequent repetition and elaboration.

Kinds of knowledge. Two kinds of knowledge are fundamental:

Declarative knowledge (knowing that). Stored as propositions in semantic networks.
Procedural knowledge (knowing how). Stored as IF-THEN rules and pattern-recognition templates.

These are often referred to in everyday language as knowledge and skill. Both declarative and procedural knowledge depend on representations of rules or information stored in memory.

Skill compilation. Through repeated practice, skills become compiled or routinized. Several procedural steps are combined into a single whole, making performance easier and leaving cognitive resources available for other parts of a complex task. Talking about or unlearning a routinized procedure can be difficult because details of task components are lost and have to be reconstructed. Automaticity is achieved when a second, simultaneous task can be performed without noticable impairment of the first task.

Meaningful encoding. Information is stored in long-term memory in ways that make it accessible for convenient retrieval.

Chunking. Information is chunked as it becomes organized into meaningful units, making it easier to remember. Chunked information fits together better and helps overcome limits to working memory.

Elaboration. People make links between material and their prior knowledge through active thought and reflection. The more connections, the more meaningful and stable the item.

Metacognition. Problem solving involves declarative and procedural knowledge and something more. That something more is called metacognitive knowledge, involving self-monitoring, self-regulation, knowing when and where to deploy your strategies and knowledge.

Motivation. Motivation is what makes people do what they do. Whereas behavioral explanations traditionally referred to instincts, drives, arousal, and reinforcement, cognitive theorists rely on models of cognitive processing and structure. Key concepts include incentives, self-efficacy, expectancy x value, success-failure attributions, performance versus learning goals, and intrinsic versus extrinsic motivation.

Experts versus novices. Experts differ from novices in a number of respects, including more domain-specific information to draw upon; more refined domain-specific performance routines; and a commitment to steady periods of deliberate practice (reflective practice with the specific intent of skill improvement).

Human development. Children's growth in knowledge and skill can be interpreted as a series of stages from concrete to abstract forms of reasoning or as accumulation of procedural and declarative knowledge about the world. Adults also grow in their epistemological understanding; this growth can also be characterized in terms of stages, moving from fixed, authoritarian views of knowledge toward views that acknowledge the important roles of interpretation and perspective. In both cases, instruction should be matched to development levels.

Conceptual change. People make sense of their worlds by reference to schemas, mental models, and other complex memory structures. Differences between encountered experience and schemas can prompt further inquiry and reflection to resolve the conflict. Instruction should help learners assimilate and accommodate new information into existing schemas and cognitive structures.

---

language, and culture? Surely tools, people, and culture are major mediators of constructed meaning (see also Chapter 5, this volume).

SITUATED COGNITION

SitCog has been positioned as an alternative to information-processing theory. It seeks to correct some of the oversights of the symbolic-computation approach to cognition, in particular its reliance on stored descriptions of rules and information, its focus on conscious reasoning and thought, and its neglect of cultural and physical context.

The terms situated cognition, situated action, or situativity enjoy no consensus among researchers. The terms are sometimes used to denote an array of related perspectives, something similar to sociocultural constructivism. As we noted at the outset, two camps of researchers are typically associated with SitCog:

- Anthropologists like Jean Lave (1988, 1991) and Lucy Suchman (1993) are interested in the cultural construction of meaning. They meld anthropology and critical theory with the socioculturalism of Vygotsky (Forman, Minick, & Stone, 1993; Newman, Griffin, & Cole, 1989; Rogoff, 1990). The Vygotsky-inspired sociohistorical school takes as its central problem the processes whereby cultures reproduce themselves across generational boundaries. "This program provides a useful contrast to the behaviorist focus on low-level behavioral responses...and to Piagetian individualism on the other" (Kirshner & Whitson, 1997, p. 5). These researchers often avoid the term situated cognition in favor of situated action or situated learning.[1] (see also Chapter 8, this volume).

- Cognitive scientists like Allan Collins, John Seeley Brown, Don Norman, and Bill Clancey are interested in cognition at individual and social levels. Because these theorists tend to work from an AI or psychology tradition, individual cognition tends to draw more attention. For them, SitCog has strong links to artificial intelligence, neuroscience, linguistics, and psychology, all fields with direct insights for understanding the individual mind.

Other perspectives have been drawn to SitCog, as illustrated by the wide variety of contributors to Kirshner and Whitson (1997). SitCog's success in attracting researchers is another sign of its promise. Contributions from ecological and semiotic perspectives, in particular, are broadening and deepening the SitCog framework (see also Chapter 6, this volume).

Integrating Levels of Scale

The stand-out characteristic of situated cognition seems to be the placement of individual cognition within the larger physical and social context of interactions and culturally constructed tools and meanings. SitCog provides a person plus unit of analysis with individual knowing and social action intertwined. "The physical context is being reunited with the social, within the thought process" (Light & Butterworth, 1992, p. 1). Bredo (1994) depicted situated cognition as "shifting the focus from individual in environment to individual and environment" (p. 29).

Suchman (1993) made this point by portraying Lave's research on cognition in everyday environments:

[T]he very premise...that schools constitute some neutral ground apart from the real world, in which things are learned that are later applied in the real world, is fundamentally misguided...[A]ll learning is learning in situ... [S]chools constitute a very specific situation for learning with their own cultural, historical, political, and economic interests: interests obscured by the premise that schools are asituational. Schools prepare students not for some generic form of transfer of things learned in schools to other settings, but to be students, to succeed or to fail, to more into job markets or not, and so forth. (p. 72)

Of course, sociologists and critical theorists have been saying as much for years. The difference is that Suchman, Lave, and others are directly challenging the insulated view of cognition that ignores these contextual factors. Social and individual are not simply different levels of study—these levels interact and are inexorably connected. Bredo (1997) described this tight coupling:

> [Writing, conversing, or thinking are] the result of dialogue... in which person and environment (ideally) modify each other so as to create an integral performance. Seen in this way, a successful person acts with the environment, shaping it to modify himself or herself, in turn, and then to shape the environment, and so on, until some end is achieved....[T]he production of a well-coordinated performance involves a kind of dance between person and environment rather than the one-way action of one on the other. (p. 29)

Designers of computer-based learning environments might argue that social and cultural factors play a minimal role because the principal interaction is between computer and individual learner. Greeno (1997) disagrees:

> The situative view...assumes that all instruction occurs in complex social environments. For example, a student studying along with a textbook or a computer tutor may not have other people in the same room at the time, but the student's activity is certainly shaped by the social arrangements that produced the textbook or the computer program, led to the student's being enrolled in the class where the text or program was assigned, and provided the setting in which the student's learning will make a difference in how the student participates in some social activity, such as a class discussion or a test. (pp. 9-10)

The principal challenge facing SitCog researchers is developing effective means of integrating levels of scale. The vision is clear, but the methodologies, both for research and for practice, are still in early stages of development. Until better tools become available, designers of learning environments should strive to be inclusive and expansive in their views, as they seek to integrate multiple perspectives in viewing the whole system rather than individual levels of their design thinking.

Constructing Meaning

As mentioned previously, situated cognition also challenges the orthodoxy concerning how meaning is constructed. Researchers in AI and perception have generally taken a neural or connectionist approach to this question. Researchers like Winograd and Flores (1986) began taking seriously the criticisms of Dreyfus (1979). The result was an internal challenge to stage- and rule-based processing from within the AI community itself. Bill Clancey has been among the most vocal questioners of stored representations in memory and rule-based knowledge systems. In the following passage, for example, Clancey (1993) argues that reflections, like other actions and thoughts, are immediate constructions:

> Every act of deliberation occurs as an immediate behavior. That is, every act of speaking, every motion of the pen, each gesture, turn of head, or any idea at all is produced by the cognitive architecture as a matter of course, as a new neurological coordination (pp. 111-112).

Clancey made some strong statements against stored representations and symbolic processing, for which he received some criticism. His most recent book (Clancey, 1997) takes a more moderate and consolidating approach, leaving room for conscious reflection and representations. St. Julien (1997) illustrated how facts, rules, and representations might play a role in a situated framework:

> People who are competent in a field, people we usually think of as experts or simply as competent, are the producers of such facts. Facts, rules, and features are first used by experts among experts. They are helpful in discussing marginal cases, cases where the usual fluid, unremarkable competence has broken down. Facts, rules, and features provide the socially agreed on framework within which the fully competent can support each other when working on a difficult problem. (,p. 7)

Although working within a situated framework, the roots of this position lie squarely within mainstream cognitive science research on concept learning. The difference is that the focus has shifted from individuals to groups and communities making use of shared rules and facts.

The debate about rules and plans has implications back to the role of instructional designer. Clancey (1995) contrasted two attitudes toward design: One rationalist or scientific, the other interactional. A rationalist view sees design in procedural or rule-based terms, with plans preceding action. You articulate the ideal up front, specify a design metric, and make adjustments for deviations as you proceed. Learning occurs through feedback regarding deviations and how adjustments are translated into redevelopment. Advocates of a systems design model for instructional development should see the parallel. Contrast that with the interactional view: What people do is created in their interactions; individual's representations orient action but do not control action. Representations include plans, formulas, algorithms, rules, and architectures. "How the plans are interpreted is itself an interactive, non-predictable process...Every behavior is an improvisation" (p. 27). "Human behavior is inherently ad hoc, inventive, and unique" (p. 28). "People do not simply plan and do. They continuously adjust and invent. Managing this process means managing learning, not managing application of a plan" (p. 39).

Clancey's (1995) interactional view has specific implications for designers:

- We as instructional designers must go into the community of the practitioner, using ethnographic methods of observation and reflection,
and become participant observers. We develop a focus on how the
community learns (pp. 33-34).

- Instructional designers must use methods of participatory design i n
which the worker participates in redesign practices with the designer
(p. 38).

The discussion on design illustrates the differences between symbolic-process-
ing and SitCog. The discussion also has further implications for how instructional designers approach the task of creating learning environments. A
fuller discussion of these issues is presented in later sections of the chapter.

Meaning Construction as a Social Activity

Thinking and meaning construction are also approached from the sociocul-
\tural camp of SitCog theorists. In this view, construction of meaning is tied
to specific contexts and purposes. People develop shared ways of responding
to patterns and features in particular contexts that Gee (1997) calls discourses.
"Discourses are sociohistorical coordinations of people, objects (props), ways
of talking, acting, interacting, thinking, valuing, and (sometimes) writing and
reading that allow for the display and recognition of socially significant
identities" (pp. 255-256). Within discourses, people can exchange thoughts
and explanations. Explanations or theories about practice tied to sociocultural
groups are called cultural models (Gee, 1992; Shore, 1996). Cultural models
are not just held by individual participants but reside also in the practices i n
which the group engages, the tools they use, and the contextual setting.

Resnick, Säljö, Pontecorvo, and Burge (1991) viewed thought and
reasoning as

> "inherently (and throughout the life space) social activities in which
> talk and social interactions are not just a means by which people learn
> to think, but also how they engage in thinking. They might say that
> discourse *is* cognition *is* discourse... One is unimaginable without the
> other." (p. 2)

Discourses and cultural models may not be physically present in the immediate context, but their impact on meaning construction is nonetheless critical.
Individuals achieve a sense of continuity over the lifespan as they interpret
immediate situations in terms of past situations they see as having relevance
to the here and now. Thus, an immediate situation can only be by reference
to the history of participants and associated groups:

We interpret a text or a situation in part by connecting it to other texts and situations that our community or our individual history has made us see as relevant to the meaning of the present one. Our community, and each of us, creates networks of connections (and disconnections) among texts, situations and activities... These networks of connections that we make, and that are made in the self-organizing activity of the larger systems to which we belong, extend backwards in time as well [as] outwards into the social-material world. (Lemke, 1997, p. 50).

Table 3.4 continues our parallel exercise, summarizing key insights from situated cognition for the design of learning environments. We confess that this table was tougher to construct than the other two: The approach is newer and, in some ways, more ambitious. Moreover, it has not been popularized and disseminated in the way the older traditions have been.

These principles are also less specific in their prescriptions for the design of learning environments. Even in their descriptive nature, however, the principles differ markedly from those in the earlier tables. A SitCog approach to learning environments pays close attention to language, activities of individuals and groups, cultural meanings and differences, tools (including computer tools and environments), and the interaction of all of these together. Assessing the potential of a given learning environment would involve understanding how these components combine in a way that results in participation in activities valued by individuals and groups.

How are instructional designers to evaluate the potential of SitCog as an aid to the design of learning environments? Sfard (1997) noted that learning is usually thought of as acquiring something—perhaps a competency, skill, or capability. SitCog theorists have operated from a different metaphor, that of participating in communities of authentic practice. Lave (1988) argued that people are principally defined by their participation in an activity as well as the roles they assume in social practice (see also Lemke, 1997). Sfard saw an upside to this participation metaphor:

The promise of the [participation metaphor] seems, indeed, quite substantial. The vocabulary of participation brings the message of togetherness, solidarity, and collaboration. [It] does not allow for talk about permanence of either human possessions or human traits... Being "in action" means being in a constant flux. The awareness of the change that never stops means refraining from a permanent labeling. Actions can be clever or unsuccessful, but these adjectives do not apply to the actors. For the learner, all options are always open, even if he or she carries a history of failure. Thus, quite unlike the [acquisition metaphor], the [participation metaphor] seems to bring a message of an everlasting hope: Today you act one way; tomorrow you may act differently. (p. 8)

Table 3.4 Situated Cognition Principles Relating to Learning Environments

Learning in context. Thinking and learning make sense only within particular situations. All thinking, learning, and cognition is situated within particular contexts; there is no such thing as nonsituated learning.

Communities of practice. People act and construct meaning within communities of practice. These communities are powerful repositories and conveyers of meaning and serve to legitimate action. Communities construct and define appropriate discourse practices.

Learning as active participation. Learning is seen in terms of belonging and participating in communities of practice. Learning is seen as a dialectical process of interaction with other people, tools, and the physical world. Cognition is tied to action—either direct physical action or deliberate reflection and internal action. To understand what is learned is to see how it is learned within the activity context.

Knowledge in action. Knowledge is located in the actions of persons and groups. Knowledge evolves as individuals participate in and negotiate their way through new situations. The development of knowledge and competence, like the development of language, involves continued knowledge-using activity in authentic situations.

Mediation of artifacts. Cognition depends on the use of a variety of artifacts and tools, chiefly language and culture. These tools and constructed environments constitute the mediums, forms, or worlds through which cognition takes place. Problem solving involves reasoning about purposes in relationship to the resources and tools which a situation affords.

Tools and artifacts as cultural repositories. Tools embody the history of a culture. They enable thought and intellectual processes and constrain or limit that thought. They also provide powerful means of transmitting culture.

Rules, norms, and beliefs. Cognitive tools include forms of reasoning and argumentation that are accepted as normative in society. Using a tool in a certain manner implies adoption of a cultural belief system about how the tool is to be used.

History. Situations make sense within an historical context, including the past experiences and interactions of participants, as well as anticipated needs and events. Cultures, through tools, artifacts, and discourse practices, embody the accumulated meanings of the past.

Levels of scale. Cognition can best be understood as a dynamic interplay between individual and social levels. Focus on one level, while assuming constancy or predictability at the other, is bound to at least partly misinterpret the situation.

Interactionism. Just as situations shape individual cognition, individual thinking and action shape the situation. This reciprocal influence constitutes an alternative conception of systemic causality to the more commonly assumed linear object causality.

Identities and constructions of self. People's notion of self—of continuing identity, separate from others yet belonging to carious groups—is a constructed artifact with many uses. People have multiple identities, which can serve as tools for thinking and acting.

This perspective affords greater flexibility in defining selves, roles, and identities. In a learning environment, this flexibility could likely contribute to
more positive risk-taking, inquiry, and appreciation of multiple perspectives.
    On the other hand, SitCog has been criticized on a number of points,
especially areas where theorists have overstated their positions (Anderson,

Reder, & Simon, 1996).   Sfard (1997), although sympathetic to situated approaches, acknowledged the difficulty situated theorists have in explaining transfer of knowledge from one setting to another:

> A persistent follower of the [participation metaphor] must realize, sooner or later, that from a purely analytical point of view, the metaphorical message of the notion of transfer does not fit into [their] conceptual frameworks.   Learning transfer means carrying knowledge across contextual boundaries; therefore, when one refuses to view knowledge as a stand-alone entity and rejects the idea of context as a clearly delineated "area," there is simply nothing to be carried over, and there are no definite boundaries to be crossed. (p. 9)

Adult educators in particular face pressure to deliver training that can transfer to job situations.   Situated theorists do not speak their language if they cannot promise some transfer to the job.[2]

Tripp (1993) highlighted another potential downside of situated approaches, issuing a warning against leaving learners to their own resources:

> In general, studies of adults who have learned languages "on-the-job" reveal a phenomenon called "fossilization." Fossilization refers to the learning of incorrect, but understandable, syntax and pronunciation which suffices for communication. Since this interlanguage allows satisfactory social interactions, the learner does not progress to a higher degree of mastery and, thus, the mistakes are fossilized and become part of the learner's permanent repertoire. (p. 72)

To the degree that authentic environments create unsupervised performance opportunities, such learning variations are liable to happen.   Some of these learning variations will be positive, whereas others admittedly negative. Designers of learning environments will want to carefully weigh the risks and benefits of authentic experiences and provide supervision and guidance as appropriate.

Communities can definitely convey wrong values, and individuals can fit in poorly or pick up messages that work against academic learning goals. Salomon and Perkins (1998) note how interactions between individual and collective learning can go bad:

> What is learned by an individual may upset or even subvert rather than abet collective ends, as with the student taking advantage of his or her team members' work or the corporate climber being more interested in personal advancement than in the overall success of the organization... In such cases, the collective has "learned," but what it has learned happens to be profoundly limiting both for itself and for the participating individuals. (p. 21)

Granting consideration to these various problems, we still see situated cognition holding great promise as a guide to the design of learning environments. In the next section, we explore how SitCog might successfully serve as an integrating framework for including multiple learning theories and multiple levels of scale. Then we turn to reflections on the appropriate role of theory in the design of learning environments.

SITUATIVITY AS AN INTEGRATING FRAMEWORK

Norman (1993) posed a nicely competitive question: Does symbolic cognition accommodate situativity, or does situativity accommodate symbolic cognition? Greeno and Moore (1993) believed that a situated approach can best serve as an integrating framework:

> [W]e see, in the present situation, a prospect of completing a dialectical cycle, in which stimulus-response theory was a thesis, symbolic information-processing theory was its antithesis, and situativity theory will be their synthesis. In the 1950s and 1960s, when the theory of symbolic information processing was being developed..., the prevailing stimulus-response theory in psychology lacked resources for analyzing and representing the complex structures involved in mental activity. A goal of stimulus-response psychology was to account for behavior as much as possible in terms of externally identifiable factors, and the structures of information and procedures were contained in a theoretical "black box." The theory of symbolic information processing has allowed us to investigate the contents of that black box in detail.

> We contend that symbolic processing theory presents another black box that contains the structure of interactive relations between cognitive agents and the physical systems and other people that they interact with.... (p. 57)

Part of what makes SitCog a contender for integration is its ability, as we have discussed, to accommodate both individual and social scales of study. Salomon and Perkins (1998) recalled the analogy of a spreading flu. Consider two levels of explanation—cell biology and epidemiology:

> Clearly, the two complement each other. Subverted cellular mechanisms figure in the invasion of individual cells by viruses, but the viruses have to arrive at individual cells to infect them. Although each process can be understood in its own right, understanding the interplay yields a richer and conceptually more satisfying picture. (p. 2)

The analogy sounds very appealing, but how far can competing theories, emphasizing different levels of scale, really fit together? How commensurable are models of individual cognitive processing with broader depictions of situated action?

Greeno believes in the commensurability of views, arguing for accommodation of behavioral and information-processing strategies within an overall situated framework. This is possible, he says, because SitCog acknowledges the various contexts where such strategies may be needed and relevant:

> [L]earning environments organized on behaviorist skill-acquisition principles encourage students to become adept at practices, involving receptive learning and drill, that result in efficient performance on tests, and learning environments organized on cognitive knowledge-structure principles encourage students to become adept at constructing understanding on the basis of general ideas and relations between concepts. (Greeno & the Middle School Mathematics Through Applications Projects Group, 1998, p. 14)

In other words, different situations will call for different tools, models, methods, and so forth. Instructional methods are thus seen as tools to be appropriated by participants within the local situation, rather than general prescriptions to be used in all learning situations. Although learning goals and purposes should always be examined critically, the specific choices of goals and activities are rightfully placed within the specific situation.

Greeno et al. (1998) contrast the three foundational learning theories, while maintaining the primacy of a SitCog framework:

> Behaviorist principles tend to characterize learning in terms of acquisition of skill. Cognitive principles tend to characterize learning in terms of growth of conceptual understanding and general strategies of thinking and understanding. Situative principles tend to characterize learning in terms of more effective participation in practices of inquiry and discourse that include constructing meanings of concepts and uses of skills. We argue here that the situative perspective, focused on practices, can subsume the cognitive and behaviorist perspectives by including both conceptual understanding and skill acquisition as valuable aspects of students' participation and their identities as learners and knowers. (p. 14)

Greeno et al. were optimistic that elements of behaviorism, cognitivism, and situativity can be combined:

> Both the behaviorist skill-oriented and cognitive understanding-oriented perspectives have informed the development of educational practices significantly, but they are often portrayed, in research literature and the popular press, as diametrical opposites, where learning according to one view precludes learning according to the other. We argue here that important strengths and values of behaviorist and cog-

nitive practices can be included in practices on the basis of the situative principles of valuing students' learning to participate in inquiry and sense-making. Situative principles can provide a useful framework for evaluating the contributions of behaviorist and cognitive practices in a larger context. (p. 15).

[I]n the situative perspective, both learning to participate in the discourse of conceptual meanings and learning basic routines of symbol manipulation can both be seen as significant assets for student participation, rather than being orthogonal objectives. (p. 17)

We cautiously agree with Greeno. SitCog, because of its holistic tendencies and preferences for rich, active environments, is well positioned to serve as a synthesis or integrating framework. It seems easier to imagine an open, holistic framework accommodating a more technical, symbolic framework than the reverse. Ultimately, we believe some way must be found to accommodate multiple levels of scale and, to some extent, competing paradigms or theories. Gould (1987, cited in Clancey, 1997) makes a similar point about the need to include both biology and culture:

We must...go beyond reductionism to a holistic recognition that biology and culture interpenetrate in an inextricable manner. One is not given, the other built upon it....Individuals are not real and primary, with collectivities (including societies and cultures) merely constructed from their accumulated properties. Cultures make individuals too; neither comes first, neither is more basic. (p. 244).

At this point, accommodating multiple levels of scale within a situated framework is not fully realized. Some camps demonstrate antipathy to a neural or psychological level of scale. We see no inherent incommensurability between a SitCog framework and many neural and information-processing concepts of individual cognition. This is an area where we would like to see further development and discussion; we are optimistic that a greater level of integration can take place between theories that are seen, at present, as competitors.

Implications for Learning Environments

Greeno et al (1998) offered what might constitute a mission statement for SitCog as an integrating framework:

We need to organize learning environments and activities that include opportunities for acquiring basic skills, knowledge, and conceptual understanding, not as isolated dimensions of intellectual activity, but as contributions to students' development of strong identities as individual learners and as more effective participants in the meaningful social practices of their learning communities in school and elsewhere in their lives. (p. 17)

We share Greeno's enthusiasm, yet a tension is emerging. Situativity can be read in two competing ways: a) as a *prescriptive* basis for design or b) as a *descriptive* basis for understanding and accommodating different purposes, tools, methods, and so forth.

On the one hand, we could look to SitCog theory to tell us what kind of methods to use to achieve active, thriving communities of practice. This view would champion certain methods as promoting learning (e.g., authentic performance in information-rich, authentic settings) while eschewing others (e.g., direct instruction or efforts to manage cognitive load). Barab and Duffy (Chap. 2, this volume) present a good example of using the theory in this way.

Alternatively, we could look to SitCog to help us understand, through observation and critique, how a given learning environment combines elements to accomplish certain goals. Is the learning environment successful in accomplishing its learning goals? How do the various participants, tools, and objects interact together? What meanings are constructed? How do the interactions and meanings help or hinder desired learning?

At first glance, the second use of the theory may seem unrelated to design. We believe, though, that a descriptive approach, although not offering a direction path to action, holds some advantages for thinking about design. First, as Greeno has shown, a descriptive use of SitCog can more easily accommodate a variety of conceptions and purposes for instruction. Because such a view does not attach itself to a clear set of instructional methods, it will likely be relevant to more learning situations. Second, because descriptive critiques start with the given situation, designers and participants may more clearly see a path toward improvement. This may help to mitigate the concern expressed by some practitioners that ideologically based approaches are just too extreme or idealistic to adopt wholesale. Finally, a less prescriptive approach will likely be more respectful of participants' values and concerns. Communities of practice represent diverse interests and political beliefs. Any learning environment meant to reflect that diversity would need to be able to incorporate varied methods, approaches, strategies, and so forth.

The two contrasting uses of SitCog theory result in an interesting irony:

- The prescriptive use of SitCog, although pursuing authentic communities of practice, runs the risk of becoming just another model to be imposed on practitioners out of context and without regarding to situational concerns.

- At the same time, the descriptive use of SitCog runs the risk of legitimating practices that run counter to authentic, situated learning.

Rather than resolve this difficulty, we hope to see some attention to both concerns. Care should be taken to respect local purposes and culture, while at the same time promoting positive values such as authentic activity within communities of practice.

A further tension exists concerning how feasible it is to control and thus design authentic learning environments. If we are reading the situated position correctly, authentic communities of practice are not so much designed, but rather emerge within existing environments and constraints. They fill ecological niches where certain opportunities open up, based upon the environment, people, tools, organizational structure and power dynamics, etc. How can we talk about designing authentic learning environments when so much of what goes into a learning environment is predetermined by constraints, or emerges based on the participants themselves?

Brown and Duguid present the issue another way. They cited a wonderful observation on the ineffability of knowledge:

> A very great musician came and stayed in [our] house. He made one big mistake... [he] determined to teach me music, and consequently no learning took place. Nevertheless, I did casually pick up from him a certain amount of stolen knowledge. (Tagore, as cited in Brown & Duguid, 1993, p. 10)

This statement suggest not only the tacit nature of important knowledge but also the near impossibility of conveying knowledge systematically, that is, by design.

Nonetheless, using situated principles, Brown and Duguid (1993) hoped that learning environments could be designed that would succeed in conveying tacit but important knowledge:

> It is a fundamental challenge for design—for both the school and the workplace—to redesign the learning environment so that newcomers can legitimately and peripherally participate in authentic social practice in rich and productive ways—to, in short, make it possible for learners to "steal" the knowledge they need. (p. 11)

> The best way to support learning is from the demand side rather than the supply side. That is, rather than deciding ahead of time what a learner needs to know and making this explicitly available to the exclusion of everything else, designers and instructors need to make available as much as possible of the whole rich web of practice—explicit and implicit, allowing the learner to call upon aspects of practice, latent in the periphery, as they are needed. (Brown & Duguid, 1993, p. 13).

Brown and Duguid seem not so eager to accommodate behaviorist and cognitivist perspectives. Yet their vision of designing situated-learning environments is also compelling. There seems to be room within the situated camp for a variety of approaches to instruction and the design of learning environments. The problem of how to design something that seems undesignable is not resolved; however, the process of design seems one of coordinating and compiling resources, then guiding participation—as opposed to prespecifying complete learning resources and activities.

FURTHER QUESTIONS ABOUT THEORY AND PRACTICE

In this section, we turn more directly to general questions concerning how theory and practice might best work together in the design and development of learning environments.

Grounded Design

Hannafin and colleagues (Hannafin, Hannafin, Land, & Oliver, 1997) are fully aware of the competing paradigms for instructional design. Moreover, they see potential strengths in different theories of learning and instruction. As a response to the plurality of perspectives, they developed the concept of grounded-learning systems design. Grounded-learning systems design is defined as "the systematic implementation or processes and procedures that are rooted in established theory and research in human learning" (Hannafin et al., 1997, p. 102; see also Chapter 1, this volume).

Following this model, ID practices (or approaches) should be grounded in *some* theory validated by some research tradition. Good behaviorally based instruction might coherently and consistently follow a Gagné-style approach, for example, whereas good situative instruction would be grounded on very different principles and values. Consistency is the key:

> A learning environment described as reflecting cognitive-information processing views of learning, yet failing to account for limitations in short-term memory, reflects a mismatch between presumed foundations and assumptions and their associated methods. A constructivist's learning environment that decontextualizes and tutors to mastery is equally ungrounded. (p. 57)

The test for legitimacy has thus shifted from using the right theory to grounding practice in the right way. Grounded practice for instructional design must be:

- based on a defensible theoretical framework
- consistent with research validating that theoretical framework
- generalizable to other cases and situations
- empirically validated through successive tryout and revision (Hannafin, et al., 1997; see Chapter 1, this volume).

The concept of grounded design is a clear attempt to accommodate multiple theories for designing sound instruction.   Many designers may find a grounded approach more realistic than the search for the one true theory. The decision about an appropriate theory to use is thus situated in the local environment.

We are somewhat sympathetic to this concept, especially its effort to negotiate a truce among theoretical positions. But we need some clarifying of the construct.   The examples given by Hannafin et al. (1997) seem to be of two different sorts:

- schools and instructional programs in operation at some site (e.g., airplane pilot schools); and

- models and related materials designed by theorists to be more broadly used by practitioners (e.g., the *Jasper* series; KIE; *Microworlds Project Builder*).

These two types of product are somewhat different. Hannafin et al. present an example of two private airplane pilot schools: one employing a directed instruction approach and one more hands-on and situational.   These pilot schools are clear examples of instruction in real contexts.   The theorist-designed models, however, are not so clearly grounded in specific sites or communities.   Although the models incorporate substantial elements of design and decision-making, we see them principally as tools to facilitate instruction rather than instruction itself.   In the usual sense of the term, instruction happens when these conceptual tools and resources get used in real settings by real people.   The instructional models cited by Hannafin are tools for the theorist (to test out and disseminate their theories) and tools for the practitioner (to appropriate and use them in specific settings).

Returning to Hannafin's example of the two pilot-training schools, we are left to wonder: Did the schools design their approaches by reference to particular theories, or did they arrive at their approaches without recourse to theory? We could imagine either scenario: Maybe the schools hired a consultant or a trainer schooled in a particular theory, or maybe a veteran pilot saved her money, started a school, and developed the curriculum in the way that seemed best. Or more likely, the training approach evolved over time, undergoing occasional revision based on a number of influences, some theory-based, some intuitive, some reflecting constraints of the business or of the teaching situation.

The idea of grounded design is a helpful construct that relates specific instructional models back to more general theories of learning.   The cognitive apprenticeship model should be consistent with its grounding theory of SitCog.   The *Jasper* Series and its associated model of anchored instruction should be consistently aligned with principles of authentic, constructivist learning advocated by its designers.   Gagné's nine events of instruction should be grounded in the behavioral or cognitive learning theory of its author.   These specific models and materials provide a concreteness and directness that practitioners find extremely helpful in converting theories to practical action. On the other hand, the same level of consistency between the details of real-life instruction and a given theory is not expected or wanted. In fact, we believe that most instructional programs in operation would be ill-served by a strong linkage to a particular theory. To explain our concerns, we return to a more general discussion of educational theories and their relation to practice.

Educational Theory-making in Cultural Context

Labaree (1998) contrasted educational knowledge with that gained in other sciences and professions. Educational research, he said, generates

- soft (as opposed to hard) knowledge that is not easily verifiable, definitive, and cumulative; and

- applied (as opposed to pure) knowledge that is more local, less generalizable, and less theoretical.

To clarify this point, Labaree offered an interesting analogy. Imagine knowledge in geographical and architectural terms. An urban discipline would accumulate knowledge in concentrated, central locations. High-rise buildings could be built on the strong foundation of secure, replicable findings. Hard sciences are like that. In contrast, education more closely resembles a rural landscape, with farmhouses and outbuildings distributed across wide open spaces. Educational knowledge is hard to build up into strong, stable structures; rather, it seems very locally distributed across settings, problems, participants, and content areas.

Shulman (1986) made a similar point about education's special epistemological status:

> Education is not a "science" in the sense of those sciences discussed by Popper, Kuhn, Lakotos, Feyerbend...[its] major focus is (or ought to be) on an artifact called "practice"...It is the marriage of theoretical knowledge with practical action which characterizes education (along with medicine, law, and other "professional fields") and requires a philosophical perspective of its own. (pp. 39-40)

The soft, applied, rural nature of educational knowledge results in some predictable effects, some good, some bad: lower status within the academy, more flexibility in determining research problems, more recurring waves of reform, more diversity in perspective, and greater influence of outside theories and frameworks. We would hope, as Shulman suggested, for greater appreciation of practical knowledge. Too often, though, the knowledge and wisdom gained from years of practitioner experience is subordinated to the structured, formal knowledge of the university researcher or textbook. Practitioners are asked to apply the knowledge or theory developed by the researcher; the practitioner role is at risk of being reduced to that of technician.

Theories in Situated Context

According to Blum (1970),

> Aristotle used theory as that kind of mental activity in which we engage for its own sake, as contemplative: to theorize meant to inspect or to keep one's gaze fixed on. To theorize was to turn one's mind in a certain direction, or to look at the world under the auspices of a certain interest. (p. 303)

But since Aristotle, theory has taken on a whole host of meanings. Thomas (1997) claimed that the lack of precision in meaning has resulted in its being equitable to nothing more than intellectual endeavor (p. 75).

Thomas' (1997) critique speaks of the hegemony of theory and argues for more "ad hocery" and anarchy in thought and method:

> [T]heory of any kind is...a force for conservatism, for stabilizing the status quo through the circumscription of thought within a hermetic set of rules, procedures, and methods. Seen in this way, theory—far from being emancipatory...—is in fact an instrument for reinforcing an existing set of practices and methods in education. (p. 76)

Why is theory harmful? The answer is that theory structures and thus constrains thought. Thought actually moves forward, Feyerabend (1993) said, by "a maze of interactions...[by] accidents and conjunctures and curious juxtapositions of events p. 9). The naïve and simple-minded rules that methodologists use cannot hope to provide the progress for which we wish. He quotes Einstein as saying that the creative scientist must seem to the systematic epistemologist to be an "unscrupulous opportunist." Holton (1995) also drew on Einstein, saying that the essence of scientific method is in the seeking "in whatever manner is suitable, a simplified and lucid image of the world. There is no logical path, but only intuition" (p. 168). In other words, Feyerabend (1993) concluded, "the only principle that does not inhibit progress is *anything goes*" (p. 14).

Although we acknowledge a more positive role for theory use than Thomas does, we believe that creators and users of theory should be more aware of ways theory can be misused in practical situations.

Theory-based or Theory-informed?

How then should practitioners make use of theory as a guide to the design of learning environments? A theory-centered approach runs the risk of putting theory in charge, with the practitioner subordinate to the ideas. This risk is most evident when speaking of applying theories to practice, as though theories were simple technologies to be applied.   Bednar, Cunningham, Duffy, and Perry (as cited in Hannafin et al., 1997) state:

> ...effective instructional design is possible only if the developer has reflexive awareness of the theoretical basis underlying the design...[it] emerges from the deliberate application of some particular theory of learning (pp. 101-102).

Although these authors do not advocate a simple application of theory to practice, theirs is nonetheless a fairly cognitive-rational position. Instructional designers deliberately apply some theory of learning. Whatever decisions or strategies they choose should be consistent with this underlying theory. The Hannafin idea of grounded practice rests on this same premise.

How else can the stance toward theory of designers and participants of learning environments be imagined? Most clinical psychologists are reportedly eclectic in their stance toward the various theories of psychotherapy. Many teachers and instructional designers take the same noncommital stance toward theory. They prefer a menu or toolbox metaphor instead of an application or consistency metaphor. Practitioners tend to be opportunistic with respect to different theoretical conceptions; they might try viewing a problem from one theoretical perspective, then another, and compare results. This stance toward theory might be termed eclectic or grab-bag, but we prefer to think of it as problem- or practitioner-centered. People, rather than ideologies, are in control. The needs of the situation rise above the dictates of rules, models, or even standard values. As we have indicated, we believe such a person-centered approach may be the most situated of approaches, even when the resulting strategies do not look wholly situated or authentic.

Sfard (1998) highlighted the dangers of narrowly applying a single theory to practice:

> When a theory is translated into an instructional prescription, exclusivity becomes the worst enemy of success. Educational practices have an overpowering propensity for extreme, one-for-all practical recipes. A trendy mixture of constructivist, social-interactionist, and situationist approaches...is often translated into a total banishment of "teaching by telling," an imperative to make "cooperative learning" mandatory to all, and a complete delegitimization of instruction that is not "problem-based" or not situated in a real-life context.
>
> But this means putting too much of a good thing into one pot. Because no two students have the same needs and no two teachers arrive at their best performance in the same way, theoretical exclusivity and didactic single-mindedness can be trusted to make even the best of educational ideas fail. (pp. 10-11)

Sfard seemed to be arguing for precisely the opposite of tidy consistency. She continued:

What is true about educational practice also holds for theories of learning....Dictatorship or a single metaphor, like a dictatorship of a single
ideology, may lead to theories that serve the interests of certain groups
to the disadvantage of others....When two metaphors compete for
attention and incessantly screen each other for possible weaknesses,
there is a much better chance for producing....a liberating and consolidating effect on those who learn and those who teach. (p. 11)

Good design of learning environments should be informed by theory but
not slave to it. Designers and participants may keep a theory in mind—or
maybe many theories at once—when considering a problem and deciding on
a course of action. But the problem, not the theory, is at the center. Local
conditions will recommend a solution—in the contextualized, contingent
reasoning of professional practice, which cannot be captured by the technical
rationality of abstract theories, research, and generalities.

Respecting Real Communities

SitCog treats culture as a powerful mediator of learning and practices, both for
students and teachers. Think about a typical problem in practice: To a large
extent, the surrounding culture and scales of community define what is possible and what is real. A school district applying a uniformly consistent Sit-
Cog-inspired teaching method will run into trouble if the broader community's values are not represented. Consistent theoretical grounding is only
possible or desirable where participants share a common ideology. Examples
might include the military, a small company, or a charter school. But even in
these cases, constituencies have this maddening tendency to diverge off the
beaten path, to seek innovation and change, to differ on even fundamental
points. Resulting instructional designs are likely to be some sort of compro-
mise, reflecting the diversity of participants and stakeholders. And rather
than a weakness for lack of theoretical consistency, we tend to see such compromises as valuable reality checks. The hegemony of theory is resisted, and
the needs of real people are accounted for. Through democratic and dialogical
processes, a local solution is found to problems, synthesizing diverse interests, beliefs, and needs, hopefully crossing ideological boundaries to include
the full community.

Our critique of theory can be applied to instructional methods as well. We
believe that instructional quality cannot be guaranteed by adherence to a particular method or strategy. Quality or effectiveness has as much to do with
relationships, contexts, and situations, as it does with method. Quality has as
much to do with how a method is realized, as with how the method is typed
or categorized. Palmer (1997) put it this way: "Good teaching cannot be
reduced to technique; good teaching comes from the identity and integrity of
the teacher" (p. 16). We realize this challenges a core tenet of traditional ID

doctrine. Unfortunately, a full discussion of the limitations of this method is beyond the scope of this chapter.

SUMMARY AND CONCLUSION

We have laid out a number of claims in this chapter concerning situated cognition. First, we presented SitCog as the latest learning theory with potential for grounding learning-environment design, following behaviorism and information-processing theory. However, although SitCog holds some advantages over previous foundations, it does not presently offer a comprehensive account of cognition. "In its more specific implications for education, situated cognition theory has yet to refine a distinct and distinctive approach" (Kirshner & Whitson, 1998, p. 27). For SitCog to fully serve as an integrating framework, a means of accommodating multiple perspectives needs to be developed, to allow inclusion of selected ideas and practices from behaviorism, symbolic cognition, and other theories, both psychological and nonpsychological.

SitCog also presents an opportunity to define the designer's role in new ways. The design task is seen in interactional, rather than rational-planning, terms. But more importantly, design and control become situated within the political and social context of actual learning environments. Rather than applying the best learning theory, designers and participants of learning environments honor the constraints and affordances of the local situation. The use of theory within such learning contexts becomes much less linear and direct. Like any tool, practitioners can find value in various theories, especially in providing alternative lenses for seeing problems. Theories, like other tools, help define the situation and are in turn defined by them. A situated view of design, then, is one that supports the worthy practices of participants and stakeholders, using whatever theories, tools, or technologies at their disposal.

NOTES

[1] Greeno et al. (1998)has another reason for avoiding the term situated cognition. Rather than a kind of cognition, situated cognition is best thought of as the only cognition: "There is not a situated way of teaching and learning ... that contrasts with nonsituated ways. All teaching and learning are situated; the question is what their situated character is" (p. 19). Clancey (1993) echoes this same point:

We are always situated because that is how our brains work. We are situated in an empty dark room, we are situated in bed when dreaming. People doing the Tower of Hanoi problem are always situated agents, regardless or how they solve the problem [Situated action] is a characterization of the mechanism, of our embodiment, not a problem-solving strategy. (p. 100)

[2]A novel way of looking at the problem of transfer has been offered by Greeno, Smith, and Moore (1993). They framed the issue more ecologically in terms of affordances and constraints that hold across situations. This is in line with the person plus unit of analysis, because affordances and constraints cannot be attributed solely to the person or the environment, but must be considered in terms of their interrelationship. According to Greeno, when the same kinds of relationships hold across situations, transfer occurs.

Adult educators have enthusiastically appropriated the idea of cognitive apprenticeships, but the model has been very unevenly applied in real settings. Whereas Collins and Brown conceived of rich, authentic learning environments, instructional products based on the model can be quite traditional and didactic in nature. Kirshner and Whitson (1998) also noted the wide array of methods seeking justification from SitCog theory, ranging from literal apprenticeships to market-driven microvouchers as an alternative to public education!

REFERENCES

Anderson, J. R., Reder, L. M., & Simon, H. A. (1996). Situated learning and education. *Educational Researcher, 25*(5),5–11.

Baker, R. L., & Schutz, R. E. (1971). *Instructional product development*. New York: Van Nostrand Reinhold.

Blum, A. F. (1970) Theorizing. In Jack D. Douglas (Ed.) *Understanding everyday life* (pp.301-319). Chicago: Aldine Atherton.

Bredo, E. (1994). Reconstructing educational psychology: Situated cognition and Deweyian pragmatism. *Educational Psychologist, 29* (1), 23-35.

Brown, J. S., & Duguid, P. (1993, March). Stolen knowledge. *Educational Technology*, 10-15.

Bruner, J.S. (1983). *In search of mind*. New York. Harper & Row.

Bruner, J.S. (1990). *Acts of meaning*. Cambridge, MA: Harvard University Press.

Clancey, W. J. (1993). Situated action: a neuropsychological interpretation. Response to Vera and Simon. *Cognitive Science, 17*, 87-116.

Clancey, W. J. (1995). Practice cannot be reduced to theory: Knowledge, representations, and change in the workplace. In S. Bagnara, C. Zuccermaglio, & S. Stuckey (Eds.), *Organizational learning and technological change.* (pp. 16-46).). New York: Springer-Verlag.

Clancey, W. J. (1997). *Situated cognition: On human knowledge and computer representations.* Cambridge: Cambridge University Press.

Cole, M. (1996). *Cultural psychology.* Cambridge, MA: Belknap Press.

Cook, D. A. (1997). Behavioral analysis as a basis for instructional design. In C. R. Dills & A. J. Romiszowski (Eds.), *Instructional development paradigms* (pp. 215-244). Englewood Cliffs, NJ: Educational Technology Publications.

Dick, W. (1987). A history of instructional design and its impact on educational psychology. In J. A. Glover, R. R. Ronning (Eds.), *Historical foundations of educational psychology* (pp. 183–200). New York: Plenum Press.

Dreyfus, H. L. (1979). *What computers can't do: The limits of artificial intelligence* (2nd ed.). New York: Harper & Row.

Feyerabend, P. (1993). *Against method* (3rd ed.). London: Verso/New Left Books.

Forman, E., Minick, N. & Stone, C.A. (Eds.). (1993). *Contexts for learning: Sociocultural dynamics in children's development.* New York: Oxford University Press.

Gagne, R. M. (1965). *The conditions of learning* (1st ed.). New York: Holt, Rinehart & Winston.

Gagné, R. M. (1987). Peaks and valleys of educational psychology: A retrospective view. In J. A. Glover, & R. R. Ronning (Eds.), *Historical foundations of educational psychology* (pp. 395–402). New York: Plenum Press.

Gee, J. P. (1992). *The social mind: Language, ideology and social practice.* New York: Bergen & Garvey.

Gee, J. P. (1997). Thinking, learning and reading: The situated sociocultural mind. In D. Kirshner & J. A. Whitson (Eds.), *Situated cognition: Social, semiotic and psychological perspectives* (pp. 37-55). Mahwah, NJ: Lawrence Erlbaum Associates.

Glaser, R. (Ed.). (1965). *Teaching machines and programmed learning II: Data and directions.* Washington DC: National Education Association.

Greeno, J. G. (1997). On claims that answer the wrong question. *Educational Researcher, 26*(1) 5–17.

Greeno, J. G., & the Middle School Mathematics Through Applications Projects Group. (1998). The situativity of knowing, learning, and research. *American Psychologist, 53*(1), 5-26.

Greeno, J. G., & Moore, J. L. (1993). Situativity and symbols: Response to Vera and Simon. *Cognitive Science, 17*(1), 49-59.

Greeno, J. G., Smith, D. R. & Moore, J. L. (1993). Transfer of situated learning. In D. K. Detterman & R. J. Sternberg (Eds.), *Transfer on trial:*

Intelligence, cognition, and instruction (pp. 99-167). Norwood, NJ: Ablex.

Hannafin, M. J., Hannafin, K. M., Land, S. M., & Oliver, K. (1997). Grounded practice and the design of constructivist learning environments. *Educational Technology Research & Development, 45* (3), 101-117.

Hilgard, E. R. (1987). Perspectives on educational psychology. In J. A. Glover, & R. R. Ronning (Eds.), *Historical foundations of educational psychology* (pp. 415-423). New York: Plenum.

Holton, G. (1995). The controversy over the end of science. *Scientific American, 273*(4), 168.

Kirshner, D. & Whitson, J.A. (1997). Introduction. In D. Kirshner & J. A. Whitson (Eds.), *Situated cognition: Social, semiotic, and psychological perspectives.* Mahwah, NJ: Lawrence Erlbaum Associates.

Kirshner, D., & Whitson, J. A. (1998, November). Obstacles to understanding cognition as situated. *Educational Researcher, 28,* 22-28.

Kliebard, H. M. (1987). *The struggle for the American curriculum 1893-1958.* New York: Routledge.

Labaree, D. F. (1998). Educational researchers: Living with a lesser form of knowledge. *Educational Researcher,* 4-12.

Lave, J. (1988). *Cognition in practice.* Cambridge, England: Cambridge University Press.

Lave, J. (1991). Situated learning in communities of practice. In L. B. Resnick, J. M. Levine, & S. D. Teasley (Eds), *Perspectives on socially shared cognition* (pp. 63-82). Washington, DC: American Pscyhological Association.

Lemke, J. L. (1997). Cognition, context, and learning: A social semiotic perspective. In D. Kirschner & J. A. Whitson (Eds.), *Situated cognition: Social, semiotic and psychological perspectives* (pp. 37-55). Mahwah NJ: Lawrence Erlbaum Associates.

Light, P., & Butterworth, G. (1992). *Context and cognition: Ways of learning and knowing.* Hillsdale, NJ: Lawrence Erlbaum Associates.

Mager, R. F. (1962) *Preparing instructional objectives.* San Francisco: Fearon.

Markle, S. M. (1965). *Good frames and bad.* New York: Wiley.

Mayer, R. E. (1992). Cognition and instruction: Their historic meeting within educational psychology. *Journal of Educational Psychology, 84* (4), 405–412.

Mayer, R. E. (1996). Learners as information processors: Legacies and limitations of educational psychology's second metaphor. *Educational Psychologist, 31* (3/4), 151-161.

Newman, D., Griffin, P., & Cole, M. (1989). *The construction zone.* Cambridge, England: Cambridge University Press.

Norman, D. A. (1993). Cognition in the head and in the world: An introduction to the special issue on situated action. *Cognitive Science, 17* (1), 1-6.

Palmer, P. J. (1997, November/December). The heart of a teacher: Identity and integrity in teaching. *Change,* 15-21.

Perkins, D. N. (1991, May). Technology meets constructivism: Do they make a marriage? *Educational Technology,* 18–23.

Resnick, L. B., Säljö, R., Pontecorvo, C., & Burge, B. (Eds.). (1991). *Discourse, tools, and reasoning: Essays on situated cognition.* Berlin, Germany: Springer.

Rogoff, B. (1990). *Apprenticeship in thinking.* New York: Oxford University Press.

Salomon, G., & Perkins, D. N. (1998). Individual and social aspects of learning. In P. D. Pearson & A. Iran-Nejad (Eds.), *Review of Research in Education, 23,* 1-24.

Sfard, A. (1998, March). On two metaphors for learning and the dangers of choosing just one. *Educational Researcher, 27,* 4-13.

Shore, B. (1996). *Culture in mind: Cognition, culture, and the problem of meaning.* New York: Oxford University Press.

Shulman, L. S. (1986). Paradigms and research programs in the study of teaching: A contemporary perspective. In M. C. Wittrock (Ed.), *Handbook of research on teaching* (3rd ed., pp. 3-36). New York: MacMillan.

St. Julien, J. (1997). Explaining learning: The research trajectory of situated cognition and the implications for connectionism. In D. Kirschner & J. Whitson (Eds.), *Situated cognition: Social, semiotic, and psychological perspectives* (pp. 261-280). Mahwah, NJ: Lawrence Erlbaum Associates.

Suchman, L. (1993). Response to Vera and Simon's Situated Action: A Symbolic Interpretation. *Cognitive Science, 17*(1), 71-75.

Thomas, G. (1997). What's the use of theory? *Harvard Educational Review, 67*(1), 75-104.

Toffler, A. (1985). *The adaptive corporation.* Aldershot UK: Bower.

Tripp, S. D. (1993, March). Theories, traditions, and situated learning. *Educational Technology, 33,* 71-77.

Winograd, T., & Flores, F. (1986). Understanding computers and cognition: A new foundation for design. Norwood NJ: Ablex.

Young, M. F. (1993). Instructional design for situated learning. *Educational Technology Research & Development, 43*(1), 43-58.

4

Revisiting Activity Theory as a Framework for Designing Student-Centered Learning Environments

David H. Jonassen

Pennsylvania State University

INTRODUCTION

Rohrer-Murphy and I (Jonassen & Rohrer-Murphy, 1999) described how activity theory may be used as a framework for designing constructivist learning environments (Jonassen, 1999) by analyzing the activity systems that are being simulated in the learning environment. Just as activity theory itself is a constantly evolving multivoiced activity system (Engeström, 1993), so are the conceptions of how it can be used to model activity systems in learning environments. Asmolov (1987) believed that "the principle of historicism.... pervades all investigations using the activity approach." That is, the development of our understanding of activity theory and its uses for designing student-centered learning environments (SCLEs) is historically mediated; it changes over time. As theoretical foundations of SCLEs coalesce (as described in this book), our understanding of how to design them also clarifies.

So, in this chapter, I revisit the activity theory framework in terms of a SCLE that we developed to support a university course in operations management. First, I describe the SCLE that was developed. Then, I describe the components and assumptions of activity theory. Finally, I analyze the activity systems for creating the environment as well as the real-world, business-related activity systems that were simulated in the environment. I continue to believe that activity theory offers a powerful framework for analyzing activity systems for the purpose of designing SCLEs and for understanding the activities of an instructional design community engaged in designing such learning environments. This belief is not without critics. S. Barab (June, 1999, personal communication) questioned whether it is possible to transmit characteristics from one activity system into another, that is, to map the characteristics of a business activity system onto a learning activity system: "One cannot embed characteristics from the outside, but instead they will emerge within the system as a result of primary and secondary contradictions that characterized the system" (see Chapter 3, pp. 76-78, this volume). This descriptive-prescriptive issue is implicit in nearly every chapter in this book.

STUDENT-CENTERED LEARNING ENVIRONMENTS

In Chapter 1 (this volume), Land and Hannafin describe the tenets of open-ended, student-centered learning environments, which are the focus of this book. They exemplify those tenets with a variety of existing learning environments. I have elsewhere described a model for designing SCLEs (Jonassen, 1999) that synthesizes the tenets and beliefs described by Land and Hannafin, though I do not presume that it is universally appropriate. Rather, it will probably be useful only in contexts where the goals of learning are consistent with nonschool-world learning, where there is a desire to simulate the sociocultural and sociohistorical context in the learning environment. That is the model that guided the construction of the SCLE that I describe next.

The SCLE was designed and developed to support a third-year course in operations management in a college of business in a major university. The goal of the environment was to introduce students to and provide them practice conducting aggregate planning. Aggregate planning is a problem-solving process where operations managers attempt to balance inventory, production, technology, and employees (human resources) with demand and sales. It costs money to hire and fire employees and hold inventory, so producing or providing the right amount of goods and services to meet but not greatly exceed sales demand maximizes profits, which is the primary goal of business in a capitalistic society. Rather than teaching all of the prerequisite knowledge, our environment immersed students in the planning process, requiring them to understand concepts and principles of aggregate planning in the context of solving aggregate planning problems. I briefly describe the components of SCLEs and exemplify them with short descriptions of our aggregate planning SCLE.

Problem/Project Space

The focus of any SCLE is the question or issue, the case, the problem, or the project that learners attempt to solve or resolve. It constitutes the learning goal and the object of the activity system represented (learning how to do something). The fundamental difference between SCLEs and direct instruction is that the problem drives the learning. In direct instruction, problems function as examples or applications of the concepts and principles previously taught. In SCLEs, students learn domain content in order to solve the problem. Thus, knowledge and learning are situated and contextually bound.

SCLEs can be constructed to support question- or issue-based, case-based, project-based, or problem-based learning. Question- or issue-based learning begins with a controversial question or a dilemma. In case-based learning, students construct knowledge and develop requisite thinking skills by studying cases (e.g. legal, medical, social work) and preparing case summaries or diagnoses. Case learning is anchored in authentic contexts; learners must think and manage complexity like practitioners. Project-based learning focuses on relatively long-term, integrated units of instruction where learners focus on complex projects consisting of multiple cases. They debate ideas, plan and conduct experiments, and communicate their findings (Krajcik, Blumenfeld, Marx, & Soloway, 1994). Problem-based learning integrates problems at a curricular level, requiring learners to self-direct their learning while solving numerous cases across a curriculum. Case-, project-, and problem-based learning represent a continuum of complexity, but all share the same assumptions about active, constructive, and authentic learning (see Chapter 2, this volume). SCLEs can be developed to support each of these, so for purposes of this chapter, I refer to the focus of the SCLEs generically as a problem.

Because the key to meaningful learning is ownership of the problem or learning goal, it is important to present learners with interesting, relevant, and engaging problems to solve. Problems should be ill-structured, so that some aspects of it are emergent. Unless some components of the problem can be defined by the students, they will have no ownership of it and will be less motivated to solve it. Students know that textbook problems are prescriptive and well-structured and therefore have little reason or desire to solve them.

Ill-structured problems emerge from practice in the field being studied. For learning how to conduct aggregate planning, we present two companies that are dealing with aggregate planning problems (one small and less complex, one large and more complex), so there are two case problems that students solve in the Aggregate Planning SCLE. The first is an accounting firm, Brilliant Deductions Tax Accounting, and the second a soft drink company, Bloat Pop, Inc. Learners are coached to attempt the less complex accounting case first.

The problem or project space in SCLEs consists of three integrated and highly interrelated components: the problem context, the problem presentation or simulation, and the problem manipulation space.

Problem Context. The physical, sociocultural, and organizational context that surrounds any problem helps to constrain and define the project. SCLEs describe important contextual elements of the activity system in which the problem is usually solved. This may include descriptions of the actors or stakeholders in the activity system, their backgrounds, beliefs, and goals, the organizational climate, and the history and cultural constraints implicit in the environment. In each problem (Brilliant Deductions and Bloat Pop), learners begin by entering into a conversation with employees of the firm (Fig. 4.1) as well as reading and listening to internal correspondence within the organization. These conversations help to establish the organizational and operational climate of the businesses. The narrative format for represent-

FIG. 4.1 Brilliant Deductions background page.

ing the problem context is realistic and illustrates the attitudes and beliefs of stakeholders in the organization.

Problem Representation or Simulation. The problem context and problem representation become a story about a set of events which leads up to the problem that needs to be resolved. The way in which the problem or project is introduced to the learner is critical to the amount of buy in by the learners. The problem presentation has to be interesting, appealing, and engaging. The purpose of the problem presentation is to simulate the problem in the context in which it is normally and naturally encountered. Why? Because understanding the context is essential to understanding the problem. The context constrains and defines the problem. Each of the icons on the side (As shown in Fig. 4.1), demand, technology, sales, human resources, and inventory represent the different aspects of the case. Clicking on the sales icon presents historical sales information for Brilliant Deductions; clicking on the inventory button provides information about available inventory, and so on. The problem for the learner is to predict demand and sales and to determine the appropriate levels of technology, inventory, and human resources to maintain.

Problem Manipulation Space. The problem or project space must also provide students with the opportunity to manipulate the problem in order to test various dynamic relations among the problem components. Students cannot assume any ownership of the problem unless they know that they can affect the problem situation in some meaningful way. So, manipulating the phenomena in a problem and seeing the results of those manipulations are important. Perkins referred to this problem component as a phenomenaria (spaces for manipulating phenomena). Phenomenaria allow students learners to test their hypotheses on reasonably faithful simulations of the environment being explored. Again, the problem presentation and problem manipulation spaces are often integrated into a seamless problem space. In the aggregate planning problem, students' solutions are worked out on a complex and multifaceted spreadsheet (shown in Fig. 4.2). They can manipulate levels for all the factors such as production rates, employees hired, or employees fired. These values are integrated into aggregate planning formulas to allow learners to test the effects of any manipulation. They continue to manipulate the variables until they have achieved what they believe to be the maximum levels.

Related Cases

Understanding phenomena is inextricably interrelated with our experiences of them. What novice business people (learners in college) lack most are experiences, because most curricula focus on transmission of concepts and abstract theories. Experiences are especially critical when trying to solve ill-structured problems. So, when learners are expected to solve problems in a SCLE, it is necessary to scaffold those experiences by providing related cases. Related cases in learning environments support learning in two important ways: by scaffolding memory through case-based reasoning and by representing complexity (multiple perspectives related to any problem).

Assumptions						
1) The maximum overtime is 20 hours (a total of a 60 hour work week) - you will need 2 employees on OT to mak						
2) Only full-time employees are allowed to work OT						
3) The owner must pay the computer fee for himself when the number of temp employees is under 6						
Will you sign the union contract (difference must be less than 50 K of part 1's Total Profit)?						
Would you recommend expansion ?					Total Profit :	
Demand (in weeks)	Week 1	Week 2	Week 3	Week 4	Week 5	Week 6
Long Form	35	40	55	65	80	80
Short Form	95	115	165	195	245	295
LongForm Accountants	2	2	3	3	4	4
ShortForm Accountants	1	2	2	3	3	4
Owner Contribribution	0.75	0.75	0.75	0.75	0.75	0.75
Total emps needed	2.27	2.78	4.20	5.10	6.52	7.18
Fire FT emps						
Hire FT emps						
Current number of FT emps	5	5	5	5	5	5
Hire temps						
Fire temps						
Current number of temps	0	0	0	0	0	0
Emps available for OT	5	5	5	5	5	5
No of emps on OT						
Revenue	$21,750	$25,500	$35,750	$36,250	$36,250	$36,250
Expenses:						
Owner	$2,000	$2,000	$2,000	$2,000	$2,000	$2,000
Req FT labor costs	$3,000	$3,000	$3,000	$3,000	$3,000	$3,000

FIG. 4.2 Section of aggregate planning spreadsheet.

The more engaging our experiences are, the richer our conscious understanding of those experiences is. The problems that have the most meaning for us are those in which students have invested the greatest amount of effort to solve. Related cases support meaning making by providing representations of the experiences that learners have not had, enabling them to consciously experience the nature of the activity systems normally involved in their solution. When individuals first encounter a problem, they are likely initially to draw on intuitive theories or personal experiences. People often try to map previous experiences and its lessons onto the current problem. By presenting related cases in learning environments, SCLEs provide the learners with a set of experiences and the knowledge that they may have constructed related to those experiences, to compare with the current problem or issue.

Related cases also help to represent complexity in learning environments by providing multiple perspectives or approaches to the problems or issues being examined by the learners. Cognitive flexibility theory provides multiple representations of content in order to convey the complexity that is inherent in the knowledge domain (Spiro, Vispoel, Schmitz, Samarapun-gavan, & Boerger, 1987). It stresses the conceptual interrelatedness of ideas and their interconnectedness by providing multiple representations of content. The ill-structuredness of any knowledge domain is best illustrated by multiple perspectives or themes that are inherent in many cases. These multiple perspectives are required for reasoning about complex problems. Multiple cases support the representation of the natural complexity in everyday problems.

Aggregate Planning Related Cases. For each of these areas of information (demand, technology, sales, human resources, and inventory), links to related cases present historical accounts and interviews with employees of companies similar to Brilliant Deductions. These related cases tell stories about how those similar companies accommodated demand, technology needs, sales, human resources, and inventory problems in their companies. By presenting related cases in learning environments, learners are provided with a set of experiences to compare to the current problem or issue. Learners retrieve from related cases advice on how to succeed, pitfalls that may cause failure, what worked or did not work, and why it did not (Kolodner, 1993). They adapt the explanation to fit the current problem.

Information Resources

In order to support their experiences of phenomena, individuals often need additional information about them. So SCLEs should provide information banks or repositories of information relevant to the problem. In direct instruction, content ideas are typically taught prior to applying them. In SCLEs, practice and knowledge acquisition are mutually supportive and therefore not sequenced. Information is made available to support practice. In order to be accessible and useful in supporting practice, information banks should be organized in ways that support the kinds of activities in which they are engaged. Enabling learners to access information that does not support understanding and practice probably will not enhance either. In fact, it often distracts the learner and impedes understanding and problem solving.

Aggregate Planning Resources. The aggregate planning SCLE provides a variety of information resources about the aggregate planning process that help the students to understand the process and its business procedures well enough to solve the problem. Students are provided text documents, graphics, and sound resources about the process. Making information available only in the context of the problem solving activity is one of the major operational differences between traditional and constructivist learning environments. Traditional instruction insists on providing all of the concepts and theory prior to applying it by solving problems, whereas SCLEs assume that information is meaningful only in the context of activity.

Cognitive (Knowledge Construction) Tools

SCLEs seek to represent the complexity of the real-world activity system it simulates. However, that complexity often calls on skills that are not in learners' repertoires prior to engaging in the problem or project. Therefore it is necessary to scaffold their performance of those activities and the emergent sense making that co-occurs with that performance. In order to do that, it is necessary to identify the activities that are involved in solving the problem or completing the mission that is embedded in the problem representation. Having identified those skills, it is necessary to build in cognitive tools that scaffold the learners' abilities to perform those tasks. Cognitive tools may be organization tools for analyzing ideas, dynamic modeling tools for creating representations of their mental models, visualization tools for helping to see phenomena in different ways, conversation tools for enabling them to build collaborative knowledge bases, or computational tools (Jonassen, 2000). SCLEs often embed a suite of tools to help learners think in appropriate ways.

Aggregate Planning Tools. While investigating all aspects of the case (demand, technology, sales, human resources, and inventory) and the related cases (described next), learners may engage in the aggregate planning process. Clicking on the Aggregate Planning icon links to the instructions for downloading and using an Excel spreadsheet to calculate costs (Fig. 4.2). The Excel spreadsheet enables students to manipulate all of the variables in the case and test the results of those manipulations. The formulas enable students to speculate by entering different values for each of the variables in the planning process. When the students complete their analysis and are satisfied with their projections, they submit their spreadsheets to an electronic grading service. Because several hundred students are typically enrolled in this operations management course, electronic scoring is essential. Prior to the use of the SCLE, this meant multiple choice questions. This SCLE provides an authentic alternative to multiple choice exams that requires learners to speculate, make inferences, and solve problems.

The aggregate planning SCLE uses a spreadsheet as its primary cognitive tool because, according to Plane (1997), managers use spreadsheets all the time for analysis. They are computation and speculation tools that are authentic to business operations.

Conversation and Collaboration Tools

A common misconception of learning environments is that they are designed to be used by individuals in isolation. To the contrary, modern technology-supported learning environments use a variety of computer-mediated communication methods to support collaboration among communities of learners. SCLEs provide access to shared information and knowledge building tools to help learners to collaboratively construct socially shared knowledge. Most problems in business are solved collaboratively, so in order to effectively simulate business activities, learners should also be required to collaborate. In order to support this, SCLEs may provide for computer conferencing, chats, UseNet groups, MUDs and MOOs to facilitate dialog and knowledge building among the community of learners.

Aggregate Planning Collaboration Tools. In the residential course, students are required to solve the problem in collaborative groups of three. The groups of students must work simultaneously in the university computer labs or in their dormitory rooms. In order to support distance learning, instructional designers have been experimenting with a variety of conversation and collaboration tools to support the aggregate planning process. The most commonly used environments have been asynchronous conferencing; however, I believe that synchronous conferencing, whenever possible, may be productive because learners are engaged in an intentional problem-solving process. Synchronous electronic communication requires intentional activity and an object of deliberation, both of which are essential components of activity theory.

In the following section, I describe activity theory and later use it as a lens for analyzing the aggregate planning process for the purpose of designing the aggregate planning SCLE in addition to analyzing the design process that I engaged in. Instructional design involves complex activity systems, as I shall show.

ACTIVITY THEORY

Activity theory is "a philosophy and cross-disciplinary framework for studying different forms of human activity" (Kuutti, 1996). It is a

• form of sociocultural analysis (virtually all human activity is embedded in a social matrix composed of people and artifacts, Nardi, 1996),

• form of sociohistorical analysis (virtually all human activity evolves over time and is distributed among individuals and their cultures),

• theory of mediated action which focuses on agents and their cultural tools, the mediators of action (Wertsch, 1998).

Activity theory has its roots in the classical German philosophy of Kant and Hegel, the dialectical materialism of Marx, and the sociocultural and sociohistorical tradition of Russian psychologists such as Vygotsky, Leont'ev, and Luria (Kuutti, 1996). Activity theory is not a methodology. Rather it is a "philosophical framework for studying different forms of human praxis as developmental processes, both individual and social levels interlinked at the same time" (p. 532). Activity theory adopts Marx's dialectic materialist view of activity and consciousness as dynamically interrelated (Leont'ev, 1972), which provides an alternative perspective to the mentalistic and idealist views of human knowledge that assume a duality of thinking and activity. Activity theorists argue that conscious learning and activity (performance) are completely interactive and interdependent. Activity cannot occur without consciousness (the mind as whole), and consciousness cannot occur outside of the context of activity.

Of what relevance is activity theory to instructional designers? Because most of the conceptions of learning that are described in this book claim that learning occurs most naturally and meaningfully in the sociocultural, activity-oriented contexts, it is important to analyze activity systems (activity structures in their sociocultural, sociohistorical contexts) as part of the instructional design process. Activity theory is a useful framework for understanding the totality of human work and praxis (Bødker, 1991a), that is, activity in context. So analyzing activity systems is essential for designing SCLEs. It is also important to use new methods of analysis for understanding the instructional design process. In most organizational contexts, instructional design is a rich sociocultural process that is far better understood through the lens of activity theory than it is through analyzing the procedure charts that have dominated the field for so long.

Before examining how to use activity theory as a framework for analyzing activity systems, I briefly describe the components of activity systems and then describe the assumptions under which activity systems function.

Activity System

Traditionally, psychologists have examined human performance as the primary unit of analysis. Behaviorists (see Chapter 3, this volume) examined individual behavioral dispositions; cognitivists examined individual mental models, cognitive structures, and explanations for their performance. Education has fostered the use of these metrics by emphasizing individual accountability in its evaluation processes. Activity theory, on the other hand, is a form of sociocultural analysis that focuses on the activity system as the unit of analysis.

Activity systems are collective human constructions that are not reducible to discrete individual actions (Leont'ev, 1974). Russell (1997) claimed

> An activity system is any ongoing, object-directed, historically-conditioned, dialectically-structured, tool-mediated human interaction: a family, a religious organization, an advocacy group, a political movement, a course of study, a school, a discipline, a research laboratory, a profession, and so on.

Activity systems are focused by the interaction of minds in the world, socially constructing and sharing meaning (Holt & Morris, 1993).

Activity systems contain interacting components (subject, tools, object, division of labor, community, and rules, as shown in Fig. 4.3) and are organized to accomplish the activities of the activity subsystems (Engeström,

1987). Activity subsystems (production, distribution, exchange, and consumption, as shown in Fig. 4.3) describe the higher order functions, interactions, and relationships between the components of the triangle (Holt & Morris, 1993).

Production Subsystem. The primary focus of activity systems analysis is the top triangle of Fig. 4.3 (the production of some object). Production of the object is oriented by the outcome or intention of the activity system. Our activity (producing a SCLE) was oriented by the outcome of engaging management students in an authentic form of problem solving. The object of the aggregate planning process is a plan for regulating the outcomes of production, hiring and firing, and inventory. The production subsystem

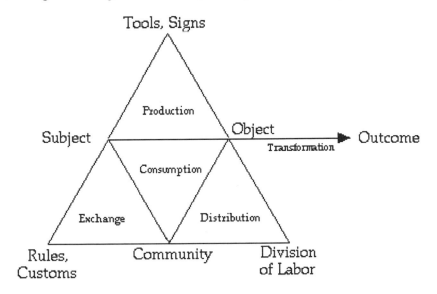

Fig 3. Activity system (Adapted from Engeström, 1987)

consists of the objects that attempt to produce the outcome of the system. Analyzing the artifacts that are generated by the activity system (outcome) is important to understanding the purpose of the system. The production process in any activity system involves a subject, the object of the activity, the tools that are used in the activity, and the actions and operations that affect an outcome (Nardi, 1996). The production subsystem is generally regarded as the most important, because in the production processes, the object of the system is transformed into the outcome, that is, the intentions of the activity system are manifest. The production subsystem consists of interactions and relationships between the subject and object that are mediated by tools and signs. Its goal is to transform the object of activity into an outcome. It is important to note that concurrent with the production of physical objects, the subject is also producing (constructing) knowledge about the activity, its components, assumptions, and contradictions. The conscious understanding is an essential part of the activity that cannot be separated from it.

Subject. The subject of any activity is the individual or group of actors engaged in the activity. Activity systems are perceived from their point of view. For example, in an ID context, the subject may be a single designer or a team consisting of designers, a manager, subject matter experts, and media producers.

Object. All activity is object-oriented. Objects of activity systems are artifacts that are produced by the system. Whether physical, mental, or symbolic, they are the product that is acted on by the subject. The transformation of the object into the outcome represents the purpose or intention of the activity. The outcome of our SCLE was learning which is facilitated by the object of the activity system, the SCLE. Whatever it is, the object is transformed in the course of activity, so it is not immutable (Nardi, 1996). Just as the object is transformed during the production process, the subject may also be transformed by the object. As individuals engage in activity systems, they are changed by those systems. Although the object of the activity might initially be a SCLE, the form and function of that object is likely to be modified as the activity unfolds.

Tools, Signs, and Mediators. The production subsystem is completed by the tools, sign systems, theories, and procedures that mediate the activity. Most generally, tools and signs are the means that actors (subject) use for acting on the object. They can be anything used in the transformation process (physical, like hammers or computers, or abstract or mental, like sign systems, programming languages, models or heuristics). The use of culture-specific tools shapes the way people act and think. For the activity of designing, tools may include the design models and methods employed (e.g. anchored instruction, case-based reasoning), the physical apparatus and tools (computers, Fax machines, telephones, video cameras), and reasoning (e.g. problem-solving skills, task decomposition, synthetic thinking) that mediate the group's activity toward designing and developing the SCLE. The tools alter the activity and are, in turn, altered by the activity. For example, using an inquiry design model will result in dramatically different instructional materials (object) than a direct instruction model. Yet the inquiry model that is used will be adapted by each new application. It cannot be applied identically in different contexts, as many traditional design models assume. Activity theory itself is a mediating tool for research and development. In the context of this chapter, it recommends an approach to analyzing situations for ID.

The tools that were used to construct the learning environment consisted of learning models, such as anchored instruction, cognitive flexibility theory, and case-based reasoning, from which several aspects of the environment were drawn. They also included methods, such as nominal group technique, for conducting needs assessment, as well as the computers, software, and programming languages like Java used to produce the environment. The tools that aggregate planners use primarily include spreadsheets and business forecasts. The tools that designers use include the ID models, communication tools, needs assessment and task analysis methods, multimedia computers, video, and so on.

Consumption Subsystem

The consumption subsystem (Fig. 4.3) describes how the subject and the surrounding community collaborate to act on the object. The consumption process represents a contradiction inherent in activity systems. Although the goal of activity systems is to transform an object, those production activities also consume energy and resources from the subject and the community in which it operates (Holt & Morris, 1993). The subject must operate within a community that reciprocally supports the production activities of the subject but also consumes effort from the subject. The consumption subsystem involves the community in which the subject exists to become involved with the production of the object.

Community. Very little, if any, meaningful activity is accomplished individually. People may perform individually in different contexts, but their ability to perform is predicated on groups of people. That is, individuals are concurrently members of different communities. The learning environment design community consists of the interdependent aggregate (e.g. designers within the organization, project managers, artists, programmers, subject matter experts, and others who contribute to the activity), designers who share (at least to some degree) a set of activities and their social meanings. They also rely on their immediate community of workers to fulfill the activity. Therefore "the human individual's activity is a system of social relations. It does not exist without those social relations" (Leont'ev, 1981, pp. 46-7).

The community consists of the individuals and subgroups that focus at least some of their effort on the object. Within activity systems, the community functions to distribute cognitive responsibility among participants and artifacts (see Chapter 5, this volume). Knowledge in any activity system is distributed among the members of the subject group and community with whom it interacts, the tools they use, and the products they create. Human cognition is always situated in a complex sociocultural world that affects individual cognition. Hutchins (1995) showed how cognitive responsibility in piloting a ship is distributed among numerous pilots, navigators, and the tools they use to pilot their ship in confined spaces. The task, like most activities, is too complex for an individual and is dependent on the personal knowledge of members of the activity system as well as the coordination among individuals and artifacts (Nardi, 1996). Activity theory and distributed cognitions, Nardi claimed, are close in spirit and may merge in time.

Again, although the goal of communities is to support the production activities, communities often consume effort and retard production. These contradictions may occur within a specific activity system or result from contradictions between activity systems. Why? Because individuals involved in a particular activity are also simultaneously members of other independent or overlapping activity groups that have different objects, tools, and social relations. Individuals naturally are caught up in some of the unrelated activities of their collaborators. Coworkers, for instance, may interact in several activity systems, such as church groups, social clubs, or coaching their daughter's soccer team, each of which engages different activities and cultures. Because people are all simultaneously members of various communities (the community in which we live, the community within which they recreate, and the professional community in which they work), they must continuously alter their beliefs and actions to adjust to the socially mediated expectations of different groups. Conflicts between roles in the various communities often arise, leading to transformational activities required to harmonize those contradicting expectations. These overlapping activity systems represent a horizontalness in activity theory dynamics.

Distribution Subsystem

The distribution subsystem ties the object of activity to the community by defining a division of labor. That is, it divides up activities according to social laws or expectations.

Division of Labor. The division of labor refers to the horizontal division of tasks between cooperating members of the community but also to the vertical division of power and status (Engeström, 1999). Most organizations in which work is done evolve both horizontally and vertically. However, organizations vary in terms of the flexibility with which their divisions of labor are administered. In some organizations, those divisions are negotiated on an activity-by-activity basis, whereas in other more vertical organizations, divisions are mandated from the top down. How flexibly any work organization can adapt to circumstances will determine the ability of the activity system to engage in different activities. That is, how work is distributed throughout the organization determines to some degree the nature of the work culture and the climate for those involved in any activity system.

Exchange Subsystem

The exchange subsystem engages the subject and two contextual components: the rules that constrain the activity and the community with which the subject interacts. It regulates the activities of the system in terms of personal needs. The exchange of personal, social, and cultural norms in any work community also determines the nature of the work culture and the climate for those involved in any activity system. In the exchange subsystem, those norms are negotiated by members of the community and become the rules by which the activity system and subject regulate their performance.

Rules. The rules refer to the explicit regulations, laws, policies, and conventions that constrain activity as well as the implicit social norms, standards, and relationships among members of the community. Rules inherently guide (at least to some degree) the actions or activities acceptable by the community, so the signs, symbols, tools, models, and methods that the community uses will mediate the process. For example, corporations that emphasize efficiency may not accept constructivist models and methods of learning to mediate the design activity. Activities are socially and contextually bound. So, any activity system can be described only in the context of the community in which it operates.

Community. The community negotiates and mediates the rules and customs that describe how the community functions, what it believes, and the ways that it supports different activities. Within the community, individuals support different activities. For example, instructional development is normally accomplished in teams. Team members have negotiated roles based on skills, preferences, or availability. Formal and informal rules evolve to guide their activity. Their assignment to those activities defines the division of labor, which is also mediated by rules and social negotiation (e.g., people in certain departments are responsible for specific activities in the process). Any work community negotiates the rules, customs, and division of labor that mediate its activity. Different communities negotiate different rules and customs.

Instructional designers also have a role in the contextually important framework of activity theory. They interpret the rules and roles of the community into a series of learning activities in which learners may assume different roles, perform different actions, negotiate different roles, and so on. When analyzing activity systems for the purpose of designing SCLEs, then, it is necessary to embed these different aspects of community—the activities and the rules, division of labor, and symbolic and social mediators that define those activities.

Activity Structure

Activity within and between subsystems consists of a goal-directed hierarchy of actions (see Fig. 4.4) that are used to accomplish the object—the activities, actions, and operations that transform the object. Activity is conscious process that consists of chains of actions that consist of chains of operations. Toward the goal of the activity "constructing SCLEs," for example, the subject consisted of the individuals and work groups that were formed at the university to work on the object (i.e. aggregate planning SCLE) through the activity of instructional design and development. That activity consisted of numerous actions: conduct needs assessment, perform task analysis, design interactions, html and Java coding, and so on. In order to accomplish those actions, designers and others performed operations, such as taking pictures with a camera, entering data into a spreadsheet, making telephone calls, and so forth. All operations are actions when they are first performed because they require conscious effort. With practice and internalization, activities collapse into actions and eventually into operations, as they become more automatic, requiring less conscious effort. The reverse dynamic is also possible: Operations can be disrupted and become actions. So the relationships among activities, actions, and operations are dynamic, as indicated by the bidirectional arrows in Fig. 4.4.

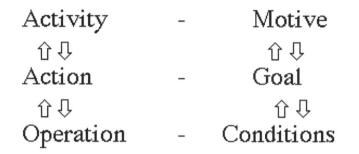

FIG. 4.4. Hierarchical nature of activities, actions and operations

The activity provides the motive for the activity system. Activity system components are oriented by the goal of transforming the object into the outcome. When all system components are oriented by the same object and process, with few contradictions between and among those components, the activity system functions more productively. Actions are completed in order to fulfill shorter term goals, while operations are mediated by the conditions under which they occur. The hierarchical nature of activity structures provides a hierarchy of motives that support activity, actions, and operations.

In order to simulate activity systems in SCLEs, it is necessary to identify the activity structures entailed by the activity. In designing the aggregate planning SCLE, for instance, we had to identify the aggregate planning activity structure. The activity of aggregate planning consisted of actions such as predicting demand for products or services, human resource requirements, and technology needs; anticipating sales; determining production and inventory levels; and balancing those factors. These actions required numerous operations including researching information, manipulating spreadsheet values, making telephone calls, and so on. Having identified the activity structure of aggregate planning, we were then able to identify the problem representation and manipulation components of the SCLE as well as antici-pate the need for cognitive tools to scaffold these actions and operations where necessary. The activity structure determines what the learners in an SCLE will be doing while learning in the activity system simulated.

Next, I elaborate some of the assumptions underlying activity systems and activity theory.

ASSUMPTIONS OF ACTIVITY THEORY

Unity of Consciousness and Activity

One of the most fundamental assumptions of activity theory is the integra-tion of consciousness and activity. Activities are the human interactions with the objective world and the conscious activities that are embedded in those interactions. Thinking is the internalized form of activity. Most educators have always assumed that it is necessary to learn about something before learning how to use it. Declarative knowledge must precede procedural. Gagne's (1968) prerequisite sequencing of instruction, for instance, claims that verbal information is prerequisite to intellectual use of ideas. Activity theory, on the other hand, claims that the human mind emerges and exists as a special component of interactions with the environment, so activity (sensory, mental, and physical) and conscious processing (learning) cannot be sepa-rated. Individuals cannot understand something without acting on it. Con-scious meaning making is engaged by activity. What individuals know is base on the interaction of conscious meaning making and activity, which are dynamically evolving. For example, instructional designers who worked on the aggregate planning environment described earlier had studied the ID process from textbooks, but their understanding of the process was shaped by the activities and knowledge constructed on this project and any others they may have worked on. And having worked on this project, their identities as instructional designers emerged through the activities of designing. Identity building, from a social constructivist perspective, provides perhaps the strongest evidence of learning. It, like other forms of meaning making, is embedded in activity. Identity building occurs when designers engage in ID activities, using the language, processes, and tools of design in different con-texts. Therefore, designers who work in different contexts conceive of them-selves and the design process differently, because the systems of people (their goals, needs, and beliefs) and artifacts change the nature of the conscious activity.

Not only do activity and consciousness coexist, they are mutually sup-portive. There is reciprocal regulatory feedback between knowledge and ac-tivity (Fishbein, Eckart, Lauver, van Leeuwen, & Langemeyer, 1990). As we act we gain understanding, which affects our actions, which changes our under-standing, and so on. This transformational process is critical to activity theory. Consciousness and activity are dynamically interrelated. As novice designers perform ID activities, they come to better understand the process, which in turn affects the way they perform ID activities, which affects their performance. That is, consciousness is embedded in the wider activity system that surrounds an individual's activities, so that changes in the physical, mental, or social conditions of a person's situation are internalized and directly reflected in the person's conscious activities. If a company implements new design processes, it redefines the designers' understanding of their job and the activities that comprise it.

Intentionality

All animals, including humans, interact with their environments and learn about their world through those interactions in order to fulfill some goal. Activity theory focuses on the purposeful actions that are realized through conscious intentions.

Before intentions are manifest in actions in the real world they are planned. Humans orient their activity to the context in which it will occur and plan their activities accordingly. Their intentions and plans are not rigid or accurate descriptions of the intended action but rather are always incomplete and tentative. Nearly every instructional design project, for instance, is adjusted, reconceptualized, and renegotiated during the design and development process. According to activity theory, intentions emerge from contradictions that individuals perceive in their environment, such as differences between what they believe they need to know in order to accomplish a goal and what they do, in fact, know at any point in time. Their intentions, however, can exist only in the context of the intended activity. The phenomenal growth of activity theory itself has emerged in response to internal contradictions in the field of psychology.

So, activity theory claims that learning and doing are inseparable and that they are initiated by an intention. What is the source of that intention? Intentions are directed at objects of activity (see the activity system model in Fig. 4.3). The object of activity can be anything as long as it can be transformed by subjects of the activity system. Objects may be physical objects (e.g., a house that is built), soft objects (e.g., computer program), or conceptual objects (e.g., a theory or model of activity that is negotiated). The object of instructional designers, for example, may be the objectives they write, the html file that they code, or the design model they use. The transformation of that object (e.g., completion of code) moves the subjects toward the accomplishment of their goal (Fig. 4.3). Because this transformation process continues to motivate activity (e.g., getting the code to work), the object of activity focuses the intended actions on the object. The transformed object is the motive of the activity.

Although a great deal of literature contrasts formal schooling with everyday social cognitive practice, schooling itself represents an activity system. Among the more significant differences in schools and everyday situations as activity systems is that the primary goal of learning activities in schools are psychic transformations, as opposed to some object or intention. Those psychic transformations are based on prerequisite skills, knowledge, and motives (Lompscher, 1999). However, when those prerequisites are not yet developed in learners, a generic contradiction arises.

> Learning actions [*not activities*] are prerequisites for acquisition of certain material, but they cannot be formed (acquired, learned) without being engaged in the corresponding material. It is impossible to learn the appropriate learning actions first and then to learn the material. The actions, content, structure, and course are determined by the object; there is no contentless or objectless formal action to be transferred to different materials. (Lompscher, 1999, p. 267-268).

Learning actions in schools are purposeless, whereas activities that give rise to learning in the real world are purposeful; they are motivated by intentions. This contradiction represents a raison détre for most of the situated and constructivist beliefs described in this book. Abstracted learning actions have no meaning. Rather, they must be defined by the object and the activity system that engage them.

Contradictions

Historically, instructional designers know that activities and activity systems change over time. Evolution and change in social structures is a natural phenomenon. What causes changes in activity systems are contradictions that emerge within them. Maturana and Varela (1987) described these as perturbations. Such perturbations or contradictions are the causes of changes in scientific theories, resulting in paradigm shifts (Kuhn, 1972). That is, activity systems are dialectic, adaptive, and self-regulating, just as this chapter is an adaptation of the earlier paper that resulted from dialectic.

As alluded to before, activity theory has emerged as an accommodation to contradictions inherent in psychology: psychic process versus object-related activity, individual versus group process, discrete act versus sociocultural phenomenon, internal versus cultural, acquisition versus construction, descriptive versus prescriptive, and goal-related versus historical-dialectic. The nature of mind has intrigued philosophers for millennia. Clearly, activity theory comes down on the sociocultural, historical side of the debate.

Social, cultural, and organizational factors in activity systems often result in what appear to be inherent contradictions. Among these is the paradox that production necessitates consumption and vice versa (Holt & Morris, 1993). For instance, most organizations involved in developing web-based distance education are continuously plagued with the contradictions caused by wanting to maintain high levels of quality, which requires more expensive interactive learning components, and the need to recover costs and make a profit. The nature of the aggregate planning process that was represented in our SCLE was the need to maintain full employment and adequate inventory without under or overproducing. The dialectic nature of the planning process requires operations managers to adjust (hire and fire, produce and go idle).

Although contradictions are usually internal to the activity system, they may also be external, as when values, beliefs, or activities of one activity system conflict with those of another. The nature of the activities performed in one or both activity systems must change.

Mediated Action

Activity always involves artifacts (instruments, signs, procedures, machines, methods, models, theories, laws, and forms of work organization). Whereas cognitive psychology traditionally has focused only on mental representations, ignoring artifacts or mediating tools and signs, "activity cannot be understood without understanding the role of artifacts in everyday existence, especially the way that artifacts are integrated into social practice" (Nardi, 1996, p. 14). This focus is one that has long been recognized in anthropological research and one that can be useful to instructional designers. Sociocultural theory does not argue that human action does not have a psychological dimension. Rather it argues that psychology is conditioned by mediating artifacts as well as cultural, institutional, and historical contexts (Wertsch, 1998).

A fundamental assumption of activity theory is that tools mediate or alter the nature of human activity and, when internalized, influence humans' mental development. Kaptellinnen (1996) argued that all "human experience is shaped by the tools and sign systems we use" (p. 10). Sociocultural analysis, as explicated by Wertsch (1998), is focused on disclosing all aspects of mediated action. He started with Burke's (1969) sociocultural components of act, scene, agent, agency, and purpose and laid out the conditions whereby nearly all human action is mediated action. In mediated action, there is an irreducible tension between the agent and the mediational means; they are synergistic, and the action is defined by the interplay of agent and mediator. Wertsch goes on to explicate the properties of mediated action, describing the transformative effects of agent on mediator on agent, the affordances of the mediators, and the internalization of the mediated action. Although his description of mind as mediated action is perhaps the clearest and most complete description of sociocultural analysis, a complete review is beyond the scope of this chapter.

Historicity

Activity is a historically developed phenomenon. That is, activities evolve over time within a culture. In order to understand the dynamics of a particular context, it is necessary to grasp the changes or evolutions of that situation over time. As indicated at the very beginning of this chapter, activity theory itself is a constantly evolving, multivoiced activity system (Engeström, 1993). That is, activity theory, like most theories, is an activity system where researchers from different disciplines contribute to a socially constructed conception. For example, cognitive psychology has undergone significant changes from the information processing conceptions that dominated work in the 1970s.

From an activity theory perspective, the process of instructional design, aggregate planning, or any activity, can only be understood by analyzing its historical development. For example, the military orientation of instruction in the 1950s and 1960s is easily interpretable if it is acknowledged that most instructional designers at that time worked for the military and accepted its beliefs and values, which in turn permeated the design processes they used. Instructional design skills, like all conscious processes, are internalized forms of activity that are common to the community in which individuals act. Activity theory focuses on the centrality of activity in a cultural theory of cognition.

Summary

Activity theory provides a different lens for analyzing learning processes and outcomes for the purpose of designing instruction. Rather than focusing on knowledge states, it focuses on the activities in which people are engaged, the nature of the tools they use in those activities, the social and contextual relationships among the collaborators in those activities, the goals and intentions of those activities, and the objects or outcomes of those activities. Rather than analyzing knowledge states as detached from these entities, activity theory sees consciousness as the mental activities that suffuse all of these entities. Concepts, rules, and theories that are not associated with activity have no meaning. Articulating each of these entities and their dynamic interrelationships is important when designing instruction, because the richer the context and the more embedded the conscious thought processes are in that context, the more meaning that learners will construct both for the activities and the thought processes.

PROCESS FOR APPLYING ACTIVITY THEORY FOR DESIGNING SCLEs

If the most appropriate unit of analysis is activity, then SCLE designers should, at least in part, analyze the activity systems for their components and dynamic relations. Task analysis in traditional ID situations most commonly consists of some form of subject matter, procedural, or prerequisites analysis (Jonassen, Tessmer, & Hannum, 1999). These forms of analysis focus either on the ideas that should be known or the sequences for performing procedural tasks or learning conceptual tasks. Those methods provide impoverished views of the complexity, interrelatedness, and embeddedness of authentic, problem-solving tasks, which are the hallmark of most constructivist and situated views of learning. Because most of the chapters in this book argue for more contextualized, embedded, socially constructive kinds of learning, the ID community needs a means for analyzing situations outside the school world in order to appropriate those attributes for use in the learning environment. I am not arguing that SCLEs should attempt to replicate the world outside of formal schools for use in schools but rather to simulate important parts of it, including the activity structure, the sociocultural context, and the mediation systems that are prominent in those activity systems. Since those attributes are such an important part of activity systems analysis, I am arguing that activity theory provides a useful lens for analyzing complex situations for designing instruction. I next describe a method where activity theory functions as a framework for designing SCLEs. The SCLE will simulate the activity system in the environment.

Although there is not an established methodology for using activity theory to design SCLEs, there are numerous precedents for using activity theory as an analytic tool. Activity theory or components of activity theory have been used to analyze activity in a broad array of domains, including information systems (Nissen, Klein, & Hirschheim, 1991), human-computer interactions (Kuutti, 1996), user interface design (Bellamy, 1996; Bødker, 1991b), network communications, education (Engeström & Middleton, 1996), politics, communities of expertise (Engeström, 1992), decision theory, activities of everyday living (Korvela, 1997; Winegar, 1992), organizational behavior (Engeström, 1987; Koistinen & Kangasoja, 1997) and anthropology and psychology (de Vos, 1986).

Methodological Assumptions of Activity Theory

Although activity theory focuses on practice, it is primarily a descriptive tool rather than a prescriptive theory. Care must be taken in generalizing the descriptive lenses of activity theory. Although Engeström (1993) believed that activity theory does not offer ready-made techniques and procedures for research, its widespread application as a lens for analyzing activity has yielded some generally accepted practices. First and foremost, whatever the focus, the activity must be studied in real-life practice with researchers as active participants in the process (Kuutti, 1991). Activity theory necessitates a qualitative approach to analysis. In designing SCLEs, it is necessary to study the in situ practices that instructional designers hope to simulate in the learning environment. In our SCLE, we examined the aggregate planning process in two corporate settings that we simulated in the learning environment.

In order to analyze learning situations, it is important that the analysis assumes certain characteristics:

- The research time frame should be long enough to understand the objects of activity, changes in those objects over time, and their relations to objects in other settings. Activities and their objects in groups of workers necessarily overlap. In our situation, we spent only a week per setting in the analysis process. More time would have undoubtedly uncovered more contradictions and implications.

- Analysts should pay attention first to broad patterns of activity before considering narrow episodic fragments that do not reveal the overall direction and importance of the activity. Because we could not simulate the full complexity of the situation, these broad patterns were sufficient for designing our SCLE.
- Analysts should use varied data collection methods (interviews, observations, video, historical materials) and points of view (subject, community, tools). The researcher needs to commit to understanding the activity system from all of these different perspectives.

The following process provides very general guidelines, not a procedure, for using activity theory as a framework for designing SCLEs.

1) Clarify the Intentions of the Activity System

In order to orient the analysis, it is necessary to first clarify the motives and goals of the activity system (Engeström, 1987). What are the goals of the activity system? What are their expectations about the outcome? The purpose of this process is to understand (a) the contextual constraints on the activities, (b) the motivations for the activity being modeled, and (c) any interpretations of perceived contradictions. In creating SCLEs, this step will provide critical information for explaining contradictions that can be introduced into the learning environment.

In the aggregate planning process, the goal of the activity system is a plan for monitoring production and inventory levels and matching human resource needs to that plan. In the aggregate planning SCLE, our goal was to develop a web-based learning environment that simulated the aggregate planning activity systems in two or more organizations. In the ID process, system goals and motives are typically articulated by a formalized process for writing objectives. The objectives, according to design models, function to orient the activity of the designers and producers. However, it can be inferred from activity theory that objective writing, as practiced in most design processes, provides an impoverished view of the goals and motives of the process they are trying to represent in instruction. The intentions of ID activities should be clarify the complexity, interactions, and intentionality of human performance. That requires a more powerful lens than objective writing.

Representing Intentions and Objects in Student-Centered Learning Environments. Many techniques may be used for collecting information about intentions, including the analyses of formal and informal documentation, user observations, interviewing, and even psychoanalyses (deVos, 1986). Although this step is not always addressed in traditional ID, activity theorists believe that it might be the most important step of the process. Given that SCLEs are designed to scaffold learning, a thorough understanding of the intentional dynamics of the activity system is critical.

The information that is collected in this stage will guide the construction of the problem space. All SCLEs are goal-directed, so clearly understanding the goals of the participants represented in the SCLE is essential. The goals will define the object of the problem that challenges learners in the SCLE. The motives will also determine whose perspectives are important to represent in the related cases. For our scenario, we examined (using observations and interviews) management problems in several organizations to determine who was involved in aggregate planning, and what their motives and expectations were. Those positions were represented in the problem space as well as the information resources in terms of personnel backgrounds, resumés, mission statements, annual reports, industry standards, and so on.

2) Analyze the Activity System Components

A primary assumption of activity theory is that activity cannot be understood or analyzed outside the context in which it occurs. When analyzing human activity, instructional must examine not only the kinds of activities that people engage in but also who is engaging in that activity, what their goals and intentions are, what objects or products result from the activity, the rules and norms that circumscribe that activity, and the larger community in which the activity occurs. This step involves defining in depth the components of the given activity, namely, the subject, object, community, rules, and division of labor.

The subject of the aggregate planning activity was the operations managers who establish the goal of the system based on the contradictions they perceive in the system. We described not only their activity structure but also how they perceived their roles in relationship to the goals of the system, that is, to minimize costs.

The object is the thing to be acted on, tangible or intangible. In our case, it was the aggregate plan. The object will be partially defined by the first step of analysis, but it needs to be explicated. The object may be a product, a communication, a theory, or any combination of elements. Clearly defining the how that plan fulfilled the goals of the organization was essential. What does an aggregate plan consist of? How far in the future does it predict? Which parameters have to be specified, and with what degree of accuracy?

The components of the activity system (subject, community, object) do not act on each other directly. Instead, their interactions are mediated by signs and tools, which provide the direct and indirect communication between the objects. Analyzing the communications over time provided important historical information about how and why their activity systems existed as they did. Therefore, we examined the role that artifacts, institutions, and cultural values played in shaping activity in these different organizations. These mediators included the computer programs (spreadsheets), aggregate planning procedures and methods, the rules of the organizations, and their forms of work organization. The most common form of tool in aggregate planning is the computer and the telephone. They were the principle enablers of aggregate planning. They make activity feasible and possible (by networking or linking) (Kuutti, 1996).

Mediators also assume the form of formal rules or models. The rules of the businesses mediated the relationship between the subject and the community or communities in which they participated. Those rules differed dramatically from business to business. The smaller accounting firm was regulated by simpler, less formal rules and methods than the larger soda manufacturer.

Representing Subject, Object, and Mediators in SCLEs. The mediators describe the kinds of models and methods that constrain activity. We reflected them in the problem representation space as well as the information resources. In both cases, however, we selected the spreadsheet as the mediator that was used to manipulate objects in that space. In the information resources, we included information about organizations and their methods of operation.

It was also important to examine the community in which the subjects work, the nature of the social interactions among participants, and the beliefs and values that define or impact the activity. Who are the agents or players in the community of practitioners? In both, e-mail and telephone conversations mediated the social interactions among employees, so e-mails and telephone conversations were used as the primary medium for representing community.

In describing the activity system, it is also important to examine the division of labor that mediates the relationship between the community and the object. The division of labor in the tax accounting firm was less hierarchical than in the soda manufacturer because there were fewer and more seasonable employees.

3) Analyze the Activity Subsystems

Not only is it important to analyze the components of any activity system, but it is also necessary to analyze the interactions and contradictions among those components. Those interactions and contradictions are manifest in the production, consumption, exchange, and distribution subsystems.

Analyzing the production subsystem involves observing how the subject interacts with tools, signs, and other mediators in order to transform the object. How does the object unfold? What effects do the mediators have on the nature of the activity? Do they change the performance, abilities, and beliefs of the subject?

When analyzing the consumption subsystem, we observed how the activity community members interact with the aggregate planners. Who did the aggregate planners rely on for information or implementation? Do community members support or impede the production process? How do they consume resources? What effects does their consumption have on the production process?

In analyzing the distribution subsystem, we examined how the businesses were organized, that is, their division of labor. Were actions and obligations of the employees formalized procedures or ad hoc? What rules or laws dictated performance? What were the expectations of the managers in relation to accountants, marketing, sales, or production? How well did the operating divisions get along?

In analyzing the exchange subsystem, we examined how norms and rules within the organization were negotiated. How did the members of the businesses regulate their performance?

While examining subsystems, we were alert to contradictions or conflicts among them. Were all the aggregate planners working together? Was their intention clear and consistent among all employees, or did units or divisions compete with each other? How much did consumption of resources affect production? How were responsibilities for aggregate planning negotiated and distributed among employees? Was it top down or participative? These contractions can seriously impede the activity.

Representing the Subsystems in SCLEs. The production and consumption subsystems are primarily modeled in the activity structure (described next). We embedded the actions and operations in the problem representation and manipulations spaces. Aggregate planners are required to research and communicate, so we simulated exchange activities in numerous conversations and interactions with various employees of each company. It was up to the aggregate planner to determine whom he or she would interact with. We embedded data collection and conjecturing actions in the spreadsheet. The distribution process is simulated in the nature of the tasks assigned to members. In our SCLE, the learners were responsible for aggregate planning activities. However, it is reasonable in SCLEs to divide roles among participants. That is, learners might assume different roles in order to experience the diversity and distribution of activities in any activity system. In SCLEs, faithful reproduction of activity subsystems is neither possible nor necessarily desirable. The designer must analyze the subsystems in any organization and determine which are important to simulate, what capabilities learners may have, and what means for simulating those subsystems will work best in the environment to imitate characteristics of the lager activity system.

4) Analyze the Activity Structures within Subsystems

Another key process is analyzing the activity structure (all of the activities that engage the subject) that defines the purpose of the activity system. Activities consist of individual and cooperative actions and chains of operations. This hierarchy of activity, actions, and operations describes the activity structure.

The activity level has been interpreted as the intentional level because it focuses on the intentions or motives (conscious needs, values, desires) as its driving force (Linnard, 1995). Examples of activities in management include developing training programs, managing employees, aggregate planning, and many others.

The action level is the functional level (Linnard, 1995) that uses planning and problem solving actions to fulfill the activities. Examples of actions in our SCLE included predicting demand, setting sales agendas, regulating staffing levels, determining technology needs, and regulating inventory. In other related activity systems, such as marketing departments, actions might include designing and implementing marketing programs.

Operations are routinized performances. Subjects conduct operations in order to complete the actions. Examples of operations include entering information into spreadsheets, making telephone calls, counting inventory, and so on.

Together, these three levels (activity, action, operation) comprise an activity structure. Activity structures describe the interrelationships of all of the conscious and unconscious thinking and performances focused on the object (e.g. the aggregate plan). Therefore, for any activity system being simulated in a SCLE, it is necessary to identify all of the actions and operations that support the activity.

This is not unlike the traditional needs and task analyses phases of ID. Defining and identifying activity structures, however, suggest purposely including an understanding of the intentionality of the action or operation for the learner. Why are people doing this? Further, it situates these actions and operations in contexts that are both external and internal (interpreted) to the individual. This decomposition of activities into its supporting actions and operations creates the depth necessary for the design of good SCLEs.

Representing Activity Structures in SCLEs. The outcomes of this stage of any activity analysis will be a description of the activities, actions, and operations that are required to solve the problem in the SCLE. The activity structure defines the problem manipulation space, that is, how will learners in the SCLE be able to manipulate the object simulated in the SCLE. This process should be repeated in different contexts. For the aggregate planning SCLE, we analyzed management problems in eight different settings. We observed how managers worked in these different settings. Analyzing different activities provided the basis for the problem manipulation space for two of the problems and a set of six related cases (examples of activities with similar activity structures). The actions available to the manager need to be added to the problem manipulation space. In the problem manipulation space, the actions the manager can take need to be operationalized. For each, what will be the result? Additionally, the activity structures will isolate the actions and operations that may need to be modeled or scaffolded in the learning environment.

5) Analyzing Contradictions in the Activity System

Every activity system is plagued by internal and external contradictions. Contradictions external to business include shifts in demand, new competitors, changes in economic conditions, inflation, interest rates, and so on. Internal contradiction between operations management, marketing, finance, and production are common in businesses. Some contradictions are inherent in the activity system such as the desire to maintain full employment and adequate inventory without under- or overproducing. The dialectic nature of the planning process requires operations managers to adjust technology, human resources, inventory, and sales.

Representing Contradictions in SCLEs. Contradictions can be reproduced as themes and perspectives represented in the related cases. They can also be portrayed in the communications (telephone calls, faxes, and e-mails) that represented the problem. Contradictions can even be represented in the mediators (spreadsheet formulas, inaccessible people or tools, or inconsistent sign systems or formalisms for denoting activities between departments or activity systems). Just as contradictions are embedded in every part of an activity system, they can be represented in every part of the SCLE.

6. Analyzing the Context

The issue that activity theory addresses most directly and that is perhaps most relevant to the design of SCLEs is contextuality. Traditional methods of task analysis focus only on the technical core of performances, ignoring the real-life, noninstructional contexts within which activities occur. Activity theory argues that decontextualized performance produces little if any understanding. Activity itself is both defined and defines context. Context is not merely the outer container in which people behave in certain ways. Rather, people consciously create context through their own objects. Context is both internal to people (involving specific objects or goals) and also external (involving artifacts, other people, and settings).

Analyzing context is essential for defining the larger activity systems within which activity occurs (subject, community, object) and the dynamics that exist within and between the subject and the mediators. The designer is seeking information in order to describe "how things get done in this context." Why? Because different contexts impose distinctively different practices.

Representing Context in SCLEs. The outcomes of these actions will describe the problem context that is modeled in the SCLE. The community of actors needs to be identified and invested with capabilities, restrictions, actions, privileges, and so on. Those attributes need to be the basis for connecting the actors and their relationships in the SCLE (described in the next step). What social relations and division of labor should be represented in the problem context? These features make the environment ill-structured, complex, and (most importantly) relevant and meaningful to learners. Analyzing the activity context will also identify the contextual elements that need to be recognized and indexed in the related cases in order to help learners to access them. What tools and mediators are used by managers? Case access or moving between cases or problems is often based on similarity of contextual elements. Finally, analyzing the context will make obvious the kinds of conversation and collaboration tools that are required to support the activity structure. What kinds of interactions are the managers allowed with other employees, outside contractors, attorneys, or others? How do they normally communicate with each of these people? What are the communication protocols?

CONTRADICTIONS IN ACTIVITY SYSTEMS

In this chapter, I describe a method for modeling activity systems in SCLEs for the purpose of engaging learners in authentic learning activities. Research described in other chapters in this book supports the intellectual benefits of engaging in complex and authentic tasks in SCLEs. However, I am not naive enough to suggest that all schools and universities need to do is to model everyday activity systems. Why? First, as Carraher and Schliemann point out (see Chapter 7, this volume), many important intellectual activities and concepts may not have reasonable everyday activities associated with them, so students could be deprived of important intellectual experiences. In this brief section, I describe another, more powerful reason, mainly internal contradictions within formal activity systems and external contradictions between the activity systems being modeled in the SCLE and the activity systems in evidence in most schools and universities.

Schools and universities may also be analyzed as activity systems. The operations management course for which the SCLE described earlier was developed is also an activity system in which the students are the subjects, the object of their activity is learning to perform in businesses, the mediating artifacts include the professor, textbooks, notetaking services, test files, computers, and so on. However,

> in the majority of classrooms real learning results do not correspond with either the expectations of society or the efforts of most teachers and learners. High rates of forgetting, low levels of applicability of knowledge and skills, insufficient of problem finding and problem solving, and aversion to school learning are often demonstrated. (Lompscher, 1999, p. 264)

Why does this occur? Largely because of internal contradictions between the object and means of learning and instruction. Professors want their students to be able to be independent problem solvers and thinkers, but the students often seek the most expedient and least demanding approaches to learning that enable them to pursue their social objectives more thoroughly. Also, the intentions of the professors to enable thinking and problem solving are contradicted by mediating artifacts, such as a content-oriented curriculum, lecture methods for knowledge transmission, and multiple-choice examinations that largely assess memorization. Students know that the real object of learning is comprehension and memorization of ideas. That object or goal contradicts the object of the SCLE we designed—to solve problems and think independently. This contradiction between real and expected learning outcomes may represent the greatest impediment to learning in SCLEs, unless the activities engaged by the learning environment are consonant with the outcomes that are assessed by the professor. The students know better.

CONCLUSIONS

This chapter describes a theory of activity-based learning (activity theory) that may be used as a framework for describing the components and their interrelationships in constructivist learning environments. "Activity theory seems the richest framework for studies of context in its comprehensiveness and engagement with different issues of consciousness, intentionality, and history" (Nardi, 1996, p. 96). Applying activity theory to the analysis of non-school world situations for the purpose of designing SCLEs involves examining and elaborating the activity structures engaged by work; the tools, rules, and symbol systems that mediate that work; and the social and conceptual context in which that work occurs. Experience in applying these methods for activity system analysis is needed for validation. Instructional designers need to resolve whether or not SCLEs that are based on an activity theory analysis might not themselves become contradictions that impede rather than support the goals of the educational activity system. Is it possible for learners to become sufficiently immersed in a representation (SCLE) of an activity system?

REFERENCES

Asmolov, A.G. (1987). Basic principles of a psychological analysis in the theory of activity. *Soviet Psychology, 25*(2), 78-102.

Bellamy, R. K. E. (1996). Designing educational technology: Computer-mediated change. In B. A Nardi (Ed.), *Context and consciousness: Activity theory and human-computer Interaction* (pp. 123-146). Cambridge, MA: MIT Press.

Bødker, S. (1991a). Activity theory as a challenge to systems design. In H.E. Nissen, H.K. Klein, & R. Hirschheim (Eds.), *Information systems research: Contemporary approaches and emergent traditions.* Amsterdam: Elsevier.

Bødker, S. (1991b). *Through the interface: A human activity approach to user interface design.* Hillsdale, NJ: Lawrence Erlbaum Associates.

Cognition and Technology Group. (1992). Technology and the design of generative learning environments. In D. H. Jonassen & T. M. Duffy (Eds.), *Constructivism and the technology of instruction: A conversation* (pp. 77-90). Hillsdale, NJ: Lawrence Erlbaum Associates.

deVos, G. A. (1986) Insight and symbol: Dimensions of analysis in psychoanalytic anthropology. *The Journal of Psychoanalytic Anthropology, 9* (3), 199-233

Engeström, Y. (1987). *Learning by expanding: An activity theoretical approach to developmental research.* Helsinki, Finland: Orienta-Konsultit Oy.

Engeström, Y. (1992). *Interactive expertise: Studies in distributed working intelligence* (Research Bulletin 83). Helsinke: University of Helsinke Department of Education.

Engeström, Y. (1993) Developmental studies of work as a testbench of activity theory: The case of primary care medical practice. In S. Chaiklin & J. Lave (Eds.), *Understanding practice: Perspectives on activity and context.* Cambridge, England: Cambridge University Press..

Engeström, Y. (1999). Activity theory as individual and social transformation. In Y. Engeström, R. Miettinen, & R. L. Punamäki (Eds.), *Perspectives on activity theory* (pp. 19-38). Cambridge: Cambridge University Press.

Engeström, Y., & Middleton, D. (1996). *Cognition and communication at work.* Boston, MA: Cambridge University Press.

Fishbein, D. D., Eckart, T., Lauver, E., van Leeuwen, R., & Langemeyer, D. (1990). Learners' questions and comprehension in a tutoring system. *Journal of Educational Psychology, 82,* 163-170.

Gagne, R.M. (1968). *The conditions of learning.* New York: Holt, Rinehart, & Winston.

Holt, G. R., & Morris, A. W. (1993). Activity theory and the analysis of organization. *Human Organization, 52*(1), 97-109.

Hutchins, E. (1995). *Cognition in the wild.* Cambridge, MA: MIT Press.

Jonassen, D. H. (1999). Designing constructivist learning environments. In C.M. Reigeluth (Ed.), *Instructional-design theories and models* (2nd ed., pp. 215-240). Mahwah, NJ: Lawrence Erlbaum Associates.

Jonassen, D. H. (2000). *Computers as mindtools for schools: Engaging critical thinking.* Columbus, OH: Prentice-Hall.

Jonassen, D.H., & Rohrer-Murphy, L. (1999). Activity theory as a framework for designing constructivist learning environments. *Educational Technology: Research & Development, 47* (1), 61-79.

Jonassen, D.H., Tessmer, M., & Hannum, W. (1999). *Task analysis procedures for instructional design.* Mahwah, NJ: Lawrence Erlbaum Associates.

Kaptelinen, V. (1997). Computer-mediated activity: Functional organs in social and developmental contexts. In B. Nardi (Ed.), *Context and consciousness: Activity theory and human-computer interaction* (pp. 45-67). Cambridge, MA: MIT Press.

Koistinen, K., & Kangasoja, J. (1997, July). *Learning to survive: how does a small multimedia company learn to master the production process?*

Paper presented at the 1st Nordic-Baltic Conference on Activity Theory, Helsinki, Finland.

Kolodner, J. (1993). *Case-based reasoning*. San Mateo, CA: Morgan Kaufmann.

Korvela, P. (1997). *How to analyze everyday activity at home?* Paper presented at the 1st Nordic-Baltic Conference on Activity Theory, Helsinki, Finland.

Krajcik, J. S., Blumenfeld, P. C., Marx, R. W., & Soloway, E. (1994). A collaborative model for helping middle grade science teachers learn project-based instruction. *The Elementary School Journal, 94* (5), 483-497.

Kuhn, T. (1972). *The structure of scientific revolutions*. Chicago: University of Chicago Press.

Kuutti, K. (1996). Activity theory as a potential framework for human-computer interaction research. In B. A Nardi (Ed.), *Context and consciousness: Activity theory and human-computer interaction* (pp. 17-44). Cambridge, MA: MIT Press.

Kuutti, K. (1991). Activity theory and its applications to information systems research and development. In H. E. Nissen, H. K. Klein, & R. Hirschheim (Eds.), *Information systems research: Contemporary approaches and emergent traditions* (pp. 529-549). New York: Elvsevier.

Leont'ev, A. (1972). The problem of activity in psychology. *Voprosy filosofii, 9*, 95-108.

Linnard, M. (1995). New debates on learning support. *Journal of Computer Assisted Learning, 11*, 239-253.

Lompscher, J. (1999). Activity formation as an alternative strategy of instruction. In Y. Engeström, R. Miettinen, & R. L. Punamäki (Eds.), *Perspectives on activity theory*(pp. 264-297). Cambridge, England: Cambridge University Press.

Maturana, H., & Varela, F. (1987). *The tree of knowledge*. Boston: New Science Library.

Nardi, B. A. (1996). Studying context: A comparison of activity theory, situated action models, and distributed cognition. In B.A Nardi (Ed.), *Context and consciousness: Activity theory and human-computer interaction*. Cambridge, MA: MIT Press.

Nissen, H.E., Klein, H. K, & Hirschheim, R. (1991), *Information systems research: Contemporary approaches and emergent traditions*. Amsterdam: Elsevier.

Russell, D.R. (1997). Rethinking genre in school and society: An activity theory analysis, *Written Communication 14* , 504-554.

Spiro, R.J., Vispoel, W., Schmitz, J., Samarapungavan, A., & Boerger, A. (1987). Knowledge acquisition for application: Cognitive flexibility and transfer in complex content domains. In B.C. Britton (Ed.), *Executive control processes*. Hillsdale, NJ: Lawrence Erlbaum Associates.

Wertsch, J. V. (1998). *Mind as action*. New York: Oxford University Press.

Winegar, L. (1992). Children's emerging understanding of social events: Co-construction and social process. In L. T. Winegar & J. Valsiner (Eds.), *Children's development within social context* (pp. 3-27). Hillsdale, NJ: Lawrence Erlbaum Associates Publishers.

5

Distributed Cognitions, by Nature and by Design

Philip Bell
University of Washington

William Winn
University of Washington

INTRODUCTION

During the 1990s, educators have proposed a number of conceptual frameworks to guide the design and use of learning environments. Each chapter in this book deals with one of these. The extent to which these frameworks are similar or different, or even new, is the question this book seeks to answer. Yet, even a superficial glance at the chapters in this book will reveal that these frameworks are, for the most part, learner-centered, concerned with learner activity, cognizant of the importance of context—including social context—for learning, and rely to some extent on nonhuman artifacts or technologies for their implementation (see also Chapter 1, this volume). The frameworks are also somewhat ill formed—a common characteristic of pretheoretic conceptions in the social sciences.

This chapter deals with distributed cognition. This way of thinking about teaching and learning exhibits the common properties of the other frameworks just enumerated, including ill formedness. Indeed, researchers are not even decided upon the name for the approach. In the literature, it is called *distributed learning* and *distributed intelligence* in addition to *distributed cognition*. However, it is not our objective in this chapter to settle the matter of names. (We use distributed cognition). Rather, we discuss substantive questions about distributed cognition that arise from our own work and from that of others.

Four such questions about distributed cognition immediately come to mind:

1. Is all cognition distributed? Is there agreement (Cole, 1991; Pea, 1995) that, generally, cognitive acts involve sharing effort and information among a person and other people or artifacts? Or are (Salomon, 1995) only some cognitive acts are distributed whereas others are the property of individuals, or perhaps even that individual cognition is a necessary precondition for distributed cognition?

2. Is cognition distributed differently in systems containing artifacts, media, and technologies than it is distributed among people? Indeed, what is the role of a nonsentient device in distributed cognition? Is it a tool that extends and amplifies the ability of humans to reason, like the devices enumerated by Perkins (1992)? Or is it a more equal partner in reasoning, like intelligent devices such as the Writing Partner (Zellermayer, Salomon, Globerson, & Givon, 1991)?

3. What roles do humans play when cognition is distributed? Can each student or novice contribute more or less equally to the learning environment, and with what consequences? Does the traditionally asymmetrical relationship between student and teacher change in a distributed learning environment?

4. How can distributed cognition systems be designed and shaped for educational purposes? Does the fact that cognitive activity is shared among a number of people and artifacts require different ways of going about designing instructional systems? Does the distribution of cognition, together with the constructivist orientation to learning and the situated nature of cognition that go along with it, have implications for the way learning environments are used and for the way teachers working in them teach?

   In this chapter, we break our discussion of these matters into two parts. First, we examine the nature of distributed cognition. We begin with a vignette that illustrates many of the issues that impinge on our understanding of distributed cognition. The vignette describes what happened in a freshman Chemistry class that one of us observed two years ago at the University of Washington. It serves as a starting point for an examination of general principles of distributed cognition made through two lenses—system theory and cognitive theory. A system-theoretic look at distributed cognition shows some of its important characteristics that can best be seen as part of a big picture. The cognitive view lets us look more closely at the details. Second, we look at how learning environments can be expressly designed to foster distributed cognition. This section, too, focuses on a case. But rather than an illustrative vignette, it is built around a research program that one of us is actively engaged in and will continue to develop. We conclude by identifying some recurring attributes of distributed cognition and pointing to some similarities and differences among conceptual and practical approaches called distributed cognition, and those called by the other names that identify the other chapters in this book.

THE NATURE OF DISTRIBUTED COGNITION

The Case of the Chlorine Isotope

Imagine, if you will, a dark and dingy chemistry lab that no one else really wants to use. There is a smell of burnt something-or-other and a vague odor of unidentifiable chemicals. There are a dozen students at work stations, each equipped with a sink, a gas supply and a networked Macintosh computer.

The topic for the day is the chemical properties and uses of a particular isotope of chlorine. Jim begins with a Powerpoint presentation that outlines the basic chemistry behind the properties of this substance. Because he does not have access to a mass spectrometer, he has provided data about the spectrum of the isotope on his web page. Students download these data into an Excel spreadsheet and simulate a mass spectrometer on their Macintoshes. They produce graphs of the spectra. There is considerable collaboration among the students, some helping others in technical matters, such as using Excel, many inspecting each others' graphs, and all conversing about their interpretations of the data. Working together is the norm in this class, it seems.

Now Jim links to the Pacific Northwest National Lab (PNNL) in Richland, Washington over the Internet and starts a CU-See Me videoconferencing session with a scientist colleague. Jim's colleague explains how he is using this isotope of chlorine to trace seepage from holding tanks on the Hanford nuclear reservation into the Columbia River. The properties that the students have discovered through their simulation are what makes the isotope particularly useful for tracing underground water movement.

Jim now makes an analysis of the isotope, using the PNNL mass spectrometer, remotely, over the Internet. The spectra from this run are displayed on each student's computer. Again, there is much inspection of each others' screens and collaborative interpretation of the data. This leads to the discovery of an unexpected discrepancy between the spectra produced by the Excel simulation and the spectra output from the mass spectrometer at PNNL. Jim and his colleague confer. The definitive data are, it seems, kept in a database in Japan. Jim connects to this database over the Web, downloads graphs of the spectra, and displays them on the students' computers. Everyone discusses the three sets of spectra, which match the PNNL data more closely than the local data, and the discrepancies are resolved.

Let us begin by mentioning the evidence for distributed cognition and related phenomena in this vignette. The students collaborated, informally, in performing their tasks and interpreting the outcomes. They used a tool—the Excel spreadsheet — to help them understand the properties of the isotope. A significant amount of cognitive effort was off-loaded onto the remotely-located mass spectrometer. For a short period, they interacted with a practicing scientist and were able to situate their work in the real-world problem of tracing radioactive seepage into groundwater. The unexpected discrepancy in data revealed the fallibility of professors, scientists, and technology to the students, allowing a view of how professionals handle such events. Recourse to yet another tool, the database in Japan, allowed the discrepancy to be resolved and the class to be brought to closure.

The Learning Environment as System

One striking characteristic of the learning environment described in this vignette is its complexity. Such complexity is typical of learning environments in which cognition is distributed among people and devices (see Hutchins, 1995). We therefore continue our analysis, at a high level of abstraction, by looking at the distributed learning environment as a system. This particular lens will give insight into the dynamics of distributed learning systems as complete entities in which, for the moment, concerns for what happens to individual learners are relegated to secondary importance.

The complexity of systems arises not so much from the number of components they may have—students, scientists, computers, mass spectrometers—but from the potential of all components to interact with each other. Because learning environments are of necessity dynamic systems, we must focus on these interactions.

Productive (as opposed to destructive) dynamic systems are self-organizing. This means that the amount of variation, or uncertainty, within them decreases over time (Von Foerster, 1982) until something close to a steady state is attained (Von Bertalanffy, 1986). In an early, important, and mostly overlooked application of system theory to education, Pask (1975, 1984) likened the self-organizing process to a conversation between two or more participants whose purpose is to arrive at "an agreement over an understanding." What is more, in Pask's theory, as in our chemistry classroom, the participants in a conversation may be two or more brains, two or more machines, or a combination of two or more brains and machines. Pask's criterion for cognitive ability is the potential for self-organization, not biology. And artifacts feature as prominently in distributed cognition systems as people (see the following and Hutchins, 1995).

The learning environment in the chemistry class exhibits most properties of a self-organizing system. The activities it undergoes exemplify a conversation that ends in understanding. At the beginning of the class, we assume that there was a high level of uncertainty about the isotope among the students or, if they had some conception of its properties or purpose, these conceptions were quite variable. In the ensuing examination of data, exchanges of information, generally conversations in Pask's usage, uncertainty is reduced. After the spreadsheet simulation, students observe that the spectra on each screen are similar. However, the attempt to verify this convergence from another source leads to a surprise. The PNNL spectra do not match those generated locally. Uncertainty and variability in the system increase again. A third set of data, deemed definitive, matches the PNNL spectra more closely than the local spectra. This leads to an agreement among what the students, the scientist, and the professor know and what the two valid sets of data show. The system attains a steady state.

This analysis suggests a number of things. The first is that, when cognition is distributed with a view to helping students learn something, students' conceptions converge toward an agreement with experts, with valid data and therefore with theory. This view is consistent with current views of conceptual change, particularly in learning science, as we shall demonstrate later. Second, a distributed learning system needs to be able to deal with unexpected events that increase the uncertainty (entropy) of the system, rather than reduce it. If it cannot, the system falls apart. Think, for a moment, of well planned lessons that have turned into disasters because neither the teacher, nor the available resources, nor the other students were able to satisfactorily answer one student's insightful question. Third, artifacts such as reference data, computers and other devices must themselves be open to change as part of self-organization. This idea is somewhat difficult to grasp. However, at the very least, artifacts, meaning mostly computers and the data they produce, should not be trusted blindly. At best, computers should be sufficiently intelligent to be active participants in the conversation, as Pask's were and as generations of intelligent systems have been subsequently.

On the other hand, these artifacts are useful sharing ideas through external representations. Pea (1995, p. 61) has made the point that intelligence can be augmented through the use of inscriptional systems, rather than symbol systems, meaning that there is an advantage to using artifacts to inscribe our ideas in the world rather than always keeping them in our heads. We will return to this idea later in this chapter.

A systems analysis of distributed cognition begs a lot of questions. To begin with, our narrative implies that a steady state is somehow the end of the matter, that there is no more to learn. Nickerson (1995) also cautions against taking what could be seen as a systems-like approach to distributed cognition, because he, too, thought it lead to oversimplification. In fact, though, mastery of a set of concepts and principles about the chlorine isotope enables the student to explore the next, currently uncertain and variable, topic. Achieving certainty about one thing furnishes the intellectual tools that allow the discovery of uncertainty in something else.

Next, our narrative implies that there are correct answers towards which the system, and the students it contains, converge. This flies in the face of some constructivists' (Cunningham, 1992; Duffy & Jonassen, 1992; see also Chap. 2, this volume) insistence that the imposition of objective goals towards which students are to move is counterproductive to the construction of understanding. Maybe what is learned from looking at distributed cognition through a systems lens applies only to topics that are generally accepted to be objectively knowable. We return to this issue in our second, more extensive case, which is concerned with students' arguments for different points of view about the nature of light.

Finally, our narrative has kept individual people and other components of a learning environment from center stage. In the next section, we turn to a closer examination of how the individual components of a distributed learning system operate.

How Distributed Cognition Works

The jump from the systems lens to the cognitive lens is not as far as one might think. Self organization has a lot in common with Piaget's (1967) concept of equilibration and generally with cognitive theories of schema development. On this view, learning is iterative. New information that a student acquires is shaped to fit with that individual's existing knowledge. Existing knowledge is itself modified to accommodate the new information.

It is not our purpose to review cognitive theories of learning. In this section, we deal rather with what is novel and unique about learning in environments in which cognition is distributed. This leads back to two of the questions we asked in the introduction: What are roles of and interactions among people and artifacts in a distributed system? What are the roles of students and teachers in a distributed cognitive system?

The Roles of the Components in Distributed Cognitive Environments

At the conclusion of his vivid and revealing analysis of how a team of navigators uses individuals' knowledge and instruments to navigate a ship, Hutchins (1995) wrote the following:

> The conduct of the activity [navigation] proceeds by the operation of functional systems that bring representational media into coordination with each other. The representational media may be inside as well as outside the individuals involved. These functional systems propagate representational state [sic] across the media. (p. 372-3)

Navigating a ship through a narrow passage into port requires the coordination of many people and devices. People use instruments to take bearings from landmarks and report them to the person plotting the ship's position on a chart. Likewise, someone reports the depth of water beneath the ship, reading from a depth sounder. One person records this information in a log and another uses a variety of plotting instruments to compute the ship's position, current course, and projected course from the log. The timing and coordination of all these actions is critical. When asked, or at critical junctures, the navigator recommends changes in the ship's heading or speed to the officer of the deck. These recommendations may or may not be accepted. If they are, they are passed to the helmsperson who steers the ship onto a new heading. In poor visibility, at night, or out of sight from land, radar and other devices are also brought into the equation.

Hutchins' analysis makes clear that communication is the sine qua non of distributed cognition. The individuals on the navigation team may indeed hold mental representations of knowledge derived from experience or from recent observations (e.g., taking a bearing), but that knowledge is useless unless it is shared. To do that, it has to be represented externally to the individual, by calling it out, in writing, or in some other way. Similarly, the devices used for measuring bearings or the depth of water must make their knowledge visible, on a dial or scale.

The second thing that Hutchins' analysis makes clear is that shared information is pooled information. This allows the best equipped person (or device) in the environment to use that information for the benefit of everyone else. In Hutchins' example, it is the ship's navigator who brings "the representational media into coordination with each other." In navigation, positions and courses are computed by using rulers, protractors, and other devices to make accurate drawings directly onto a chart. At one point, even, Hutchins (1995) states, "A navigation chart is an analog computer" (p. 61). The chart and the tools that are used to compute with it are devices that support problem-solving. They are tools for thought, as Salomon (1979) has called them.

A third characteristic of distributed cognition that Hutchins' account points to is that the components of a distributed system must rely on each other to get the job done. In navigating the ship, no one person is in possession of all the information needed to make a decision. Indeed, even the navigator makes only recommendations to the officer of the deck, who may have additional information that could lead to the choice not to accept the navigator's recommendation. The human participants in the activity must trust each other, for the most part without the opportunity to validate that trust by checking with another source of information. Ironically perhaps, it is the instruments whose reliability is called into question. The accuracy, limits, and degree of reliability of the navigating instruments are known and documented (for example, Hutchins, 1995). Backup systems and human skill are available if a component fails.

These three characteristics are also evident, in different degrees, in our Chemistry class. The importance of communication is clear, among students, the professor and the scientist, as well as between the students' computers and the professor's web site, and the PNNL mass spectrometer and the Japanese database. Pooling the information from the devices and the people is also necessary for learning to occur. And the presence of a backup, when a component proves unreliable, is necessary and prudent.

We have concentrated on a single, but telling, example. It is also important to note that Hutchins' account is one among many. Similar ideas are to be found in the study of networking problems in an engineering company (Rogers, 1992), the study of airline pilots (Hutchins & Klausen, 1996) and air traffic controllers (Halverson, 1992).

The Status of Artifacts: Tools or Teachers? We turn now to a closer look at the role of devices, mostly computers, in distributed cognition. In our examples so far, artifacts have served to extend human capabilities. Perkins (1992) enumerated a number of ways this can happen. Information banks (such as the database of spectra in Japan) extend individual's memories by providing access to all manner of databases on all imaginable subjects. Symbol pads (like the Excel spreadsheet or the course plotter's log) extend their ability to communicate by providing a variety of ways for individuals to record their thoughts, as text, or graphics, or in another format. Microworlds (like the Excel simulation) make it easier for us to experiment with models of pieces of real or imaginary worlds, whether by controlling the behavior of a virtual turtle by giving it commands in LOGO (Papert, 1983), by manipulating the values of parameters in a computer model of Newton's laws of motion and observing the consequences (White, 1988), or by changing the amount of air pollution in a virtual environment and observing the consequences at regular intervals in the future (Jackson, Taylor, & Winn, 1999). This suggests that cognition is best understood in terms of a person's internal cognitive capability plus the augmentation by external devices. We must therefore consider not just the cognitive activity and capability of the person but of the person plus (Perkins, 1995) or of cognitive effects *with* technology, as Salomon, Perkins, and Globerson (1991) put it.

If artifacts make individuals smarter and more productive while they are using them, there is evidence that they also have a more lasting effect. Salomon et al. (1991) referred to this as effects *of* technology (as opposed to effects *with* technology) and claim that working with artifacts leaves a cognitive residue that can usefully support intellectual activity, in the absence of the artifacts themselves, at later times.

In the late 1970s, Salomon (1979) provided evidence that using media as tools for thought led to our internalizing the symbol systems of those media. Extensive television watching improved scores on tests of spatial ability. Modeling relevant cognitive operations through video production techniques, such as zooming (Salomon, 1974) and irising (Bovy, 1983), improved performance on tasks where the selection of details in context was a useful strategy. In short, casual exposure to media and deliberate modeling of a medium's symbolic processes had a direct and predictable effect on cognition.

A decade later, Salomon (1988) proposed something similar for computers, which he called AI in reverse. He claimed that internalizing the symbolic processes of computers would add to the repertoire of a person's cognitive skills, just as exposure to media would. This is amply illustrated in an intelligent word processor called the Writing Partner (Zellermayer, et al., 1991). Briefly, the Writing Partner guides students by presenting questions in a window that pops up on the screen while they are writing. The questions are appropriate for the kind of writing the student has planned to do and cover many aspects of the writing process, for example, rhetorical purpose, "Do you want your composition to persuade or describe?"; audience, "Is the reader a novice? Remember that he or she may need some basic facts about the topic"; elaboration, "What else do I know about this?", and many others (Zellermayer et al., 1991). These questions were clearly intended to give meta-cognitive guidance—that is, to make students think about the writing process, not simply to prompt them about what to do. The overall purpose of the Writing Partner is to move students from being knowledge-tellers to knowledge-transformers, a distinction that has theoretical roots in the work of Bereiter and Scardamalia (1987) and Hayes and Flower (1986).

Research using the Writing Partner has shown a number of things. First, subjects who received both solicited and unsolicited metacognitive guidance recalled writing-related metacognitions two weeks after working with the program. Zellermayer et al. (1991) gave this finding as evidence that the metacognitive strategies had been internalized. They also reported that students who had used the Writing Partner wrote better essays on a subsequent occasion in the absence of the tool. This provides evidence for a lasting effect, or cognitive residue, that arose from using the program.

The work of Salomon and his colleagues, cited briefly in this section, tells us two things about the status of artifacts in distributed learning environments. First, they extend and support intellectual capabilities while they are being used. Individuals benefit in two ways from this. First, they can offload some cognitive work to devices that are more efficient at performing certain tasks than humans are, like calculators, spreadsheets, and marine charts. This allows individuals to direct more cognitive effort to other activities that only they can do well. Second, exposure to artifacts, whether they have been designed to help us internalize and develop cognitive skills, like the Writing Partner, or not, like television, leaves a residue that can serve individuals well when they must perform tasks in the absence of the tool.

DISTRIBUTING COGNITION BY DESIGN

So far, we have made no particular distinction between natural and contrived distributed cognition systems. We now move to an examination of how distributed cognition systems can be designed and used. In so doing, we adopt a rather different perspective on distributed cognition, introducing new ideas, and picking up again on some of the issues we have already discussed, but from the pragmatic point of view of using distributed cognition to help students construct understanding.

Evidence from other theoretical perspectives that are at least somewhat sympathetic with the distributed cognition perspective—most notably the situated and ecological psychology frameworks (see also Chap. 3 & Chap. 6, this volume)—leads us to conclude that there are natural distributions of cognitive activity that occur when individuals or groups engage in intellectual activities in naturalistic settings. We give as examples Hutchins' navigators and, up to a point, the chemistry students in our earlier vignette. However, cognition can also be distributed by design, as it is in the case of the Writing Partner. Pea (1995) noted the possible benefits of design and invention orientations as powerful features of a distributed cognition framework. Rather than just providing detailed descriptions of individuals and groups interacting with the sociomaterial surround, it is possible in our role as educators to seek to be designers and shapers of such distributed activity for the sake of some intellectual outcome for the participants involved (Salomon, 1995).

Instructional designers are sometimes unaware of the depth of their influence in the artifacts they create (see Pea, 1995, for a discussion of LOGO in this regard). Indeed, because the distributed cognition perspective provides us with a general analytical frame for understanding—in an increasingly detailed manner—how people intellectually engage with the sociomaterial surround, it might be concluded that educators have been designing for the distribution of cognition for quite a while already, albeit in a tacit manner.

For example, the use of physical manipulatives as part of early mathematics instruction could be considered a case of designing for distributed cognition. The denominations (and often the physical structure) of the manipulatives provide specific conceptual scaffolding to children as they represent and operate on specific numerical (see also Chapter 7, this volume). Another broad category of research and innovation we might focus our attention on involves the structuring of productive group work in classrooms through participant structures and mediating artifacts (Webb & Palincsar, 1996 provide an overview of much of this work). Forms of socially distributed cognition that hinge on a division of labor model seem to connect with the more cooperative forms of group learning in contrast with forms of collaborative learning that potentially highlight a coordination of distributed activity within a coordinated partnership between individuals (see Linn & Burbules, 1993, for a discussion of cooperative vs. collaborative learning).

These examples allude to the near ubiquity and high degree of variability for situations of distributed cognition (Salomon, 1995), but we bring them up currently to highlight the designed nature of these educational innovations involved in promoting and supporting distributed cognition. In many circumstances, instances of highly distributed cognition are impromptu and emerge directly from the system—as in the classic cottage cheese measurement example (Lave, 1988). In educational settings, instructors are often interested in promoting new intellectual practices, modes of inquiry, and patterns of understanding. Whether instructors are interested in understanding how to promote some degree of numeracy through engagement with manipulatives, how to scaffold productive social interactions in the classroom, or how novice navigators learn to guide a sea-faring vessel through a narrow channel (see also Lave & Wenger, 1991), these represent empirical instantiations of designed structures that shape human activity to educational ends. In other words, the distributed cognition perspective need not just be a descriptive analytical frame, but we argue that the field should be moving toward understanding how it can be more of a prescriptive frame that guides the design of innovative learning environments.

When Salomon (1995) identified the two broad classes of distributed cognition that we discussed previously, he also discussed issues of design for each perspective. First, he described situations of distributed intelligence that focus on off-loading an individual's cognitive burden onto designed systems, warning that they may not promote important internalization of central aspects of the off-loaded aspects. A prototypical example of this class of design might be a CAD system for architects that stores and accumulates information and properties relevant to a design. Second, for situations where there are more targeted cognitive outcomes for groups and individuals, learning environments can be constructed to reciprocally scaffold students in specific cognitive practices. In these instances, the designed system (or package) is used to engender and promote an important cognitive practice, as with the Writing Partner, rather than simply accomplishing a specific end in and of itself. As an example of this latter class of distributed cognition, we describe later in the chapter how a classroom learning environment was designed that involved knowledge representations to support students' scientific debate and learning.

From the perspective of educators who seek to design and promote productive distributed learning environments, the following sections highlight some motivating commitments for such a distributed perspective before moving to a more detailed description of one such learning environment.

Heightened Attention to the Sociomaterial Context

As we already asserted, the primary theoretical and methodological commitment of the distributed cognition framework is that it argues for shifting the designer's unit of analysis away from that of the individual engaged in cognition-in-the-mind to a consideration of individuals engaged in cognitive activity within social and material contexts (Salomon, 1995). That is, the sociomaterial context is taken to shape the cognitive work being accomplished by the individual (or individuals) in crucial, interactive ways (Hutchins, 1995). They are crucial in the sense that it makes more theoretical sense to talk about the complex interactions between the components in the system than it does to isolate or ignore the components as non-interacting features of the setting.

This perspective brings heightened attention to the cognitive phenomena that occur in naturalistic settings. Whether the cognitive phenomena observed in such settings map back to phenomena investigated in less naturalistic settings (e.g., psychological laboratories) remains largely an open empirical question. Yet there is reason to believe, because of the heavy interaction between individuals and the sociomaterials context, that the cognitive phenomena in naturalistic and less naturalistic settings will be different to some significant degree (cf. Hutchins, 1995).

It is also worth noting that the distributed cognition perspective is sympathetic to views of learning that attend to individual as well as to social aspects of meaning construction and knowledge refinement (Driver, Asoko, Leach, Mortimer & Scott,1994; Linn, 1995; Palincsar, 1998). Distributed cognition is perhaps most different from a social constructivist perspective in that it also attends to the manners in which individuals interact with the material world in significant ways.

Intellectual Artifacts Afford Distributions of Cognitive Activity

From an ecological psychology perspective, physical objects support specific types of interactions with those objects (Gibson, 1979; Chapter 6, this volume). In other words, objects can be characterized by their affordances, some of which result from the intentional act of design, others being perhaps best described as unanticipated consequences (Norman, 1988). In that these object-affordances are strewn throughout the material contexts through which we move, they become features of the distributed cognition systems of interest here. That is, components can become interacting features of a distributed cognition system through their affordances, whether designed for or fortuitous.

In educational arenas, instructors are often interested in not just physical affordances of objects but the cognitive affordances of specific types of intellectual artifacts, which can be physical or technological. For example, in the case we present later in the chapter, we describe how a knowledge representation software tool can afford (and sometimes scaffold) specific types of cognitive activities for individuals and groups. We are interested in what sorts of intellectual moves and goals are supported at a group level as well as individual aspects of students' learning through engagement with such artifacts.

Technology Affords Distributed Interaction and Collaboration

New highly interactive and networked media provide a motivating force for pursuing a framework, like distributed cognition, that is sensitive to the prospects of meaningful interaction and collaboration at a distance (Pea, 1994; Pea & Gomez, 1992; Scardamalia & Bereiter, 1991). These are specific technological forms of more general system designs that support forms of distributed or collective intelligence. As people hear more about virtual communities, coordinated-networked curriculum, distributed multimedia, virtual collaboration, immersive environments, and ubiquitous computing, they are in need of integrative, theoretical perspectives like distributed cognition that can serve to structure their understanding of how to make use of those new technologies (Implications of New Media, 1995).

The work that has been performed in the growing field of computer-supported collaborative learning (CSCL) perhaps best typifies the exploration of the new possibilities represented by the emerging technologies (Koschmann, 1996; Pea, 1994). In such work, there is a desire to build learning environments to support a range of distributed cognitive work — communities of learners, conceptual learning conversations, and knowledge-building communities. Instructional designers are just in the initial stages of exploring the commonalities and discontinuities between the variety of CSCL activities that are afforded by the new technologies and how best to design them.

Design as a Central Feature of a Scientific Program

As we already mentioned, the distributed cognition perspective represents a shift toward more closely investigating cognitive activities in naturalistic settings. This parallels the shift in the empirical investigation of educational innovations undertaken by those subscribing to the design experiment approach (Brown, 1992; Collins, 1992; diSessa, 1991; Linn, 1990). Design experimentation provides a foundation for the design and formative refinement of educational innovations through detailed empirical inquiry into the use of those innovations in naturalistic learning settings, usually classrooms. Almost always, there is a system of interdependent components (e.g., software learning environments coupled with specific activity structures) that make up the designed innovation. They are then perhaps best described as being package-like with regard to their successful use in classrooms. The instructional materials depend on the pedagogical strategies used by the teacher which may in turn depend on the epistemological beliefs of the students. Their success depends on sharing knowledge and on the interdependability of the package's components.

It appears, therefore, that there is a natural synergy between the distributed cognition perspective and the design experiment approach to innovation in that they are both focused on understanding the cognitive interaction between components of a complex system in naturalistic settings. For example, researchers have studied how the distribution of expertise has played out in the design of communities of learners (Brown, et al., 1995). Whereas distributed cognition can serve as solely a descriptive lens onto human activity as it naturally occurs, it might also provide an important lens onto dimensions of educational innovation where design is incorporated as a central feature of the scientific endeavor. It can help instructional designers understand the systemic interactions involved in the cognitive system as they design, use, study, and refine these innovations.

We now present a case that illustrates many of these ideas. It shows how a designed distributed cognitive environment works in the real world.

The Case of Using Argument Maps To Shape Classroom Debates

The following case of distributed cognition comes from an eighth-grade physical science classroom where students are engaged in a lively classroom debate about the nature of light. Working in pairs, students have spent the last seven days analyzing pieces of empirical evidence from the Web related to everyday and scientific aspects of the debate. Before working on this project, students spent more than four weeks exploring different properties of light and vision through hands-on laboratory activities (Linn, 1992). In this classroom, computers are primarily used as learning partners—aspects of the software scaffold students' inquiry and promote their reflection and refinement of knowledge. Learning partners can be considered a specific genre of learning technology, in contrast to other genres such as direct instruction or exploratory learning environments.

In this particular culminating debate about light, students discuss and make sense of about a dozen pieces of evidence in their small group. As they do so, they construct a visual argument map—a form of knowledge representation—using a software tool called SenseMaker intended to make their understanding of the collection of evidence readily visible (Bell, 1997). As shown in Fig. 5.1, SenseMaker allows students to construct arguments by categorically and spatially relating the same set of Web-based evidence (represented as dots) with differing scientific claims about the topic (represented by boxes). Evidence that supports a conceptual claim is placed within a box; boxes can be hierarchically nested to indicate theoretical components that are related. Students either create their own conceptual frames or borrow them from a frame library in the software.

As part of this argument construction process, students also embed conceptual capital into their arguments by composing a written explanation for each piece of evidence regarding how it should be tethered to the various perspectives. In 80% of their explanations, students are applying or suggesting causal ideas about the evidence (Bell, 1998). This theorizing capital that students have embedded into their arguments gets cashed-in in dynamic ways when they present their argument during the classroom debate. Each student pair ends up creating a visual argument for their position about the nature of light that they have printed out along with their notes for use during the debate. There is quite a bit of variability in the arguments even though they center around common pieces of evidence.

Students' use of the argument representations to shape their knowledge-building discourse is the centerpiece of this distributed cognition system. Their individual and small group work on the arguments really pays off during the classroom debate. As each group takes turns presenting its arguments to the class, the SenseMaker argument of that group is web-cast on the computer screens located throughout the classroom. This technique allows each group in the audience to easily compare their own argument map to that of the presenting group.

Students generate questions after a group's presentation, often by indexing the argument map of the presenting group. Although the argument maps are rather simple knowledge representations, they serve the purpose of shaping the discourse of the students in productive ways. It is worth noting that the classroom debates are student-centered conversations with student comments typically accounting for 90% of the talk. Imagine a group presenting the argument shown in Fig. 5.1. After they describe the evidence that most strongly supports their position on the nature of light, they are asked a flurry of questions sequentially from students located around the room who have been investigating their argument map. Why had they categorized a specific piece of evidence as supporting a particular theory? Why did they not categorize two evidence items together given how similar they were? What did they really mean by a conceptual frame they had created in their argument? These conversations unfold and build on earlier aspects of the discourse in interesting ways. Specific pieces of evidence become regular items of discussion that are returned to from group to group. Students bring up alternative explanations and discriminate between them by making connections to earlier classroom experience or other life experiences. Groups start to describe changes they would anticipate making to parts of their maps, given what they have subsequently learned.

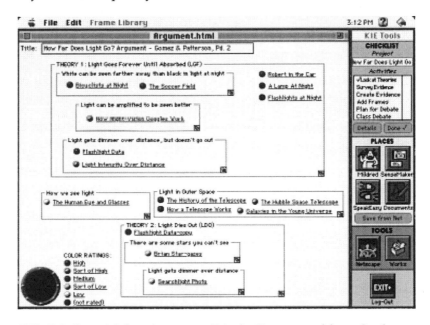

FIG. 5-1: SenseMaker Argument Jointly Constructed by a Student
Pair for Use in the How Far Does Light Go? Classroom Debate

The web-cast argument maps were a distribution of different perspectives and theorizing about the debate. By making group thinking visible in this manner, it was possible to encourage the students to expand and refine the range of ideas they were considering in relation to the debate topic. When students asked questions based on some simple feature of an argument map, or a difference between it and their own maps, they would often conceptually unpack the relevant evidence explanation and share different perspectives.

This case highlights several design lessons associated with an intellectual partnership form of distributed cognition. It is therefore important to review how these classroom communities came to successfully use the SenseMaker tool. In fact, there were many important changes made within those communities and to the educational objects involved in the innovation that enabled the students to construct their arguments. The designed system was refined over the course of five classroom trials—and necessarily so. We now identify central features of the design along specific theoretical categories.

Arranging Epistemological Forces

DiSessa (1995) called for a heightened awareness of the epistemological forces that shape the design and use of technology systems, although such a perspective is of use for the broader learning environment in general. In the case we just presented, web-casting the argument maps during the debate qualitatively shifted the discourse compared to previous classroom trials. Because the SenseMaker tool strategically employs some degree of epistemic fidelity with scientific argumentation (i.e., coordinating empirical evidence with scientific claims, relating specific conceptual ideas, elaborating different theoretical alternatives, and more), students are supported in focusing on scientific aspects of the arguments created, presented, and discussed. Without such scaffolding, students rarely spontaneously coordinate evidence with theory-based conjectures during argumentation (Kuhn, 1991). When they do consider evidence, they often preferentially focus on individual items (Driver, Leach, Millar, & Scott, 1996). The argument maps highlight the salience of the evidence to the theoretical issues of the debate, and they scaffold students' consideration of the entire set of evidence rather than just individual items. In other words, the designed system shapes the students' engagement in the debate at an epistemological level. Argument maps become a representation of their understanding, and scientific criteria for argumentation are promoted for their consideration.

Knowledge Representations as Inscriptional Systems

The use of SenseMaker as a knowledge representation tool in those classes amounted to the gradual adoption of a new inscriptional system by these students and their teacher, as described by Pea (1995). In our specific case, students were inscribing arguments that represented their understanding. This involved a coordination of new products to be articulated (warrant-based evidence explanations and conceptual claim frame configurations), new practices associated with those products (evidence sense-making, frame-building, argument comparison), and new epistemological commitments (ideas as constituent and relatable objects within arguments, using personal knowledge to influence how an individual explains evidence, evidence explainable by multiple theoretical positions, and more). This coordination required far more of the students than the simple convergence on right answers, suggested by the system-theoretic approach to distributed cognition described above. In some sense, moreover, students were developing a specific new form of literacy by learning to make use of the argument maps. This included central aspects of the tool, practices, and norms associated with their knowledge representations.

Although it is beyond the scope of this chapter to provide a detailed sense of how the students developed an understanding of this new inscriptional system, the process did involve a significant concerted effort consisting of an introductory, three-day debate project, teacher modeling of appropriate practices associated with the maps, and frequent classroom discussions about metalevel aspects of the maps (e.g., why an evidence item might be appropriately placed in multiple theoretical frames). These facilitating supports that allowed for the successful use of the argument maps were identified through successive classroom trial and refinement mostly around the SenseMaker tool itself, which remained largely the same from trial to trial (Bell, 1998).

Creators of artifacts and other representational objects often load them with intelligence (Pea, 1995). In this case, students were loading their argument maps with conceptual and metaconceptual detail (e.g., criteria-based critiques of evidence) that could be used to shape the discourse during the classroom debates. The maps became resources for conversation and elaborated argumentation. It is important to note that it was necessary to refine the design of the intervention in order to shape how students elaborated their argument maps. Student arguments during the early trials were not as conceptually focused and elaborated as in the final trial.

Fostering the Development of Students' Metaknowledge

Related to the design focus on inscriptional systems, it was found to be highly beneficial (if not necessary) to encourage students to develop metaknowledge associated with the use of the inscriptions for the specific purposes of the debate. Through various aspects of the designed innovation, students were introduced to criteria for the evaluation of the maps (e.g., categorizing similar evidence items consistently within the maps) and to the subtleties of the practices associated with their use (e.g., how to compare features of different argument maps and how to conceptually unpack the contributing influences on their structure). Students were indeed learning how to make use of argument maps for the purposes of a debate, but they were also developing metaknowledge about the purposes, criteria, and practices associated with knowledge representations.

CONCLUSIONS

Characteristics of Distributed Cognition

Our discussion of distributed cognition allows us to identify some characteristics that seem to be present when it occurs. We briefly summarize these here. In doing so, we suggest at least partial answers to the four questions we posed in the introduction to this chapter.

Distributed cognition requires the sharing of cognitive activity among the components of a system. Such sharing means that students are accorded more autonomy. The balance of power among students and teachers shifts in favor of the students. System components might include other people as well as physical or digital artifacts (devices, technologies, or media). The possibilities for distributing cognitive systems have been increased by emerging network-based and ubiquitous computational devices. Given that the nuanced features and practices of these distributed systems are likely to be theoretically important, significant research will be needed to fully understand what they contribute to knowledge construction.

There is a system-level coordination of effort within a distributed cognition system. Often, there is an attempt to make progress toward a common goal or there is at least a shared understanding of how the components of the system might productively interact in order to make progress. It follows that for a distributed cognitive system to succeed, information must be shared between the components in meaningful ways. This has two consequences. First, effective communication among all components of the system is essential. Second, the cumulative wisdom of the system does not reside in any one person or artifact, though all individuals ultimately have access to that wisdom. The whole is truly greater than the sum of the parts.

In order for individuals to share information in a distributed system, ideas must be represented in forms that are external to the individuals. For example, student ideas can be externalized and made visible to a group through their knowledge representations. More generally, distributed cognition highlights the use of different inscriptional systems for recording and distributing within these systems.

Artifacts can scaffold new capabilities while individuals make use of them. That is, aspects of cognitive work can be off-loaded onto the artifacts in ways that afford new types of reasoning than what is possible without use of the artifacts. Such systems can be said to augment our capabilities. Individuals might also internalize aspects of these artifacts as they make use of them and thereby the use of an artifact can leave some sort of cognitive residue with the individual. In ways that are not well understood, people incorporate aspects of these artifacts into their thinking. An epistemological issue is what knowledge gets changed or refined as a result of the use of an artifact. Learning persists and transfers to some later cognitive activity.

Distributed learning environments hinge on questions about the nature of individual and group learning and about the knowledge (or ways of knowing) that is in question. Appropriate epistemological forces can be marshaled into action through the design of the system. Students can be encouraged to make their own thinking visible through inscriptional systems, exchange perspectives through debate-focused participant structures, and work toward a more integrated understanding of an issue through the application of more scientific criteria that are highlighted by the tools being used.

Successful classroom interventions that support distributed cognition are package-like in nature. The outcomes are systemic effects of the package, not of particular components in the intervention. Once instructional designers develop a detailed understanding of how these packages need to be designed for use in particular settings, they will be able to learn about the diffusion of such innovations by bringing them to new settings and studying how the necessary system needs to change (or not) for use in the new context.

Some Things Distributed Cognition Shares with Other Approaches

Our review of distributed cognition has also identified some characteristics that it shares with other approaches to learning, described in the other chapters of this book.

An important characteristic of distributed cognition is that it describes the construction of knowledge, aligning it generally with constructivist perspectives on learning (see Chapter 2, this volume). The distributed perspective sets itself apart from constructivist views by pulling the socio-material context into theoretic consideration.

There is a natural synergy between the distributed cognition perspective and cognitive activity as it occurs in real world settings. Distributed, in reference to cognition, often refers to distribution among people and artifacts in the real world rather than a contrived world. When aspects of this socio-material context are interpreted as centrally related to cognitive work being accomplished, distributed cognition shares a number of the attributes of theories of situated cognition. However, a distributed cognition view need not automatically forsake a focus on the internal representation of knowledge and on the transfer of knowledge from one setting to another.

When cognition is distributed, it frequently operates on the basis of the natural affordances of the components to which it is distributed—a feature that bears resemblance to aspects of an ecological psychology perspective (see Chapter 6, this volume). In the classic cottage cheese problem (Lave, 1988), the solution would not apply had the problem been to divide quantities of orange juice rather than cottage cheese. Aspects of the sociomaterial context constrain and afford particular cognitive moves in these settings by the participants. In educational settings, this quality highlights the importance of the designer for supporting specific forms of cognition and learning.

The way in which distributed systems are designed and implemented has a lot in common with the implications for design of the other chapters in this book. Generally, there is a growing interest in understanding how to support important forms of cognition and learning in naturalistic settings. In these activities, it is common for students to be actively engaged in sustained inquiry, sense-making, and knowledge-building in ways that are sensitive to the practices of the discipline. Other epistemological and pedagogical aspects of the subject matter are frequently brought into consideration in terms of what it means to know mathematics, history, or science. These features of design knowledge are not the purview of just the distributed cognition perspective, of course. What might not be shared with other frameworks is the focus on the package-like nature of successful educational innovations from the distributed cognition perspective that results from the focus on the learning environments as systems.

REFERENCES

Bell, P. (1997). Using argument representations to make thinking visible for individuals and groups. In R. Hall, N. Miyake, & N. Enyedy (Eds.), *Pro- of CSCL97: The Second International Conference on Computer support for collaborative learning.* Toronto, Canada: University of Toronto Press.

Bell, P. (1998). *Designing for students' science learning using argumentation and classroom debate.* Unpublished Doctoral Dissertation, University of California at Berkeley.

Bereiter, C., & Scardamalia, M. (1987). *The psychology of written composition.* Hillsdale, NJ: Lawrence Erlbaum Associates.

Bovy, R.C. (1983, April). *Defining the psychologically active features of instructional treatments designed to facilitate cue attendance.* Paper presented at the meeting of the American Educational Research Association, Montreal, Canada.

Brown, A. L. (1992). Design experiments: Theoretical and methodological challenges in creating complex interventions in classroom settings. *The Journal of the Learning Sciences, 2*(2), 141-178.

Brown, A. L., Ash, D., Rutherford, M., Nakagawa, K., Gordon, A., & Campione, J. C. (1995). Distributed expertise in the classroom. In G. Salomon (Ed.), *Distributed cognitions: Psychological and educational considerations* (pp. 188-228). Cambridge, England: Cambridge University Press.

Cole, M. (1991). On socially shared cognitions. In L. Resnick, J. Levine, & S. Behrend (Eds.), *Socially shared cognitions.* Hillsdale, NJ: Lawrence Erlbaum Associates.

Collins, A. (1992). Toward a design science of education. In E. Scanlon & T. O'Shea (Eds.), *New directions in educational technology.* New York: Springer-Verlag.

Cunningham, D. (1992). Assessing constructions and constructing assessments: A dialog. In T. Duffy & D. Jonassen (Eds.). *Constructivism and the technology of instruction: A conversation* (pp. 35-44).Hillsdale, NJ: Lawrence Erlbaum Associates.

Implications of new media for K-12 education. Hearings before the U.S. Congress, House of Representatives, Joint Hearing on Educational Technology in the 21st Century, Washington, DC. (1995, October) (Testimony of C Dede).

diSessa, A. A. (1991). Local sciences: Viewing the design of human-computer systems as cognitive science. In J. M. Carroll (Ed.), *Designing interaction: Psychology at the human-computer interface*, (pp. 162-202). Cambridge, England: Cambridge University Press.

diSessa, A. A. (1995). Epistemology and systems design. In A. A. diSessa, C. Hoyles, R. Noss, & L. Edwards (Eds.), *Computers and Exploratory Learning*. Berlin, Germany: Springer Verlag.

Driver, R., Asoko, H., Leach, J., Mortimer, E., & Scott, P. (1994). Constructing scientific knowledge in the classroom. *Educational Researcher, 23*(7), 5-12.

Driver, R., Leach, J., Millar, R., & Scott, P. (1996). *Young people's images of science*. Milton Keynes, UK: Open University.

Duffy, T., & Jonassen, D. (1992). Constructivism: New implications for instructional technology. In T. Duffy & D. Jonassen (Eds.), *Constructivism and the technology of instruction: A conversation*. Hillsdale, NJ: Lawrence Erlbaum Associates.

Gibson, J. J. (1979). *The ecological approach to visual perception*. Boston: Houghton Mifflin.

Halverson, C. A. (1992). *Analyzing a cognitively distributed system: A terminal radar approach control*. Unpublished Masters thesis, University of California at San Diego.

Hayes, J. R., & Flower, L. A. (1986). Writing research and the writer. *American Psychologist, 41*, 1106-1113.

Hutchins, E. (1995). *Cognition in the wild*. Cambridge, MA: MIT Press.

Hutchins, E., & Klausen, T. (1996). Distributed cognition in the airline cockpit. In D. Middleton & Y. Angstrom (Eds.), *Communication and cognition at work*. Cambridge: Cambridge University Press.

Jackson, R., Taylor, W., & Winn, W. D. (1999, April). *Peer collaboration in virtual environments: An investigation of multi-participant virtual reality applied in primary science education*. Paper presented at the annual meeting of the American Educational Research Association, Montreal.

Koschmann, T. (Ed.). (1996). *CSCL, theory and practice of an emerging paradigm*. Mahwah, NJ: Lawrence Erlbaum Associates.

Kuhn, D. (1991). *The skills of argument*. Cambridge, England: Cambridge University Press.

Lave, J. (1988). *Cognition in practice*. New York: Cambridge University Press.

Lave, J., & Wenger, E. (1991). *Situated learning: Legitimate peripheral participation*. Cambridge, England: Cambridge University Press.

Linn, M. C. (1990). Establishing a science and engineering base for science education. In M. Gardner, J. G. Greeno, F. Reif, A. H. Schoenfeld, A. diSessa, & E. Stage (Eds.), *Toward a scientific practice of science education*, (pp. 323-341). Hillsdale, NJ: Lawrence Erlbaum Associates.

Linn, M. C. (1992). The computer as learning partner: Can computer tools teach science? In K. Sheingold, L. G. Roberts, & S. M. Malcom (Eds.),

This year in school science 1991: Technology for teaching and learning (pp. 31-69). Washington, DC: American Association for the Advancement of Science.

Linn, M. C. (1995). Designing computer learning environments for engineering and computer science: The scaffolded knowledge integration framework. *Journal of Science Education and Technology*, 4(2), 103-126.

Linn, M. C., & Burbules, N. C. (1993). Construction of knowledge and group learning. In K. Tobin (Ed.), *The practice of constructivism in science education* (pp. 91-119). Washington, DC: American Association for the Advancement of Science.

Norman, D. A. (1988). *The psychology of everyday things*. New York: Basic Books.

Nickerson, R. S. (1995). On the distributions of cognitions: Some reflections. In G. Salomon (Ed.), *Distributed cognitions: Psychological and educational considerations* (pp. 229-261). Cambridge: Cambridge University Press.

Papert, S. (1983). *Mindstorms*. New York: Basic Books.

Palincsar, A.S. (1998). Social constructivist perspectives on teaching and learning. *Annual Review of Psychology, 49*, 345-375.

Pask, G. (1975). *Conversation, cognition and learning*. Amsterdam: Elsevier.

Pask, G. (1984). Review of conversation theory and protologic (or protolanguage), *Educational Communication and Technology Journal, 32*, 3-40.

Pea, R. D. (1994). Seeing what we build together: Distributed multimedia learning environments for transformative communications. *Journal of the Learning Sciences, 3*(3), 285-299.

Pea, R. (1995). Practices of distributed intelligence and designs for education. In G. Salomon (Ed.), *Distributed cognitions: Psychological and educational considerations* (pp. 47-87). Cambridge, England: Cambridge University Press.

Pea, R., & Gomez, L. (1992). Distributed multimedia learning environments: Why and how? *Interactive Learning Environments, 2*, 73-109.

Perkins, D. (1992). Technology meets constructivism: Do they make a match? In T. Duffy & D. Jonassen (Eds.). *Constructivism and the technology of instruction: A conversation* (pp. 45-56). Hillsdale, NJ: Lawrence Erlbaum Associates.

Perkins, D. (1995). Person-plus: A distributed view of thinking and learning. In G. Salomon (Ed.), *Distributed cognitions: Psychological and educational considerations* (pp. 88-110). Cambridge, England: Cambridge University Press.

Piaget, J. (1967). *Six psychological studies*. New York: Vintage Books.

Rogers, Y. (1992). Ghosts in the network: Distributed troubleshooting in a shared working environment. *In Proceedings of the conference on computer-supported cooperative work*. New York: Association for Computing Machinery.

Salomon, G. (1974). Internalization of filmic schematic operations in interaction with learners' aptitudes. *Journal of Educational Psychology, 66*, 499-511.

Salomon, G. (1979). *Interaction of media, cognition and learning*. San Francisco: Jossey-Bass.

Salomon, G. (1988). AI in reverse: Computer tools that turn cognitive. *Journal of Educational Computing Research, 4*, 123-139.

Salomon, G. (1995). No distribution without individuals' cognition: A dynamic interactional view. In G. Salomon (Ed.), *Distributed cognitions: Psychological and educational considerations* (pp. 111-137). Cambridge, England: Cambridge University Press.

Salomon, G., Perkins, D., & Globerson, T. (1991). Partners in cognition: Extending human intelligence with intelligent technologies. *Educational Researcher, 20* (3), 2-9.

Scardamalia, M., & Bereiter, C. (1991). Higher levels of agency for children in knowledge building: A challenge for the design of new knowledge media. *The Journal of the Learning Sciences, 1*, 37-68.

Von Bertalanffy, L. (1986). *General system theory*. New York: Braziller.

Von Foerster, H. (1982). *Observing systems*. Seaside, CA: Intersystem Publications.

Webb, N. M., & Palincsar, A. S. (1996). Group processes in the classroom. In D. Berliner & R. Calfee (Eds.), *Handbook of educational psychology* (pp. 841-873). New York: Macmillan.

White, B. (1988). *Thinker Tools: Causal models, conceptual change, and science education* (BBN Technical Rep. No. 6873). Cambridge, MA: Bolt, Beranek & Newman.

Zellermayer, M., Salomon, G., Globerson, T., & Givon, H. (1991). Enhancing writing-related metacognitions through a computerized writing partner. *American Educational Research Journal, 28*, 373-391.

6

Agent as Detector: An Ecological Psychology Perspective on Learning by Perceiving-Acting Systems

Michael F. Young
University of Connecticut

Sasha A, Barab
Indiana University

Steve Garrett
University of Connecticut

Many thinkers in the field of learning psychology have contributed to a modern consensus in favor of learning by doing. Of course, Dewey (1963) must be thanked for introducing this idea. But more recently instructional designers have expanded the technology for creating learning environments that foster the design and creation of products in the service of learning abstract content and conceptual information. Vygotsky's (1978) ideas challenged us to provide scaffolding for relative novices, and Lave's (e.g., Lave & Wenger, 1990) descriptions of situated learning and legitimate peripheral participation in communities of learners elaborated the culture in which successful learning can occur. But behind this consensus of the outcomes of instructional design (ID) lies fundamental differences regarding the underlying psychology.

Clearly learners are motivated by internal goals when learning by doing (e.g., to produce quality work), and clearly learners perceive external achievements of success (e.g., rewards and grades). When learning by doing, learners are solving problems, thinking creatively, and making logical arguments. And learning by doing (especially well suited to teams) is a social process in which meaning is negotiated, goals emerge from social processes, and success is taken within context. These can be viewed respectively as internal motivations, external reinforcers, and social constructivist concepts. Because these things can be explained from multiple perspectives, psychologists hoping to understand these observations weight their relative importance very differently based on their favorite theory. And that brings us to our discussion.

From the perspective of an ecological psychologist, the unit of analysis is the agent-environment interaction. Problem solving and motivation are not a product of learners' internal cognitions (information processing) nor are learners simply victims of environmental selection. Rather, they emerge as a result of an intentionally-driven agent (self-organizing system) interacting with an information-rich environment. It is this statement that we unpack within the remainder of this chapter.

Our presentation takes for granted an appreciation by the reader of the information processing and behaviorist perspectives of learning-by-doing. An ecological psychology (ecopsych) perspective is quite different from these, and it is the subject of debates that come down to fundamental assumptions (e.g., Cognitive Science, 1993). It is a perspective with which many readers may be unfamiliar, so we hope that we will be given some initial leeway to define the starting assumptions that frame our key ideas. Cognition (how people think and learn) is explained in terms of the relationship between learners and the properties of specific environments, particularly the affordances for action they have (Gibson, 1977, 1986; Young, 1993). It becomes impossible, and irrelevant, to separate the learner and the material to be learned from the context in which learning occurs (Lave, 1988). Said the other way, if learning occurs at all, then it occurs in situ, with the goals and intentions of the learning driving the perceiving and acting of an agent within that context. As such, an analysis of cognition and learning requires an understanding of complex dynamics (interactions), and it cannot be driven by observations of static states (e.g., memories, learning styles, or achievement levels) of the agent (learner) at a particular time. So from the start we are into an arena of complex dynamic systems for which linear, mathematical models are incomplete. We are operating at a level just short of philosophy, but beyond individual psychology, that can only be appreciated by comparing it with similar developments that are occurring in parallel across disciplines (e.g., Capra, 1996; Swenson, 1996).

Traditional information processing models create artificial dichotomies that prove to be difficult to avoid. Once mind-body dualism is assumed, an individual is compelled toward confusing dichotomies that lead to beliefs that there exists authentic (vs. inauthentic) learning environments, situated (vs. unsituated) learning, meaningful (vs. unmeaningful) problems, and anchored (vs. adrift) instruction.

For example, the Cognition and Technology Group at Vanderbilt (CTGV, 1990) described the role of videodiscs they produced as potentially "situating instruction in videodisc-based problem-solving environments" (p. 6). Although not intended by the authors, such descriptions create a misleading conception that some learning and thinking is situated and some is not (CTGV, 1990, 1993; Greeno, 1989). However, with an ecopsych perspective, all learning is situated. In fact, there is nothing special about meaningful or authentic learning. If anything is learned, it is meaningful to that individual in some way. No learning is inauthentic if learning occurs at all. When students are acting on goals they adopt, their actions are authentic even if the goals are not central to the information being learned. This does not mean that environments do not differ with respect to the potential learning that could occur from their affordance structure. There are clearly differences such that instructional designers can contrive environments to optimize the benefits of pursuing certain goals within them. But wherever learning occurs, it can be considered authentic, situated, and meaningful (see also Chapter 3, this volume).

A final note, Greeno (1998) attempted a synthesis of the multiple learning psychology perspectives, which he has titled situativity. Situativity puts behavioral and information processing cognition into a broader perspective using elements of ecopsych. But this synthesis retains many of the properties of information processing, including internal mediating variables; "the situative perspective emphasizes ways that social practices are organized to encourage and support engaged participation by members of communities and that are understood by individuals to support the continuing development of their personal identities" (p.11). We distance ourselves from this attempt at synthesis and instead provide what we believe to be a more radical perspective based purely on lessons derived from ecopsych.

KEY IDEAS OF PERCEIVING-ACTING SYSTEMS

Person as Detector—the Perceiving-Acting Cycle

At times our view of learning, from an ecopsych perspective, has led us to make controversial statements designed to incite debate, such as, "there is no memory," and, "intelligence is not a property of individuals, but emerges from the interaction of agent with environment." These statements are indicative of our emphasis on perception over memory. Our statements arise from the use of a different metaphor for a thinking person—people are sophisticated detectors of information. Contrast this with information-processing's favorite metaphor: People are sophisticated information processors (taking in, storing, and retrieving information). So instead of computers as the model for thinking, we prefer to compare people to control systems like thermostats. Thermostats are simple signal detectors that can be tuned to detect different temperatures. People, we contend, are information detectors that can be tuned to detect different types of information—and the environment is full of interesting information to be detected.

Because our analysis rests on a continuous dynamic agent-environment interaction, we cannot be restricted to a linear model of thinking (input-storage-retrieval). Our analysis assumes a perceiving-acting cycle that is the result of a working detector. It is this perceiving-acting cycle that allows for the coupling of individual and environment (Gibson, 1986; Kugler, Shaw, Vicente, & Kinsella-Shaw, 1992) and for the development of a theory of cognition that does not require the inclusion of mediary variables. It involves an individual who detects (perceives) information (based on the constraints imposed by intentions) and acts, thereby transforming the environment so that new effectivity-affordance relationships can be perceived and acted on.

We argue that the information that is detected within the context of this cycle (system) allows an individual to stay apprised of affordances in the environment without recourse to mediary concepts so central to the information processing perspective. Ecological psychologists have amassed evidence to support the contention that the environment is punctuated by qualitative regions of functional significance for an individual with reciprocal effectivities. This research has examined environmental affordances with respect to crawlable surfaces (Gibson, 1986), sittable heights (Mark, Balliet, Craver, Douglas, & Fox, 1990), steppable heights (Pufall & Dunbar, 1992; Warren, 1984), passable apertures (Warren & Wang, 1987), and time to contact (Kim, Turvey, & Carello, 1993). Implications of this research are that it is not necessary to posit inferences to symbolic calculations on the part of the observer; what is needed is a better understanding of the environmental affordances and how the user becomes apprised of these possibilities for action.

It is essential that an individual acknowledges this cycle as a system that loses its function of providing direct information about the environment (and its affordances) to the learner if perception and action are treated individually. In fact, it has been shown that if the individual is not given ample opportunity to engage in action (e.g., restricting head or body movement), then detection of environmental affordances is extremely limited even when looking at the same environmental information (Warren & Wang, 1987). In this way, perception is always for some goal, leading to some action, that provides a change in the information to be detected. Change is an essential element, the essence of a dynamic system. Change (variance) and stability (invariance) are critical information to be detected and acted on.

Here we would like to take the liberty of defining two key terms used previously: *affordances* and *effectivities*. Affordances are the properties of an environment, specified by the information field, that enable action. Effectivities are the abilities of an individual to take action. It is essential to understand these terms as mutually defined and codetermined. A doorway is passable (affordance) only for an agent with the ability to pass through it (effectivity). Therefore, one person, walking, may detect the affordance of a particular doorway (potential for action), whereas for another, in a wheel chair, such an affordance might not exist because they lack similar effectivities (abilities to act).

Dynamics

Because our analysis rests fundamentally on dynamics, we must distinguish the types of dynamics that interest us. First, the dynamics of information within the environment are of critical interest. For example, Gibson's (1986) notion of invariance (within an information field) across situations leads to an ecopsych description of cognitive psychology's concepts of schema and scripts. Stated simply, from an ecological psychology perspective, a script is seen as the invariance detected across similar situations, not stored in memory but detected on the fly. Our understanding of learning by doing leads us to describe activity as paths or trajectories within state spaces, applying principles of nonlinear thermodynamics (created for energy fields) to the nonlinear dynamics of intentionally driven systems, individuals or groups (Kugler, et al., 1992). Detection of invariance across experiences with objects leads to direct perception of the concepts of information processing like squareness, a reinterpretation of what is commonly considered an abstraction stored in memory as a prototype or exemplar. Similarly, detection of invariance across restaurant experiences leads to the direct detection of goal sets associated with particular action, a reconceptualization of schema theory ideas such as restaurant scripts (Schank & Abelson, 1977). Note the active verb here is detection, not understanding, processing, or recall.

As the perceiving-acting cycle unfolds over time, the intentions of the agent lead it toward a goal. But we must distinguish the complexity of even this basic statement, because it is by no means linear or unitary. First, the goal or end state of the system is more accurately described as a region within the state space, allowing for multiple correct answers (paths) that satisfy the goal constraints (see Shaw & Kinsella-Shaw, 1988, for a detailed description of the Ω-cell, a mathematical description of the border constraints imposed by goal adoption). Also, there is rarely one correct path or trajectory of interest, and this is more accurately described as a collection of tendencies from among a distribution of paths. The bottom line, though, is that understanding the dynamics of the flow field of information and its relation to the perceiver (e.g., detecting invariance) is where an ecopsych description of cognition begins.

We assume that learners are, indeed, intentionally driven systems, having goals and intentions that themselves emerge from an interaction between agent and environment. But as complex systems, they can be driven to pursue multiple intentions simultaneously. Therefore, there are also dynamics of intentions (Kugler et al., 1992). That is, each learner has goals that change in priority as he or she interacts with the environment. Then, once a particular goal takes priority, there are the additional dynamics that unfold as the learner acts to move toward that goal. These are the intentional dynamics that are best understood by ecological psychology (e.g., Turvey & Shaw, 1995). Therefore, there are both the dynamics of intentions (changing goals) and intentional dynamics (the playing out of the perceiving-acting cycle as a learner works toward any particular goal). It is this set of dynamics, not simply internal states or external rewards, that best captures the coupled interactions continually unfolding between person and environment.

People are intentionally-driven systems. This means that somehow goals emerge from a perceiving-acting system dynamically interacting with the environment. Relative to intentional dynamics, there has been less discussion on the dynamics of intentions. Where goals come from is a tricky question, but at least the inklings of an answer can be given simply: They are perceived from interacting with an information-rich environment. A full decryption of the direct perception of goals requires some nontraditional mathematics concepts such as a germ (see Shaw, 1987). Added to this are the concepts of compactified fields that reveal hidden nested levels of complexity as they are perceived in more detail. Perhaps the best analog to this is an ill-structured problem that dynamically reveals subproblems only after work on the overall problem has begun. There is a set of nested goals that individuals are pursuing at any given time. Said another way, people move along trajectories toward goals within several space-times (e.g., you may have goals you are currently pursuing as your read this sentence including being a good student, working toward a career, and getting the meaning of the text). Although you are somewhere along all these paths, it is not until the moment of this occasion that an ecopsych account of your behavior can be fully specified. The dynamics of intentions (changing goals) are interesting because they provide an opportunity for new goals to be introduced (by teachers or engaging environments), a process that is fundamental to an ecological psychology version of instruction (Barab, Cherkes-Julkowski, Swenson, Garrett, & Shaw, 1999).

Codetermined Interactions

Perhaps the most common stumbling block to understanding the ecopsych perspective is fully appreciating the inherent nature of codetermination of concepts. Key ideas from ecopsych are often interpreted as stand alone properties (of the individual or of the environment), leading to the misapplication of information processing or behaviorist analyses to these ideas. Take for example the idea of affordances (Gibson, 1977). This idea has been explained elsewhere as the properties of the environment that permit certain activities (Greeno, 1994). But it is only the properties of the environment for a specific agent acting within space-time, not all agents or for all times. An affordance is not an inherent property of the environment, only of its relationship to a specific agent, with specific goals and abilities (termed *effectivities*), on a specific occasion. A common example is that a door knob has the affordance of turnable. But it only has this affordance for an agent with the ability to turn the handle (certain dexterity and hand shape, etc.). A doorknob does not have the turnability affordance for a dog (no hands) or even an infant (insufficient strength)—agents that do not have the effectivity of turning handles. So an affordance is codetermined by properties of the object in relation to the properties of the agent. This idea of codetermination leads to an important description of terms as duals that can be described more precisely and modeled mathematically (Shaw, Kadar, Sim, & Repperger, 1992).

Within the concept of affordance also lurks the idea of intentionally driven systems. Although a doorknob may have the affordance turnable for normal adult humans, our perspective suggests that a person may only detect that affordance when they have a relevant goal (e.g., getting out of the room). This situational analysis means that although information specifying an affordance may potentially be available (along with a nearly infinite amount of other information), only agents with particular intentions are expected to pick up (or detect) such information on a given occasion. This more complicated analysis of an idea like affordance is one thing that sets the ecopsych perspective apart from linear models of cognition that place emphasis on the side of the learner or of the environment. Dynamic systems whose properties are codetermined are central to the ecopsych perspective on learning and thinking.

Affordances are a handy term from ecopsych to describe the regularities of the environment that are meaningful (in relation to adopted goals) to a learner. Meaningful here refers to the detection of the affordance due to its specification for action, an action that will move the learner toward the adopted goal. Meaning in this sense is not the product of reflection or something imposed by calculation and appraisal made on otherwise meaningless sense information or done abstractly inside the head. For ecopsych, what is perceived has meaning in it from the start—directly perceivable as a consequence of action.

Because affordances and effectivities are duals (co-determined), it is not as simple as it may seem to say that the information side of the equation (affordances) and the control side (effectivities) are equivalent to potentials for action specified by the environment (affordances) and potentials to act associated with an agent (effectivities). This would leave both components as unrealized potentials, and no dynamics would ever emerge. So there is something more than a simple ability to act that we wish to convey with the term effectivity. Rather than solely being long-term stable properties of an individual (e.g., compare the term spatial ability or mechanical ability), effectivities are assembled in a particular situation (constrained within space-time) given a particular intention. To use Shaw's words, affordances propose whereas effectivities dispose (Barab, Cherkes-Julkowski, Swenson, Garrett, & Shaw, 1999). Effectivities have the added property of dissipating the potential by actualizing it in a particular instance.

Relative experts, then, can be described as more advanced detectors: They are able to detect affordances that are there for all to see but not detected by relative novices. Garry (1993) referred to this as the ecological view of selective attention. In her research, both forensic scientists and Macintosh aficionados (expert Macintosh users) were shown a crime scene and then provided with a follow-up description that contained misinformation about one of the objects (in this case, what was previously shown as baking soda was described as sugar). This substitution was noted by the forensic scientists but overlooked by the aficionados. The phenomenon occurred in the reverse when both groups were given misinformation with respect to an object (that is, a screen saver) expected to have higher saliency to the Mac aficionados. She concluded that specific objects will have a higher *attensity* (the probability that information will be detected by the observer) to one individual as a result of his or her particular skill (prior tuning) and current goals and intentions. We argue that experience within the environment (the dynamics of perception-action) can lead to improvement, or tuning, of the detector—that is what we will call learning.

Learning as the Education of Attention and Intention

The critical role of intention in learning is that it sets the focus of attention; thus, it isolates the learner's focus from other potentially distracting influences and directs it toward those environmental affordances that relate to the task at hand—hence, it serves as an attractor around which behavior can organize (Shaw et al., 1992). This concept of intention goes beyond the notion of desire (i.e., motivation).   From an instructional perspective, there are clearly potential dangers of increasing motivation when the learner cannot share the instructional intention. Without learner-adopted intention, motivation (in this case arousal) may take on the appearance of frenetic scurrying in multiple directions; behavior becomes energized without organization. As such, learning to problem solve requires prior education of intention (e.g., learning, adopting, valuing a particular task intention) before there can be the requisite education of attention (e.g., selecting the tools for achieving an identified target; Barab et al., 1999).

But even given a shared intention, the attention of a relative novice may need to be tuned to pick up the relevant information from an information-rich environment. In describing the metaphor of the intentional spring, Shaw et al. (1992) depicted a hypothetical situation in which the goals (intentions) of one person, the instructor, can be transferred to a second individual, the student, by coupling their action with a mechanical pulley device, and in which the attention of the student can be tuned through scaffolding. This coupled system provides a context for continuous assessment by and for both agents. Figure 6.1 reproduces their conception of the physical system of the intentional spring that closely couples an instructor with a student. This system establishes a double duality (a dual of duals that can be mathematically described) by linking the perception-action of the instructor with the perception-action of the student. The instructor (left) has a goal (pulling the spring to the target length as labeled in the figure), which is transferred to the blindfolded student (right) by repeated trials. On trials where the student is short, the instructor nudges the spring further to reach the goal, and on trials where the student is going to go too far, the instructor stops the spring at the target length. Eventually, the instructor is able to fade control and simply monitor passively. In one sense, this is the ideal situated assessment scenario. Feedback is provided continuously to the student by the instructor (to learn the goal), and the instructor receives continuous input from the student (to decide when to fade the scaffolding or guidance). This is the kind of seamless assessment possible with one-on-one tutoring and the preferred unit of analysis from an ecologically valid assessment (Young, Kulikowich, & Barab, 1997). Note that in this double duality not only is information shared, but also controlled (perception-action), so that implicit in the instructor's feedback is guidance for attention (e.g., pay attention to amount of arm extension) as well as guidance for intention (what is the intended goal). Coupling of this sort provides a modeling strategy for the education of attention and intention, information and control, perception and action.

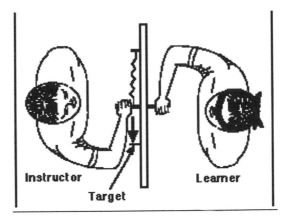

FIG. 6.1. Top view of intentional spring task. From the "intentional Spring: A Strategy for Modeling Systems That Learn to Perform Intentional Acts," by R.E. Shaw, E. Kadar, M. Sim, and D.W. Repperger, 1992, *Journal of Motor Behavior,*   24 (1), pp.3-28. Reprinted with permission.

Using the intentional spring as a metaphor, we can state that learning by doing can be enhanced by guidance from a relative expert. Such scaffolding can be added or removed based on the judgment of the instructor. But reliable judgment must be based on reliable feedback regarding student performance. Drawing on the intentional spring, though, it can be determined that it is not just outcome data (knowledge of result) that is needed, but also process information as the perception-action cycle unfolds. The instructor in the intentional spring can determine from the force and speed as they approach the target that an overshoot is likely and begin to provide guidance by applying resistance. Waiting for the overshoot to occur is too late to provide the needed guidance to improve performance on the next trial. Although it has been stated elsewhere (e.g., Young, 1993), determining how to apply scaffolding and when to remove it is the challenge of classroom education. The intentional spring is a productive metaphor for encouraging the close coupling of instructor with student, as they work on an authentic tasks together, in the spirit of Lave's legitimate peripheral participation (Lave & Wenger, 1990), Vygotsky's social constructivism (see Bruner, 1986), and the instruction of cognitive apprenticeship (Collins, Brown, & Newman, 1989).

However, these latter references are given as touchstones for similar concepts and not to infer an information processing understanding of them. The close coupling described by the intentional spring yields a modeling strategy that can improve the technology of providing scaffolding by quantifying and describing such scaffolding (determined by the treatment gradient—see Shaw et al., 1992). The expert in this model need not be a person but could be a computer model of the ideal solution trajectory. In an intentional-spring system, movement away from the ideal path can fully specify the treatment gradient, allowing the amount of scaffolding needed to be accurately specified (Shaw, Effken, Fajen, Garrett, & Morris, 1997). Once realized, imagine what an asset such a system could be to a teacher as he or she circulates among several problem-solving groups attempting to provide guidance where needed.

Figure 6.2 illustrates the nested couplings within the intentional spring strategy. At the lowest level is the coupling of the student with the learning situation (agent-environment interaction), which could take place through an interface in the case of interactive technology, or the interface could include a tool such as a golf club, automobile, or other work tool shared between relative novice and relative expert. Adopting a task goal would initiate the student's interactions with the learning situation and begin the student on an intended path.

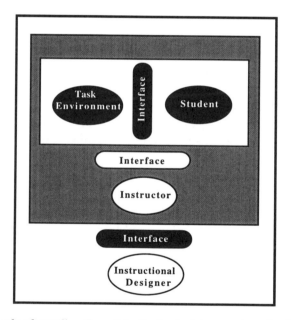

FIG. 6.2 Nested levels of coupling.From "An Ecological Approach to the On-Line Assessment of Problem-Solving Paths," by R.E. Shaw, J.A. Effken, B.R. Fajen, S.R. Garrett, and A. Morris, 1997, Instructional Science, 25, pp. 151-166. Adapted with permission.

At the middle level of analysis, an instructor is coupled to the student-environment system. Because of this coupling, the instructor can both detect perturbations (deviations off of intended path specified by the treatment gradient) from the student and can initiate corrective nudges (perturbations) to the student in the form of hints and questions (scaffolding) in a problem-solving task. Shaw et al. (1997) used a golf lesson as another intentional spring example to illustrate this technique in a perceptual motor task. The instructor can place his or her hands on the student's grip while he or she is swinging the golf club and thereby receive and apply corrective feedback during the task.

At the highest level, the instructional designer can be coupled to the instructor-student-learning situation system and can evaluate the trajectories generated by the designed learning situation for actual occasions. Unfulfilled objectives or difficulties are perturbations (deviations off of intended instructional goals) detectable to the instructional designer who could then evaluate and alter (corrective perturbation) the designed learning situation.

Key to implementing this strategy would be the quantification of the perturbations across the levels that would yield the information gradient of the treatment potential (the amount of required perturbation to restore the goal-path). Said another way, describing the learning situation from the ecopsych perspective enables the amount of scaffolding needed to be quantified based on the deviation of the system from the intended path. Further, the nested nature of agent-environment systems enables the same analysis to be applied to the student system (by the teacher) and to the teacher system (by the designer). The intentional-spring metaphor provides a strategy that has formal grounding and is intended to be generic to all goal-directed systems of which learners, teachers, and instructional designers are members.

To summarize, the intentional spring provides an example of how education of intention (the target goal) and education of attention (nudges by the instructor to slow or speed up) work within the perception-action cycle to tune the learner. No memory or symbolic representation is necessary to mediate the direct perception and action involved in intentional behavior in this example. Intention is passed to the learner by repeated trials along with guidance of attention to the relevant information to be picked up from the environment. Any distortion from the intended goal path creates a treatment gradient that can specify the direction and amount of correction need by the instructor. Here, we learning is created without the baggage of storage and retrieval mechanisms. The newly tuned detector need not retrieve information in order to act, rather by detecting new affordances for action coupled with the ability to act, the system can now perform in a way that it could not previously.

It is worth noting that the key attributes of the intentional spring are consistent with instructional techniques that are known to be effective: practice and feedback. It would be difficult to name two more powerful educational variables. Within the intentional spring there is an ecopsych description of how these powerful variables, practice (repeated trials) and feedback (the double duality of coupled perception-action), operate to enhance learning (the tuning of intention and attention).

The Fascination with Automatic Performance

The information processing model represents skill acquisition as a production system (e.g., Anderson, 1983) in which a list of conditional actions are built up (if-then statements) and assumed to be compiled and stored in the nervous system as an automatized routine. When an individual assumes all forms of knowing can be captured in explicit propositional structures, chained together, and rotely memorized, the memorization of rules designed to represent the relevant knowledge becomes primary, with practice a necessary but secondary process that strengthens the rule structures and eventually compiles them. Once enough practice is completed, the compiled rules are assumed to be sufficient for the learner to transfer to all appropriate situations outside the learning context. From this perspective, skilled performance of highly compiled rules is deemed automatic and so is rather boring.

But ecopsych is fascinated with automatic (skilled) performance. From this perspective, knowing is epistemic contact with an individual's world and depends not on rules but on active perception (Turvey & Shaw, 1995). For ecopsych, robust learning occurs when the dynamic unfolding of perception-action produces accurate performance despite varying conditions and circumstances unique to each situation. To explain how such performance is possible requires a more parsimonious starting point, a dynamic agent-environment interaction.

Driving a car is such an interaction that most of us have experienced. Many routine activities of driving a car become so automatic that an individual can find himself or herself daydreaming of other things while navigating familiar routes. Clearly there are some very basic perception-action skills that many people master to such a level so that steering, braking, turning, and so forth. are fluently performed in low stress situations. This is a very tuned system. The general ability is to attend to information that specifies potential upcoming action choices (positive or negative affordances) before it is too late to take action. However, the extent to which this skill can be developed should not be taken for granted. Perception-action tuning supports the basic coordinations that underlie the routine driving skills, and therefore, it is logical to assume that the more time spent driving the more attuned and adept a driver should become in dealing with the typical situations (Schiff & Arnone, 1995).

But what of the emergency situations of avoiding a collision? Instead of focusing on the normal reactive abilities that people develop with routine experience, we would rather focus on the question of how to extend an individual's anticipatory skills, something that seems to be taken for granted in driving except at a very rudimentary level. We are making a general simplifying assumption that many (not all) accidents that occur could in principle have been avoided. If there could be a magic virtual camera that captures an accident event on film from multiple vantage points, and the event could be replayed, then in principle, it would be possible to identify the information that could have specified the upcoming collision. If the best perspective is taken for specifying the collision and then that perspective iteratively shifted so that the driver experiences the event from multiple perspectives, it then might be possible to extend a driver's anticipatory window. With enough exposures of stereotypical accident events (a generator set), we anticipate that people would become tuned to perceive a broader class of situations and shift their readiness potential to an earlier occasion, thereby moving them out of a localized reaction space to a more global anticipation space. This education of attention (information specifying potential collisions) is actually paired with the education of control under the education of intention (prioritizing goals that lead to accident avoidance).

Consider an instructional design for the simulation example of the magic virtual camera. Over repeated trials, the novice driver is placed in a simulated crowded rush-hour highway (a complex social dynamical system) with the ability to perceive and act in different scenarios in which the other drivers have an intentional set of cooperation or competition based on the actions of the novice driver. The crowded highway system would take on different elastic or nonelastic characteristics based on established parameters, with the elastic system better able to absorb perturbations. These parameters would be tied to individual drivers' intentional sets as given by their actions: how closely an individual follows another car, how willing he or she is to change hi or her speed and position to accommodate another driver's situation (e.g., merging, lane changing, etc.). Given information about the performance of the traffic system, the novice driver would be able to tune his or her attention to the affordance of driving interactions that, in turn, would enable a higher order readiness potential to develop. Note that repeated trials and close coupling of feedback to actions are essential.

Simply knowing that certain characteristics in human nature may create certain hazards (enough to pass a multiple choice driver's test) may not be enough. This factual awareness, if it can be engendered, may need to be situated in a context where the possible action, decision, choice outcomes can be simulated, thus connecting a driver's actions to situations where that action could cause problems. In general, cooperation may be a better mode than competition on the public highways. However, just telling a new driver this or having him or her memorize this statement may not have the appropriate value without the intentional context. Rules of safe following distance, acceleration and braking patterns, and communication and signaling behavior should have situated value that grounds and connects an individual's actions and intentions to the collective system in which the individual is taking part or preparing to take part. It should be noted that tying the goals of instruction to the value of information and control variables from the learner's perspective, instead of prescribing a list of rules to be memorized to pass a test, is the essence of situated learning.

Ecopsych is a powerful alternative to the information processing model that can guide the understanding of cognition and the development of instructional environments. To illustrate the uniqueness of this approach, we next consider two common educational topics: problem solving and motivation. As stated earlier, from the ecopsych perspective, problem solving and motivation must be viewed as emergent properties of perceiving-acting systems. These are not the only topics that we could choose, and other examples of the re-interpretation of classic information processing data, such as expert-novice differences, are emerging in the literature (e.g., Vicente & Wang, 1998).

PROBLEM SOLVING AS AN EXAMPLE

Problem solving is an activity that historically has been studied from an information processing perspective. Mathematical or riddle-style puzzles are posed to individuals who are observed to sit for awhile thinking, then report a solution to the problem. This is the problem solving described by Polya (1985) and others (e.g., Bransford & Stein, 1984). Often individuals are asked to think aloud as they work through the solution. The results of such research clearly do not apply to group problem solving. Here, the military, business community, and scientific community (e.g., NASA) seek to understand how teams of individuals can collaborate to reach a solution that would have been impossible for any single individual to create (e.g., Segal, 1995). In the social problem-solving setting, the contributions of each individual are tracked from the perspective of messages transmitted from one person to another.

In contrast, Young and Barab (1999) created a model of problem solving, specifically anchored instruction that begins with a video problem (see CTGV, 1990, 1992, 1993). Problem solving has also been defined from an ecopsych perspective (e.g., Shaw et al., 1997). Rather than taking a strictly individual or strictly social perspective, problem solving is described using concepts from ecopsych as a dynamic interaction between agent and environment. As shown in Fig. 3, each of the four middle terms (anchor problem, goal adoption, constrained search path, and the transfer situation) must be understood as resulting from the interaction between individual and environmental components, represented by the top and bottom rows respectively. Therefore, an anchor problem, for example, cannot be thought of as simply the presentation of a specific problem but rather as a situation defined by aspects of the goals of the problem solver and the context in which it is introduced. These attributes, although discussed separately, are mutually coconstructed. Moving to the next step, whether a goal presented by an instructional designer in a particular anchor video is adopted and acted upon must be understood in the context of the individual's effectivities (abilities within this particular problem-solving context) and other personal goals (dynamics of intention, such as I'm hungry, stressed by midterm exam preparation, and solving this problem for extra credit in my Intro Psych class), as well as other environmental affordances and social dynamics (outside the problem itself) at the time. It is possible that some viewers never adopt the goals established in an anchor situation, and their performance must be interpreted in light of the goals and intentions they were pursuing during the problem-solving session (e.g., getting food, getting good grades, figuring out what it takes to get an A in class). When the instructional goal is not adopted, the instructional sequence has failed in the education of intention and, as a result, failed to educate attention.

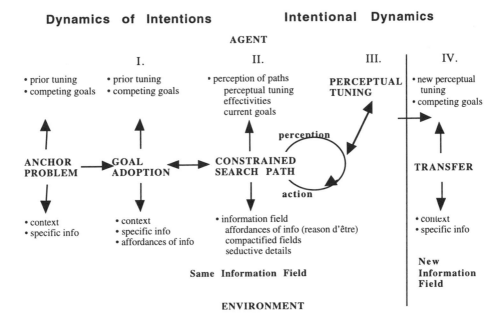

FIG. 3. Young-Barab description of problem solving.

Once the anchor problem is presented, the embedded goal is adopted (to some extent). This in turn constrains the problem solving by directing attention throughout the perception-action process. At a later time (right side) the resultant perceptual tuning enables detection of new affordances (transfer of learning) given a different information field.

Part II of our framework (refer to Fig. 3) is based on the assumption that adoption of the goal will constrain an individual's search through an environment with goal-relevant affordances by directing the perception-action cycle. This assumption is founded on theories of intentional dynamics (Shaw, Kugler, & Kinsella-Shaw, 1990). Shaw (1987) argued that goal-directed systems are not merely self-directed toward goals, but are directed by goals. These goals set up a path, or a bundle of virtual paths (mathematically described as a germ), to be perceived and acted on by the individual. Shaw, reviewing the work of Weir (1984), stated, "a goal is not a designated final state to be reached by a system but a distinctive way for the system to reach a final state over one of several optional paths, given goal variation" (p. 243). In other words, as an individual using goal-tinted lenses perceives an information field (i.e., a navigational path in the hypermedia), he or she detects fields of compactified information constituting goal paths that afford the satis-faction of the problem.

We argue that well designed anchors are problems that are consistent with one of the raisons d'être (reasons for being) of the material to be learned. For example, if an individual wanted to teach learners about chemistry he or she would first choose one of the situations chemistry was intended to address (e.g., creating stronger metals for swords or developing safe foods) and select that as the learning goal. It is in this manner that anchors have an opportunity to facilitate the learner in detecting one of the raisons d'être of the material he or she is learning in the service of addressing the anchor problems. This is another example of the education of attention (seeing the reason for scientific knowledge) by the education of intention (adopting a goal from an anchor video).

It is in Part II of our framework (Fig. 3) that choice paths in the problem space are constrained by goals. The perception of alternative goal paths is mediated by prior perceptual tuning and effectivities in relation to the current information field and its respective affordances and compactified fields. The specific solution space (the set of possible actions to be taken) generated by an individual is co-determined by prior tuning of the information field presented by this particular problem. By acting on this information (i.e., making choices) the individual changes aspects of the information field (i.e., computer screens, videodisc segments, or the room in which he or she is standing), thereby altering his or her perceptual experience. This perceiving-acting cycle, relative to the goal, constrains an individual's perception of choices to specific environmental information relative to the task at hand. This reciprocal process allows the individual to perceive new paths and implement the appropriate actions. Although the perception-action loop is continuous, eventually the goal is satisfied, and the individual can again be characterized by the dynamics of intentions in the early part of our descrip-tion as new anchors and new goals emerge.

Part III (Fig. 3) indicates that perception-action, as a dual experience, changes the learners (attunement) so that they now become different detec-tors, attuned to finer details and having accompanying finer effectivities. Gibson (1986) argued that perceptual tuning alters an individual so that he or she is not simply the same person with more information but rather a new perceptual system. His or her new perceptions regarding specific aspects of the world allow him or her to interact with the environment differently. What was previously unnoticed now has a greater intensity as he or she learns more about these topics.

Applying the intentional spring ideas to this description can be done usefully from at least two perspectives. First, the flow from left to right of the problem-solving process represents an unfolding of the intentional spring process, with Part I (goal adoption) establishing a shared information space, essentially representing the student and teacher grasping the intention spring handles. Part II (constrained perception-action) is equivalent to the support-ing guidance given by the instructor during repeated trials early in the spring process that eventually is faded to a supportive resource in Part III as attention and intention are tuned. In Part IV, the student and teacher are decoupled, and the student functions independently (transfer) based on his or her new attunement.

The intentional spring can also be applied to the problem-solving description by focusing in an up-down way on the vertical arrows indicating agent-environment interactions. This can be discussed for the different levels of nested systems described in Fig. 2. Take the broadest system (that includes the instructional designer) as an example. Parts I and IV become most central, whereas Parts II and III become an unobserved black box of interactions between student and instruction. Here, over repeated trials (multiple environments designed and implemented) the instructional designer is tuned to detect how goals (contrived by the designer) adopted by problem solvers (Part I) produce transfer (Part IV). As analyzed with the intentional spring, the learner-environment interactions suggested by the vertical arrows represent the coupling with the designer that produces improved designs.

Note that this description of problem solving as perception-action does not rely at all on symbolic representation of problem elements to be acted on by problem operators stored within a cognitive problem space. Information is not stored and retrieved from memory and applied to the problem at hand. Transfer is not a product of identification of similar elements, and learning is not the abstraction and encoding of problem solutions. Rather, with a fascination for automatic performance, our description posits the problem solver to be like an expert driver, responding automatically to the information environment in which he or she finds himself or herself. End state goals (solutions) are established by the adoption of the problem-solving intention, and progress toward the goals is guided by the perceiving-acting system as it picks up the affordances for goal-related action within the current environment (virtual, anchored instruction, or authentic real world instruction, see also Chapter 2, this volume).

MOTIVATION AS ANOTHER EXAMPLE

Many ideas that are central to information-processing analyses of thinking and learning rest on the premise that mediating variables are inside the heads of learners. Things that are attributed to being inside the head include intelligence, motivation, schemata, memories, expectations, beliefs, attitudes, metacognitive processes, and executive controls to name a few. These mediating variables are attributed with causal powers that explain behavior (action) or lack thereof (inaction). For example, if a learner fails to act in what is deemed an exciting learning environment, they are said to be unmotivated. This, then, allegedly explains in large part why they failed to act. The ecopsych perspective eliminates this mediary set of concepts that are inside the agent's head. Instead, properties of an interaction between an intentionally driven learner and an information-rich environment explain why actions occur or not; said succinctly, it is the coupling of individual and environment that is critical.

External Motivation (Rewards)

Consider as an example a weight-loss program in which dieting is prescribed, and weekly meetings of the participants feature weigh-ins and group discussions. Success in this situation can (and often is) be described as a result of external motivation. Successful dieters are given stars on their weekly weight-loss charts and applause and attention from their fellow dieters when they report their weekly weight loss at the meeting. Here, it is concluded that the environment has selected dieting behavior by providing rewards that increased the likelihood of future dieting behaviors. The token economy of stars may be designed using behavioral principles to ensure concrete as well as intangible rewards to influence dieting behaviors.

Internal Motivation

In contrast, information processing theorists would posit an intervening variable at work inside the dieter's head. Successful dieters, who maintain their diet beyond the tricks and toys (they would say) of behavior modification, would be empowered with more intrinsic forms of motivation. Inside each dieter's head would lie a force that energizes, strengthens, and directs behavior toward a weight loss goal. Such a force resides within the heads of people and functions independent of the contexts and information fields within which the person is acting. Therefore, in the case of weight loss, it can be argued that the goal to lose weight became realized because this force built up within the dieter to the point that dieting behavior was impelled to occur. Further, it is believed that this internal force can be measured by Likert-scale self reports and manipulated directly (through modeling, verbal persuasion, and the like), so the perception-action of the situation need not even be addressed. Simply increase the student's motivation, and surely they will engage in behavior.

Motivation as an Agent-Environment Interaction

From an ecopsych perspective, both conceptions of motivation (internal and external) are inadequate. External motivation leaves the person a victim of his or her material (energy-based) environment (specifically the schedules of reinforcement in which he or she is acting). External motivation omits the key idea that intentional agents are better described as driven by information fields rather than energy fields and thus often act to achieve a goal despite punishing conditions and overwhelming obstacles. Internal motivation creates an imaginary force propelling an agent to act. The force is somehow independent of the current environment, such that a student can be characterized as motivated or unmotivated regardless of the class, activity, or situation he or she is in. Yet, both conceptions seem to be providing something that the other lacks.

However, motivation can best be viewed as an agent-environment interaction. In this way, it is tied to the current situation while being connected to an agent's internal states as described by his or her goals and intentions. Consider again the diagram of problem solving shown in Fig. 3, specifically the perception-action cycle that follows goal adoption and is marked as part II of the Figure. Here, an agent with a goal is interacting within an environment. That environment may afford progress toward the goal to a greater or lesser degree. To the extent that the environment affords progress toward the goal, the agent will appear motivated. Said another way, an agent who is in an environment that affords actions toward his or her currently adopted goal can appropriately be described as motivated. It is the close coupling of goals with environmental affordances that is more accurately described as motivating.

Any dieters who find themselves in an environment that affords them an opportunity to lose weight will be able to act toward this goal and will appear motivated. Environments that afford dieting include homes with healthy food in them, group settings in which people are regularly providing good information about dieting, and rooms with fellow dieters that indirectly (symbolically) contain information for acting in a way consistent with dieting (even semiotic artifacts such as stars on a chart). Likewise, any dieters who find themselves in an environment that does not afford dieting activity (e.g., at a tasty buffet every night for a month) may become frustrated or may even act in a way inconsistent with dieting. Either way, they will aptly be considered unmotivated. In these cases, the ecopsych description is that agents are acting within the constraints of the information field that specifies toward (or away from) their diet goals.

In short, motivation, like problem solving, can best be described as an interaction arising from an intentionally driven agent perceiving and acting within an information-rich ecosystem. When the environment is conducive to action toward an adopted goal, it is a motivating environment and a motivated agent that appear. But, it is the interaction that is best characterized as motivated. Motivation is more of a process, or at least a dynamic state of affairs, that arises at the moment of the occasion from the close coupling of goals with an environment that affords rapid movement toward them. Continuing to draw on this dieting example, we next clarify a few pointed questions that help illuminate our conception of motivation from the ecopsych perspective.

What About Dieters Who Say They Have a Goal But Fail to Act?

It is easy to find failed dieters and even wanna-be dieters. The latter are of interest because they challenge the description of motivation as an interaction given previously. They appear to have adopted a goal to diet, and yet, even given an environment that affords progress toward the goal, they often fail to act. This can be explained by the dynamics of intentions. Agents generally have many (often competing) goals (operating on multiple space-time scales). It is imperative to understand the goal that an agent has currently adopted to understand behavior in a given situation. It is plausible to propose that some individuals who say they have a goal to diet have competing goals to enjoy the taste of food when they are hungry, to distract themselves when they are worried, even to achieve some self-destructive end. In which case, the action of eating will be the result (given an environment that affords the action), and movement away from the dieting goal will be achieved.

But even when these competing goals are absent, some well intentioned dieters in environments that support dieting (e.g., healthy houses with salads prepared in the refrigerator) still fail to maintain dieting behaviors. That is, the eating goal reemerges. Consider the case of a dieter who wisely suppresses the physiological need to eat by frequent eating healthy fruit snacks. Where else could this eating goal come from? The environment contains compactified fields, eating affordances and their duals, and getting food effectivities. Seeing a doughnut commercial, hearing a passing ice cream truck, and other information in the environment can cause an eating goal to reemerge. Once this dynamic change of intention takes place, the new eating goal produces a new perceiving-acting system tuned to pickup eating affordances of the environment instead of the dieting affordances that are still there. Gibson (1986) referred to this as seeing the world through goal-tinted glasses. Therefore instead of considering how easy the pre-made salad is to get in the refrigerator, the dieter is now considering how easy it is to buy a doughnut at the corner store. The boundary conditions that constrain the situation expand with the adoption of the eating goal such that a new goal path trajectory results.

What About Dieters Who Go Too Far and Continue to Act After the Goal is Achieved?

Similarly, there are dieters who do not stop with the achievement of reasonable dieting objectives and continue to starve themselves. This too appears to present a challenge to an analysis of motivation as arising from a match between an intentionally driven agent and an environment that affords action. Again, the dynamics of intentions could provide an answer. Because agents generally have many (consistent) goals, there will be occasions when acting toward one goal (dieting) produces progress toward other goals (becoming a more popular person, increasing athletic speed, or even achieving a body image portrayed in a magazine). Although initially the actors may not have perceived the relationship of some actions with movement toward these other goals, acting toward the dieting goal may reveal information to the perceiver regarding progress toward these other goals. For example, losing a little weight may result in feedback information in the form of praise and acceptance from peers or favorable comparisons to a covergirl supermodel. Now the affordances for action of the current environment, once used to achieve the diet goal, can be used to achieve these other goals as well. The adoption of new goals within the dynamics of intentions leads to a renewed perception-action cycle (e.g., continued dieting).

What About Optimal Performance as Opposed to Simple Motivation?

Although it is possible to describe too much or too little dieting, optimal performance is what is most wanted. Here the example of dieting is not as useful, but we can conclude our discussion of dieting by observing that successful dieters adopt goals with clear objectives, they operate in ecosystems that afford actions that move them toward their dieting objectives, and their environment also provides an opportunity for frequent feedback as to progress toward the objectives. The additions of a clear objective and an environment that affords frequent feedback are critical elements to optimal performance. These elements take on particular meaning from the ecopsych perspective as they are also elements of the intentional spring example of tuning of attention.

Csikszentmihalyi (1990) discussed optimal performance and coined the term flow, referring to "the state in which people are so involved in an activity that nothing else seems to matter" (p. 4). Whereas Csikszentmihalyi preferred an information processing description of this phenomenon, we view this simply as the tight coupling between the adopted goals of the individual and the affordances of the environment. Flow may be simply the experience of having a goal toward which the current information field permits direct and perceivable progress over an extended time frame. The closer the coupling of the affordances of the current situation with the adopted goal, the more an individual can become immersed in a perception-action cycle directed toward a single goal and experience flow.

The final word on motivation is that from an ecopsych perspective, it is not a force inside a person's head that energizes behavior but rather a property of the agent-environment interaction. Some of what has been studied as motivation is simply the dynamics of intentions: As an agent adopts a new goal, he or she becomes motivated, at least in cases where the agent is operating in an ecosystem that affords progress toward the adopted goal. Said another way, asking people if they are motivated to diet is essentially asking if they have adopted weight loss goals. Once a goal is adopted, people will appear more or less motivated based on the dynamics of intentions (among several competing goals, which goals are currently being acted on) and the match between the affordance of the current environment and those goals. However, this risks oversimplifying the dual nature of affordances and effectivities. Detecting an affordance brings with it a detection of a goal, and having an effectivity controls what information (specifying affordances) is picked up in any given circumstance.

CLOSING

There are many new concepts introduced by ecopsych to describe dynamic interactions between agents and their environments: affordances and effectivities, perception and action, education of attention and intention, dynamics of intentions, intentional dynamics, all of which produce a jargon-filled treatise of ideas that is difficult to approach or apply readily. The emphasis on interactions, assumptions of self-organizing systems, and acceptance of complex nonlinear dynamics as fundamentals to the ecopsych perspective can put off unfamiliar readers to the point of dismissing the ideas out of hand. Yet, these ideas have had significant impact on research and ID activities to the point where they are becoming difficult to ignore. They are credited with contributing to the literature on situated learning (Brown, Collins, & Duguid, 1989; Greeno, 1989, 1997, 1998) and are fundamental to anchored instruction (e.g., CTGV, 1990, 1993).

For a moment, throw aside the concepts of memory, storage, and retrieval of information, and think of students as sophisticated information detectors instead of complex symbol manipulating information processors. Think of ID as the process of creating environments that afford meaningful authentic activity that tunes novice perceivers to the affordances for action of tools used by communities of mathematicians, physicists, musicians, and artists. Consider the potential to quantify scaffolding by mathematical descriptions of treatment gradients detected during automatic performance. Now consider that many students do not have goals for which these tools afford much action, so they must be led to adopt new goals (the education of intention). Descriptions of learners as detectors lead us to prefer student immersion into new environments through a well written novel, a good video, or a virtual reality that can create interactions in which new goals emerge. Clever instructional designers can detect the affordances of these contrived environments and use them to encourage students to adopt new goals (build a bridge, design a robot, help a character solve an everyday problem). Those clever designers can also create learning environments that afford progress toward these new goals, environments that are so closely aligned with the goals that they encourage optimal performance. We have found thinking in this way to be liberating and we hope others will indulge in the enterprise with us.

REFERENCES

Anderson, J. R. (1983). *The Architecture of Cognition.* Cambridge, MA: Harvard University Press.

Barab, S. A., Cherkes-Julkowski, M., Swenson, R., Garrett, S., Shaw, R. E., & Young, M. (1999). Principles of self-organization: Ecologizing the learner-facilitator system. *The Journal of the Learning Sciences, 8*(3&4), 349-390.

Bransford, J. D., & Stein, B. S. (1984). *The IDEAL problem solver: A guide for improving thinking, learning, and creativity.* New York: Freeman

Brown, J.S., Collins, A, & Duguid, P. (1989). Situated cognition and the culture of learning, *Educational Researcher, 18*, Jan-Feb, 32-42.

Bruner, J. (1986). *Actual Minds, Possible Worlds.* Cambridge, MA: Harvard University Press.

Capra F. (1996). *The web of life.* New York: Anchor Books.

Cognition and Technology Group at Vanderbilt. (1990). Anchored instruction and its relationship to situated cognition. *Educational Researcher, 19,* 2-10.

Cognition and Technology Group at Vanderbilt. (1992). Technology and the design of generative learning environments. In T. M. Duffy and D. H. Jonassen (Eds.), *Constructivism and the Technology of Instruction: A Conversation.* (pp. 77-90). Hillsdale, NJ; Lawrence Erlbaum Associates.

Cognition and Technology Group at Vanderbilt. (1993, March). Anchored Instruction and situated cognition revisited. *Educational Technology, 33,* 52-70.

Cognitive Science (1993). Special Issue: Situated Action, *17* (1).

Collins, A., Brown, J. S., & Newman, S. E. (1989). Cognitive apprenticeship: Teaching the crafts of reading, writing, and mathematics. In J. Larkin (Ed.), *Knowing, learning, and instruction: Essays in honor of Robert Glaser.* Hillsdale, NJ: Lawrence Erlbaum Associates.

Csikszentmihalyi, M. (1990). *Flow: The psychology of optimal experience.* NY: Harper & Row.

Dewey, J. (1963). *Experience & education.* New York: Collier Macmillan.

Garry, M. C. C. (1993). *Susceptibility to memory distortions as a function of skill.* (Doctoral Dissertation, University of Connecticut, 1993). *Dissertation Abstracts International, 54,* 1731.

Gibson, J. J. (1986) *The ecological approach to visual perception.* Hillsdale, NJ: Lawrence Erlbaum Associates.

Gibson, J. J. (1977). The theory of affordances. In R. E. Shaw & J. Bransford (Eds.), *Perceiving, acting and knowing: Toward an ecological psychology.* Hillsdale NJ: Lawrence Erlbaum Associates.

Greeno, J. G. (1989). A perspective on thinking. *American Psychologist, 44,* 134-141.

Greeno, J. G. (1994). Gibson's affordances. *Psychological Review, 101*(2), 236-342.

Greeno, J. G. (1997). On claims that answer the wrong question. *Educational Research, 26*(1), 5-17.

Greeno, J. G. (1998). The situativity of knowing, learning, and research. *American Psychologist, 53*(1), 5-26.

Kim, N. G, Turvey, M. T., & Carello, C. (1993). Optical information about the severity of upcoming contacts. *Journal of Experimental Psychology: Human Perception and Performance, 19,* 179-193.

Kugler, P. N., Shaw, R. E., Vicente, K. J., & Kinsella-Shaw, J. M. (1992). Inquiry into intentional systems I: Issues in ecological physics. *Psychological Research, 52,* 98-121.

Lave, J. (1988). *Cognition in Practice.* Cambridge, MA: Cambridge University Press.

Lave, J. & Wenger (1990). *Situated learning: Legitimate peripheral practice.* New York: Cambridge University Press.

Mark, L. S., Bailliet, J. A., Craver, K. D., Douglas, S. D., & Fox, T. (1990). What an actor must do in order to perceive the affordance for sitting. *Ecological Psychology, 2,* 325-366.

Polya, G. (1957/1985). *How to solve it: A new aspect of mathematical method* (2nd ed.). Princeton, NJ: Princeton University Press.

Pufall, P., & Dunbar, C. (1992). Perceiving whether or not the world affords stepping onto or over: A developmental study. *Ecological Psychology,4,* 17-38.

Schank, R C., & Abelson, R. (1977). *Scripts, plans, goals, and understanding.* Hillsdale, NJ: Lawrence Erlbaum Associates.

Schiff, W., & Arnone, W. (1995). Perceiving and driving: Where parallel roads meet. In P. Hancock, J. Flach, J. Caird, & K. Vicente (Eds.), *Local applications of the ecological approach to human-machine systems.* Hillsdale, NJ: Erlbaum.

Segal, L. D. (1995). Designing team workstations: The choreography of teamwork. In P. Hancock, J. Flach, J. Caird, & K. Vicente (Eds.) *Local applications of the ecological approach to human-machine systems.* Hillsdale, NJ: Lawrence Erlbaum Associates.

Shaw, R. E. (1987). Behavior with a purpose [Review of the book *Goal-directed behavior*]. *Contemporary Psychology, 32,* 243-245.

Shaw, R. E., Effken, J. A., Fajen, B. R., Garrett, S. R., & Morris, A. (1997). An ecological approach to the on-line assessment of problem-solving paths. *Instructional Science, 25,* 151-166.

Shaw, R. E., Kadar, E., Sim, M., & Repperger, D. W. (1992). The intentional spring: A strategy for modeling systems that learn to perform intentional acts. *Journal of Motor Behavior, 24*(1), 3-28.

Shaw, R. E., & Kinsella-Shaw, J. M. (1988). Ecological mechanics: Aphysical geometry for intentional constraints. *Human Movement Science, 7,* 155-200.

Shaw, R. E., Kugler, P. N., & Kinsella-Shaw, J. M. (1990). Reciprocities of intentional systems. In R. Warren & A. Wertheim (Eds.), *Perception and control of self-motion,* Hillsdale, NJ: Lawrence Erlbaum Associates.

Swenson, R. (1996). *Spontaneous order, evolution, and natural law: An introduction to the physical basis for ecological psychology.* Hillsdale, NJ: Lawrence Erlbaum Associates

Turvey, M. T., & Shaw, R. E. (1995). Toward an ecological physics and a physical psychology. In R. L. Solso & D. W. Massaro (Eds.), *The science of the mind: 2001 and beyond* (pp. 144-169). New York, NY: Oxford University Press.

Vicente, K. J., & Wang, J. H. (1998). An ecological theory of expertise effects in memory recall. *Psychological Review, 105*(1), 33-57.

Vygotsky, L. S. (1978). Internationalization of higher psychological functions. In M. Cole, V. John-Steiner, S. Scribner, & E. Souberman (Eds.), *Mind in Society: The development of higher psychological processes.* Cambridge, MA: Harvard University Press.

Warren, E. H. (1984). Perceiving affordances: Visual guidance of stair climbing. *Journal of Experimental Psychology: Human Perception and Performance, 10,* 683-703.

Warren, E. H., & Wang, S. (1987). Visual guidance of walking through apertures: Body-scaled information specifying affordances. *Journal of Experimental Psychology: Human Perception and Performance, 13,* 371-383.

Weir, M. (1984). *Goal-directed behavior.* New York: Gordon & Breach.

Young, M. F. (1993). Instructional design for situated learning. *Educational Technology Research and Development, 41*(1), 43-58.

Young, M. F., & Barab, S. (1999). Perception of the raison d'etre in anchored instruction: An ecological psychology perspective. *Journal of Educational Computing Research, 20*(2), 113-135.

Young, M. F., Kulikowich, J. M., & Barab, S. A. (1997). The unit of analysis for situated assessment. *Instructional Science, 25*(2), 133-150.

7

Lessons From Everyday Reasoning in Mathematics Education: Realism Versus Meaningfulness

David W. Carraher
TERC

Analúcia D. Schliemann
Tufts University

INTRODUCTION

One of the key challenges of mathematics education, regardless of whether an individual makes use of computer technology, is to give proper attention to pedagogical issues, questions of teaching and learning, including how students' previous understanding serves as a foundation for future development.

Consider, for example, the following issues:

- Why are many students puzzled by the fact that multiplication does not always increase a quantity nor does division necessarily diminish it? Does it help to think about how integers work? Or should rational numbers be introduced without appealing to intuitions about whole numbers?
- Can advanced mathematical ideas be grounded on students' everyday understandings about quantities? Or does quantitative thinking impede the learning of abstract concepts? Is it a crutch to be discarded as soon as possible?
- Early mathematics instruction focuses heavily on numbers as counts (cardinality of sets). How can instructors introduce numbers as ratios, given that representations of ratios typically use sets of countable items? (It is no wonder that students prefer 4/6 of a bag of candy to 2/3 of a bag of candy. The numerator tells them how many candies they get!)
- How should instructors bridge arithmetical and algebraic understanding? Or should these be treated, as they often are, as distinct forms of reasoning best learned at different stages in schooling?

Clearly these types of issues will not be clarified by placing computers in the classroom and hoping for the best. It depends on how new knowledge relies on former knowledge yet still requiring adjustments, accommodations, and even sharp breaks with present understanding. It depends on social issues, such as how discussions are handled in classrooms, and on the social roles students and teachers adopt in learning and teaching.

We believe that everyday mathematical understanding can constitute a solid basis for the development of more advanced mathematical activities in school and for the meaningful learning of conventional symbolic systems. We also believe that for most students advanced mathematical reasoning will rest on how they think of quantities as being interrelated. This theme cuts across many topics in mathematics, including number operations (how quantities are joined and removed, multiplied, and divided), measurement (how units of measure can describe the magnitude of target quantities), conversion across units (how many of unit A there are for every unit B), vector composition (how quantities are joined in 1-space, 2-space, and n-space), graphs (how to visually depict the way variations along one quantity dimension are associated with variations along another quantitative dimension), and elementary algebraic notation (where describing relations among constant and variable quantities foreshadows notation for describing relations among mathematical constants and variables).

But there are many ways to interpret thinking in terms of quantities, including the view that children have to think about concrete, palpable objects in order to grasp mathematics. Lest our views be mistakenly identified with such naïve physicalism, we place the discussion in a larger perspective.

It is important to provide a social analysis in consonance with a cognitive one. Because technology does not act directly on learners, but only exerts an influence by virtue of the social activities and contexts in which it is employed, introducing technology into the mathematics classroom ultimately entails questions such as the following: What is the teacher's role; what are the students trying to achieve in the tasks, and does this correspond if at all to the curriculum goals; how do children generate evidence for their conclusions; how does this relate to mathematical proof; do the activities engender or require a frame of mind different from nonclassroom situations; how does describing problems in their own words bear on their mathematical understanding; and how is it possible for students to develop an autonomy of thinking as opposed to relying on the teacher's word as to whether an answer is correct.

In this chapter, we briefly review some of the main findings of studies of everyday cognition, in particular those focusing on how people use and understand mathematics in everyday activities. After this we look at some specific examples of how children's emerging mathematical understanding and interpretation of mathematical notation draw on what they know and intuit about quantities. We also point out how technology can play a role in children's learning mathematics, provided there is a clear notion of the issues they are grappling with.

EVERYDAY COGNITION AND THINKING ABOUT QUANTITIES

During the 1970s, 1980s, and 1990s, a growing body of studies of everyday cognition brought into discussion questions about the educational relevance of everyday experiences and of learning that takes place outside of classrooms. As systematic studies of everyday cognition have increasingly emerged, there has been a growing interest in the theoretical implications and educational relevance of the empirical findings.

The bulk of everyday cognition research focuses on mathematical competence (see reviews by Carraher, 1990; Nunes, 1992; Nunes, Schliemann, & Carraher, 1993). The three main areas of everyday mathematics studies are measurement, geometry, and arithmetic.

Measurement is a common mathematical activity in everyday life among groups with limited access to school instruction. Gay and Cole (1967) found that Kpelle rice farmers experienced in estimating the volumes of rice performed better than U.S. students in volume estimation tasks. Saxe and Moylan (1982) described a system widely used by the Oksapmin of Papua New Guinea for measuring the depths of string bags. deAbreu and Carraher (1989), Acioly (1994), and Grando (1988) described the system of measures and formulas used by unschooled farmers in northeastern and southern Brazil to calculate the areas of plots of land. In a survey study, Saraswathi (1989) asked illiterate, semiliterate, and literate adults in India to describe linear dimensions of objects, distances, or events. Those interviewed were more prone to use standard units when working with certain dimensions (heights, depths, distances, short lengths, and area) than with others (medium lengths, girth or perimeter, diameter, incline, and rainfall), which were more often described according to body measures or nonspecific descriptions. The majority of the those interviewed knew how to use multiple measuring systems to describe objects or distances but chose one or the other depending on their previous exposure to and experiences with the situations under discussion. For measuring time, they used movements of the sun, the moon, or stars, and time-measuring devices based on shadows or on finely calibrated water containers for reckoning time in addition to western measures such as hours and minutes of time pieces.

Shortly after the metric system was introduced in Nepal, Ueno and Saito, market sellers invented artifacts and rules for measuring and for converting between old measuring systems (based on volume) and the metric system (in this case, based on weight) encouraged by the government. The fact that the traditional system was more adequate for the varying wetness (and hence weight) of equal volumes of rice is consequential. Despite certain limitations due to the approximate nature of their calculations, the systems of measurement developed in everyday activities allow unschooled individuals to obtain meaningful, and often more useful, answers for their needs than is the case for students. For instance, in a study with Brazilian carpenters, Schliemann (1985) showed that experienced carpenters with limited schooling develop better approaches to deal with measurement and computation of volume than do carpenter apprentices enrolled in mathematical classes meant to teach them how to compute area and volume. Similarly, Scribner (1984, 1986), in her investigation of practical reasoning among dairy workers, found more flexible and effort-saving arithmetic strategies among workers than among students.

Concerning geometry, Zaslavsky (1973) provided an overview of the use of geometrical concepts in the design of African geometrical patterns. In Mozambique, Gerdes (1986, 1988a, 1988b) showed use of geometrical concepts and patterns among fishermen, house builders, and basket weavers who have no access to the procedures and representations of mathematics as it is taught in schools. Harris (1987, 1988) provided examples of geometrical reasoning among women doing needlework or working with textiles at home and in factories. Millroy (1992) found extensive use of geometrical concepts, such as congruence, symmetry, and straight and parallel lines, in everyday work among South African carpenters.

Besides measurement and geometry, arithmetic has been the most widely analyzed area of knowledge in everyday cognition studies. In her pioneering study of everyday mathematics, Lave (1977; see also Reed & Lave, 1979) showed that Liberian tailors use procedures to solve arithmetic problems based on manipulation of quantities, as opposed to the symbolic manipulation taught in schools. Such procedures, developed at work, ensure that no big mistakes with serious practical consequences occur. Analysis of street sellers' and school children's oral strategies for solving arithmetic problems across contexts shows that understanding of the decimal system and of proportional relations—two main aspects of mathematical knowledge traditionally thought to be learned in schools—may develop as a result of activities in everyday settings.

Understanding and use of the properties of the decimal system among people with restricted school experience was documented by, among others, Carraher (1985), Carraher, Carraher, and Schliemann (1982, 1985), Schliemann and Acioly (1989), and Schliemann, Santos, and Canuto (1993). Solution to proportionality problems and understanding of proportional relations independent of school instruction appears mainly when problems requiring multiplication are orally solved in order to determine the price of items people buy or sell. Street sellers' solution to proportionality problems, although based on repeated additions, shows an understanding that two variables, namely price and number of items sold, are proportionally related (Schliemann, Araujo, Cassunde, Macedo, & Niceas, 1994; Schliemann & Carraher, 1992). Carraher (1986) documented the understanding of proportionality in the everyday activities of construction foremen who have to deal with the relationship between measurement in the blueprints and the actual size of walls. Use of proportional reasoning is also described by Schliemann & Nunes (1990) among fisherman, by Schliemann and Magalhães (1990) among Brazilian illiterate cooks, and by McMurchy-Pilkington (1995), who analyzed the work of New Zealand's Maori women engaged in planning and preparing traditional meals for large groups of tourists.

It would be misleading, however, to suggest that people's understanding of these topics in any way rivals that of professional mathematicians. The differences are so vast and numerous as to make such a comparison embarrassing. For example, young Brazilian street vendors consistently worked out correct answers for arithmetic problems presented as part of their working activities (Nunes, Schliemann, & Carraher, 1993). Their approach, however, varied widely depending on how problems were presented: They used what might be termed mental arithmetic with problems presented as they occur out of school, whereas they favored written school-associated solutions when problems were presented of the sort encountered in school. The research revealed that they solved arithmetical problems using representations that appeared not to rely on generating and parsing written notation as taught in school. Their success out of school seems to depend, instead, on their understanding of how quantities can be composed and decomposed from other quantities. Interestingly, the steps through which street vendors pass in solving arithmetic problems entail breaking up and reassembling quantities in ways that do not strictly parallel the school algorithms. Nonetheless, their approach adheres to the most basic properties of arithmetic (associative and distributive laws, for example) and thereby produces the same, correct answer as those means explicitly taught in school.

What initially was understood to be peculiar to certain people alienated from the educational system in third-world countries, is now taken as representative of a more general phenomenon. Not only is mental arithmetic (or oral mathematics, street mathematics, or informal mathematics) more widespread than originally thought, it corresponds to ways of reasoning central to the mathematical thought of all people. Lest it seem that we are alluding to some sort of culturally transcendental or natural knowledge that people harbor deep in their minds despite their cultural transmission through schooling, let us make clear that we are really talking about knowledge grounded in activity and thought about quantities. But before doing this, we need to appreciate that this range of abilities embraces far more than feats of calculation, mundane or otherwise.

One of the hallmarks of everyday mathematics is flexibility: Rather than follow step-by-step prescribed procedures, the mental mathematics of vendors, as well as the mathematics of other workers in everyday work situations, involve a fluency with decimal groupings and constant attention to the meaning of the situation, the practical concerns that gave birth to the problems, and the adequacy of solutions to the problems at hand. The same person may solve a series of problems through apparently diverse sorts of composition and decomposition (doubling and halving, canceling out equal amounts of units and so on), often making use of shortcuts that the particular values in the problem seem to afford. It makes a difference whether an individual is dealing with relations among familiar quantities or those with which a person has little experience, even though one set of problems may be formally identical to another set. This must be understood well in order to make sense of a number of findings.

The understanding of proportionality problems at work can be transferred to new contexts, but it is not guaranteed (Schliemann & Magalhães, 1990). A group of maids and cooks reasoned proportionally about money problems. Roughly, this corresponds to an appreciation of an increasing monotonic function between two variable quantities (amount and price) as well as a constant rate (unit price) that allows an individual to infer one quantity's value from knowing the other. The subjects in the study quickly extended proportional reasoning to the context of recipes (which they were not otherwise inclined to treat in a strictly proportional way but, rather, by increasing in a rough fashion one quantity as the other was increased) and even to some extent to the analysis of problems entailing mixtures of chemical substances in a medicinal context. An experimental control of the order of conditions (problem contexts) made it clear that one context could raise the likelihood of (i.e. prime) problem solving in another context. Incidentally, we suspect that a recipe context can prime reasoning about chemical mixtures because there is a sense in which both entail the challenge of mixing components according to a carefully prescribed combination (or rate). In this study, the mere sequencing of a familiar context (recipes) by another less familiar context (thinking about pharmaceutical mixtures) was enough to prod a significant number of subjects into extending their reasoning to the new context.

It would be naïve to suppose this as a general mechanism for promoting transfer in school. If an instructor wishes students to attribute similarity to apparently unrelated situations (the number of ways of making sandwiches with different breads, fillings, and spices and, say, the number of ways of ordering experimental and control conditions in an experiment), he or she may have to invest considerable effort in exploring the nature of combinatorial events as well as in exploring the logic of experimental control.   The reason that a sandwich filling can correspond to an experimental treatment condition has nothing to do with what sandwiches look like or even what we do with them.   In a sense, some situation-bound properties of the examples must be overlooked in order to appreciate their status as examples of mathematical structures and relations.

The findings of everyday mathematics studies led researchers to replace conceptions of cognition as an individual's general ability with approaches that conceive of knowledge and learning as part of the social context where cognition takes place (but as we just suggested, the ties to particular contexts do not rely on increased scrutiny with regard to the appearances of things).   These findings informed educators that children who show difficulties in school tasks may have developed, through informal learning, a wealth of strategies and understandings that may be relevant to school knowledge.   Moreover, their results suggest that the immersion of mathematical activities in meaningful, socially relevant situations, where concepts and relations are used as tools to achieve relevant goals, constitutes a fruitful approach to the development of meaningful solutions and mathematical understanding (see also Chap. 2 and Chap. 8, this volume).

THE RELEVANCE OF EVERYDAY MATHEMATICS

For years, cognitive developmental psychologists have argued that mathematical knowledge begins before, and hence outside of, school.   To some this may be inherently senseless: how could they be learning without being taught?   Well, we know there is some teaching about mathematics before school.   For example, children are taught how to count using our system of numerals, but early mathematical learning owes much to the child's own efforts as well as to the fact that children grow up in a society where certain cultural activities (such as buying and selling) and artifacts (e.g. money) play a prominent role. It is difficult to explain succinctly the nature of this mathematical knowledge and experience. Indeed, Piaget, the most prolific observer and theorist of children's pre-school mathematical competence, faced considerable difficulty in making the argument that advanced mathematics ultimately harked back to thinking about actions-- actions originally resident in the physical world but eventually in mental activity itself that could be performed in the absence of concrete materials (Beth & Piaget, 1961).

It now seems clear to us that Piaget was right in one very important respect: much of children's understanding about number arises from how they come to understand and reflect upon physical quantities.   However, it is not, as Cassirer (1923) pointed out and Piaget later championed, that mathematical thought consists in a direct abstraction of knowledge from the physical properties of objects. Mathematical knowledge builds on inferred invariants despite the appearance of things.   Piaget's classic example was the invariance of number despite the physical spacing of objects of two equal sets. A child with a concept of number appreciates that it doesn't matter whether two sets of objects do not match in the extent of physical space they sweep out: a stretched-out collection of objects can have as many as a scrunched-together collection.

We understand number conservation not as a threshold that separates preoperational from operational children but, rather, as an illustration of how early mathematical knowledge is interwoven with thinking about physical quantities. We treat this as a theme that flows through much of mathematical development, never being fully resolved, much in the way that the particulate versus wave theory of light constitutes a tension rather than a problem with a clear-cut solution.

The reason the quantitative underpinnings of mathematics cannot be isolated is that there is so much that can be gained by trying to ground thought in the experience of space and action in space. The Euclidean axiom that a part is less than a whole (of which it is part) is appealing because it corresponds to much of what is learned from everyday experience. Certainly, in most cases, parts cannot be larger than wholes.

Nonetheless, these deeply rooted intuitions need to be set aside from time to time. It turns out that directed numbers and vectors are two significant topics of mathematics where this axiomatic belief must be set aside. (A sum may be smaller than any of its components in both of these cases.) One response to such counter instances is to abandon the grounding in quantities altogether. But this is unacceptable. For one thing, advanced topics in science and mathematics can be grasped meaningfully in terms of composition and decomposition of quantities. In this way, for example, many of the fundamental ideas of analysis of variance can be understood as the simple addition and subtraction of variance. Much confusion subsides when high school or university students finally understand that a large part of the information and computation regarding ANOVA can be reduced or eliminated by thinking of how quantities join together to make up other quantities. It is not that advanced statistics reduces to ideas from early childhood. Substantial adjustments must be made so that former knowledge can take into account new problem situations. But it is far easier, and in the long term far more fruitful, for students to reconcile new knowledge with what they already know than to approach each new topic as a thing to be learned totally afresh and unconnected to their previous experience.

This line of thinking goes totally against the grain of arguments that educators should bring to the classroom activities similar to those from out-of-school contexts or that apprenticeship training should replace teaching (see for example, Chap. 2, this volume). Engaging in everyday activities such as buying and selling, sharing, betting, and so on, even if simulated, may help students establish links between their experience and intuitions already acquired and topics to be learned in school. However, we believe it would be a fundamental mistake to suggest to educators that schools should attempt to imitate or reproduce out-of-school activities in classrooms (see Schliemann, 1995). First, through discussion an instructor can establish rich links to out of school activities without actually reenacting them in the classroom. In so doing, the activities become objects of reflection and public discourse in fundamentally new ways. However, in addition to this, it must be recognized that children require a range of activities that enrich and complement the activities they partake in outside of school. Schools may provide access to a variety of symbolic systems and representations essential for establishing links between concepts and situations that would otherwise remain unrelated. To achieve this, educational agents need to create situations where symbolic representations act as tools for achieving goals of a very special nature. The goals of classroom activities are different from, and probably no less complex than, goals in other, out-of-school settings. Strangely, cognitive psychology's traditional emphasis on individuals' abilities has provided researchers with disappointingly few insights into the nature and use of goals in classrooms and how they differ from goals in out-of-school situations.

The relation between lived experience and the development of scientific knowledge is a subtle one. If, as argued before, mathematical ideas acquire meaning by virtue of their ties to everyday situations, how can insr apprec hope that students will come to understand concepts such as infinity, groups, rings, and so forth, that seem to bear only a tenuous relation to daily experience? Must mathematical knowledge be directly tied to daily experience at every turn? Fortunately, research has made some headway in these matters. For example, authors observed years ago that fractions can be introduced in ways consistent with what students already know about integers (Braunfeld & Wolfe, 1966; Weckesser, 1970). Researchers and educators of many persuasions have given special attention to the role of quantitative thinking in mathematical under-standing (Bell, Fischbein, & Greer, 1984; Freudenthal, 1983; Fridman, 1991; Koba-yashi, 1988; Piaget, Inelder, & Szeminska, 1952; Schwartz, 1996; Vergnaud, 1982). They have begun to understand how to separate issues of cardinality from rela-tive magnitude (Carraher, 1996; Carraher & Schliemann, 1991). Teaching studies carried out in the former Soviet Union (e.g., Bodanskii, 1991) and recent analyses in the United States (e.g., Schliemann, Carraher, Pendexter, & Brizuela, 1998) provide many insights into how to bridge arithmetical and algebraic under-standing. They demonstrate that elementary schoolchildren can understand and solve algebra problems that most educators would not dare to hand to students before their ninth year of schooling.

Frege (1953) showed that Mill's belief that mathematical knowledge ulti-mately rested on the perception of physical objects was doomed even for the simple case of integer addition. The situation can only be bleaker for higher order concepts. An upshot of this is that psychological theories need to make allowance for conceptual objects and relations that are not directly translatable into physical objects and actions. Abandoning physicalism opens the way for studying the relations between concepts that otherwise would have little in common. Consider, for example the concepts of measurement and division. To an experienced mathematician, these concepts are intimately intertwined: A dividend is like a measured magnitude, a divisor is like a unit of measure, a quotient corresponds to how many times the unit of measure fits into the target measure, and the remainder corresponds to the quantity that is left over (Carra-her, 1995). To elementary school pupils, division and measurement may appear to be different, perhaps even unrelated concepts and operations. How do dispa-rate elements of knowledge become integrated into more general, abstract wholes?

We suspect that for people to understand such concepts as embodying similar relations, they will draw on what they know about comparing magni-tudes and determining how many times one magnitude is contained in another. This is neither the direct result of experience nor a matter of subjects projecting their ideas directly onto the object. However, once the work of integration has been achieved, it may well appear that the individual's daily experience with dividing provided a meaningful basis for understanding measurement, just as his or her experience in measuring might appear to play a role in understanding more clearly the nature of division.

Because the development of mathematical knowledge takes considerable time, researchers may arrive at different conclusions about the role of daily experience in the emergence of mathematical knowledge, depending on the time framework adopted. If we focus on the time period when children are taught to do division and measurement, the knowledge acquired in one set of situations may appear isolated from and irrelevant to the knowledge acquired in another set of situations, thus leaning toward a strict situated cognition type of analysis (see Chapter 3, this volume). If, on the other hand, a much wider period of time is scanned, knowledge acquired in one type of situation may ultimately make substantial contributions in other domains (Carraher & Schliemann, 1998).

We should be highly skeptical of attempts to classify concepts as concrete or abstract, as if these were fixed properties inherent in the concepts themselves. So called concrete knowledge acquired in everyday, familiar situations may ultimately play a fundamental role in the development of abstract knowledge. Furthermore, as Cassirer (1923) convincingly showed, general concepts are powerful not by their detachment from particular instances and situations but on the contrary, by their usefulness in explaining and illuminating a wide range of particular phenomena. The abstract is thus inextricably bound to the concrete. We have coined the phrase *situated generalization* (Carraher, Nemirovsky, & Schliemann, 1995; Carraher & Schliemann, 1998) to capture this meaning.

A similar analysis could be initiated regarding the development of knowledge in societies over long periods of time. It is well known that everyday activities such as farming, commerce, and astronomy played a fundamental role in the slow emergence of mathematics as a field of scientific inquiry (Kline, 1990). But just as a college student's knowledge of mathematics cannot be reduced to the sum of former everyday experiences that made such intellectual achievements possible, the field of mathematics cannot be reduced to the circumstances that gave rise to its emergence. Once knowledge assumes higher forms, it tends to behave in ways relatively autonomous from its origins. This is true for the individual learner; it is also true for the scientific community as a whole, which receives, as a legacy from former generations, the symbolic tools for formulating and thinking about problems thenceforth. Scientific and mathematical reasoning is always indebted to its origins in human activity without becoming enslaved to it.

A First Example: Division With a Remainder

Now let us consider some examples from early mathematics in which thinking about relations among quantities (and how they relate to written mathematical notation) lies at the heart of the matter students are trying to resolve. We begin with an example from the topic of division, exploring how it entails understanding the way four quantities—a dividend, divisor, quotient, and remainder—are interrelated and what this has to do with the process of dividing. Then we proceed to an example involving a simple equation for describing the relation between two quantities. Although they are drawn from two separate areas of the curriculum, we believe they shed light on students' struggle to reconcile thinking about quantities and describing relations among mathematical objects. The first example also clarified to us how children might benefit from having symbolic representational tools that help them visualize the quantitative relations they are attempting to articulate.   In this sense, the Visual Calculator, which we introduce in the second empirical example, arose from a theoretical analysis of studies in everyday cognition and early mathematical understanding.

We know that, from their everyday experience in the context of sharing or distributing things, even young children understand the idea that the remainder is the part of the original quantity that is left over. When computing long division results, however, the meaning of the remainder is often a puzzle for school-children. They do not know what quantity the remainder represents, and they fail to understand how the remainder relates to the decimal representation when divisions are performed in a calculator.

What follows is an example of an activity analyzed by Carraher and Schliemann (1991) in which children engaged in discussion, use, and reflection about mathematical properties and symbols using their previous understandings and new discoveries as tools to play a software game that was extremely motivating for them. An important feature of the activity is that it seemed to provide the proper environment for meaningful reflection about mathematical relations and symbolic representations even though the objects children deal with had no physical referents or material embodiments in the physical world.

The two students in this episode are Pedro and Taís. They have been working with the software, *Divide and Conquer*, designed by Carraher (1991). The software is structured around the division identity, that is, division with a remainder. The basic idea behind division with a remainder can be simply stated: Any natural number, A, can be expressed as an integral multiple of any nonnegative integer, B, added to some other integer, R, such that $A = B^*Q + R$, where Q is a partial quotient. For instance, the number 37 can be expressed as an integral number of 8s, namely, four 8s plus the remainder, 5. The students' involvement in the task is triggered by the puzzle they have to solve, namely to break a code determining which of the 10 digits from 0 to 9 stands for each of 10 random letters displayed on the computer screen. To help them break the code, they can ask the computer to perform divisions with a remainder. The results shown by the computer, however, are also partially coded according to the conventions of cryptarithmetic. The students must reflect on the relations between the numbers displayed in order to find out solutions.

In the following excerpt, Pedro and Taís are coming to realize that division in the *Divide and Conquer* game does not always give the same result as division by a calculator. Let us listen to their discussion about the two types of division. They start with division with a remainder, working within the limits of everyday multiplication and division, where nearly always only whole numbers are dealt with. For the purposes of this analysis, we leave aside the issues of code-breaking and focus instead on the process of division with a remainder, for this is what the two students did in the passage in question.

Pedro and Taís have just noted that 89 divided by 2 will yield 44 remainder 1 on the computer (although, as we said, possibly in encrypted format):

Interviewer (suggesting an idea that is obviously false, because the computer displays a remainder of 1): If I divide (89 by 2) on the calculator, I get the same answer, right? (Pointing to 44.5 on the calculator.)

Taís (shaking her head): No, I think that (on the computer) 1 was left over and here (pointing to the right part of the answer, that is, to .5) it's half of one.

Taís incorrectly interprets the .5 as a remainder—"what is left over"

Interviewer: This point-five is half of 1?... Do you think it's the same thing, Pedro?

Pedro: (is) 5 half of 1? Does 1 have a half?

Pedro appears to be perplexed by the notation; he interprets the 5 as greater than 1; then he wonders whether 1 can have a half.

Interviewer: Explain it to him Taís.
Taís: I thought like this. Here (in *Divide and Conquer*) it gave 44 with 1 left over and there (on the calculator) this point-five is one half. Forty four and one half and (the computer) had 44 remainder 1.

She sees the results as discrepant.

Pedro: Ah! Now I get it. One half of 1 is one half, and that's equal to 5.

Pedro seems uncertain about the meaning of the 5 in the present context but is willing to agree with Taís that it means one half.

Interviewer (moving to another example): And now, 80 divided by 7 gave 11 remainder 3 (on the computer). Now let's try it out on the calculator.
Pedro : It's going to be point, um, five (on the calculator).

Here begins another calculation to compare between the computer and calculator.

Pedro transposes the former example incorrectly to the case at hand.

Interviewer: Why are you telling me it's going to be (11) point five?

Pedro: Because half of 3 is 1 and a *half*. (Calculator shows 11.428571 as the answer.)

Pedro seems to think that the remainder on the calculator will be half of the remainder on the computer

Pedro: This thing here (.428571) is half of 3.

He sticks to his hypothesis, even though he cannot really understand the decimal notation. The interviewer attempts to get the students back on the track.

Interviewer: Really?...Are we dividing in half or not? (...) Isn't the problem 80 divided by *seven*?
Taís: I can't explain that.
Pedro (persisting): It must be half of 3.
Taís: No way! All this (.428571) can't be half of 3.

Now Taís seems to think that this big number (.428571) must be greater than 3.

Pedro: So...? I though that this here (.428571) taken three times would give 3, but that's not right.

Pedro seems to regard the fractional part as a piece of the remainder, 3, from division with a remainder; this is in keeping with the former example, where the .5 was taken to be half of the remainder 1. Although .5 is half of 1, the fractional part a quotient does not relate to the remainder in this general way.

Second *Interviewer* (continuing): So where

does this (.428571) come from?...

Students: (no reply)

First *Interviewer*: You are saying that that is a little piece of three, but what piece is it?

Interviewer tries to reestablish the conversion, picking up at Pedro's last comment.

Pedro: That 7 has got to have something to do with it.

E: What do you think it has to do with it?
Pedro: This here (.428571), seven times, gives us the 3.

The fractional part is treated as part of the quotient, not the remainder. If the fractional part is multiplied by the divisor you will obtain the remainder: this is correct.

(Excerpted from Carraher & Schliemann, 1991, pp. 28-29).

Pedro stumbles at a number of points in the interview. For example, he seems to not understand much about the notation for the decimal fraction that corresponds to 3/7. That is, he does not seem comfortable with decimal notation. However, despite this limitation, he seems to have discovered that the fractional part of the quotient, when multiplied by the divisor, will return the value of the remainder of integer division. He would certainly not explain his understanding in these terms. He seems to be explaining only a particular case. But his explanation draws on, or perhaps better, is assembled from a more general sort of knowledge. Even if Pedro does not yet understand all the conventions involved in the decimal number notation, he now shows a grasp of the relationships among the mathematical objects involved in the two kinds of division. He achieves this in part through his own efforts but also due to the collaboration and scaffolding provided by his colleague and the interviewers (see Chap. 5 and Chap. 8, this volume).

As the dialogue seems to show, numbers without explicit reference to physical objects or their associated quantities can nonetheless be meaningful. Yet, we are convinced that Pedro and Taís were attempting to make sense of the situation by figuring out how the quotient and remainder quantities are derived from the dividend quantity and divisor.

The following diagram (Fig. 7.1) serves to clarify some of the relations Taís and Pedro were dealing with. The upper part of the diagram depicts division with a remainder, the division that the program *Divide and Conquer* was using. Note that not all of the dividend is divided. Only 77 units are divided. The remainder, 3 units, does not take part in the division; in that sense they are left over. In the bottom half of the diagram, what corresponds to division on the calculator can be seen. All of the original dividend is broken into seven parts. Each of the chunks of 11.428571 are precisely one seventh of 80 (if the very small rounding off error involved in the computation is iterpre). Seven times the quotient should yield an amount equal to the original dividend. This does not happen in the case of division with a remainder.

It happens that the fractional part, 0. 428571, corresponds to the difference between the quotient in the second case and the (partial) quotient in the first case. That little piece, ts th refers to the tiny extent by which the quotient exceeds the partial quotient, will indeed produce the remainder 3 if we multiply it by the divisor 7. That Pedro could explain this in the absence of any diagrams is truly remarkable!

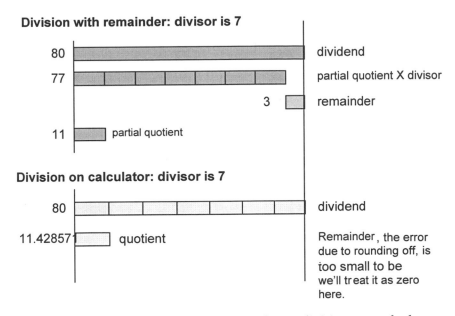

Figure 7.1. Illustration of division with a remainder vs. division on a calculator.

A Second Example: The Visual Calculator

The division example of Pedro and Taís demonstrates just how complex are the relations are among the four basic objects of division, totally apart from the problem of interpreting decimal notation. The fact that quantitative relations can be visually expressed has captured our imagination for some time. It is not that pictures speak for themselves, but rather, pictures and diagrams allow the isolation of diverse elements of a problem and discussion of how they fit together. Indeed, this explains in part why vector diagrams are well accepted within the mathematical community. Although vectors and tensors can be handled through computation alone, the diagrams help visualization of the relationships in convenient ways.

We present here some initial research that has been inspired by our previous studies on quantitative reasoning. In it we employ vector diagrams that were developed to help students visualize and discuss the relations among quantities. First, we describe the software environment, called *The Visual Calculator*, that was designed to help students and teachers engage in grounded discussions about quantities. Then, we look at an example of two middle school students using the software to solve a problem structurally similar to the well known professors and students problem from algebra research. Finally, we analyze how a 5th grade class solved a problem posed by two members of the class using visual information provided by the software on how quantities interrelate. We conclude with brief remarks on the role of technology in supporting the discussion.

The Visual Calculator™ was developed to help students visualize and discuss what happens to quantities when subjected to arithmetical operations of multiplication, division, addition, and subtraction (see Carraher, 1993, 1996, and Carraher & Schliemann, 1993). The software makes use of students' deeply rooted intuitions about the meaning of operations. For example, adding is represented in the software as joining. Subtraction can be thought of as removing or taking away. But even such basic intuitions must undergo adjustments when operations are modeled. For example, subtraction is not a distinct operation. It is composed of two operations: inverting (a subtrahend quantity) and joining (with the minuend quantity). It may not be immediately clear to the reader whether subtraction should be represented in this nonconventional way; however, there are advantages to viewing the operations -C + A and A-C as equivalent operations rather than as addition and subtraction, respectively, as conventional wisdom dictates. This admittedly entails questions of when to introduce children to negative quantities and vectors. We have clearly opted for an early introduction of such concepts instead of presenting more simplified models that must later be undone.

Multiplication and division can be introduced in ways that build on the intuitions that multiplying makes bigger and division makes smaller. If a quantity is multiplied by 3 and then the result divided by 7, a quantity smaller than the original quantity is obtained. Multiplying made the quantity bigger, and the division made the resultant quantity smaller. The overall effect of the two operations is to produce a quantity smaller than the original (see Figure 7.2 below). Now if the original quantity is multiplied by 3/7, the result is the same length as (read: equal to) that produced by the two integer operations. In fact, multiplying by 3/7 can be thought of as shorthand for the two operations of times 3and divided by 7.

This may be obvious or even trivial to those of us who have developed sturdy intuitions about rational operations. However, there is no reason to suppose that middle school students will quickly come to the same conclusions. The important thing is that students can be given conditions to mull over and discuss, to compare and set up tests, and carry out the steps in their own reasoning. How they do this, how they coordinate their understanding of integers with their emerging understanding of rational operators, merits careful research.

Multiple Units. A classic adage for teaching about fractions has been that you should not compare different units. This advice is motivated by the desire to avoid potentially confusing descriptions such as $2/3 = 1/2$, where the first term

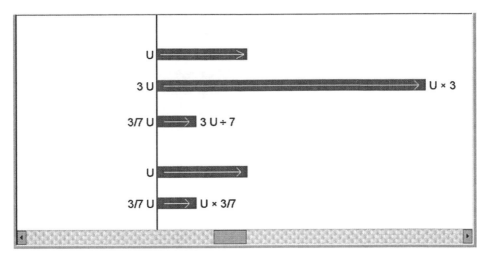

Figure 7.2. Visualization of multiplication and division in the *Visual Calculator*.

refers to one unit, and the second term refers to another unit (50% greater than the first unit). Unfortunately, this constraint, and the convention to not specify the unit in notation, hides from view important connections between units of measure, variables, and functions. These connections are much more salient when a more robust and explicit notation, such as 2/3 A = 1/2 B is adopted. The resemblance to algebraic equations is not mere coincidence. We are consciously attempting to use descriptions of relations among physical quantities to serve as precursors to relations among variable quantities and, ultimately, mathematical variables. The uncanny similarity between this notation and algebra can prove to be very useful for placing arithmetical and measurement situations in an algebraic context.

A unit of measure is any quantity that a person has decided to name (normally by a letter) and use repeatedly to describe the magnitude of various things. Multiple units of measure can be represented in the *Visual Calculator* and called by their respective names rather than referring to them indiscriminately as units. At first, a name refers to a particular line segment. However, because line segments can be replicated and will keep the same name as the original, the name can quickly take on the role of a measure in a given unit.

When a student decides to give a quantity a name, the software automatically creates a ruler in units of that magnitude. As instantiated in the software, a ruler looks more like a grid that cuts vertical lines throughout the space; it is not restricted to a number line sitting on the *x*-axis. This feature holds the potential for uniting number line and part-whole models of fractions, which research has shown to be very difficult for students to reconcile (Booth, 1986). In addition, multiple rulers can be simultaneously present on the screen. This encourages students and teachers alike to refer to how the different units relate to one another.

In an interview with two 5th grade students, Pilar and Sharmin, the students created units of P (Pilar) and S (Sharmin) and displayed both rulers at once (see Fig. 7.3 and Fig. 7.4).

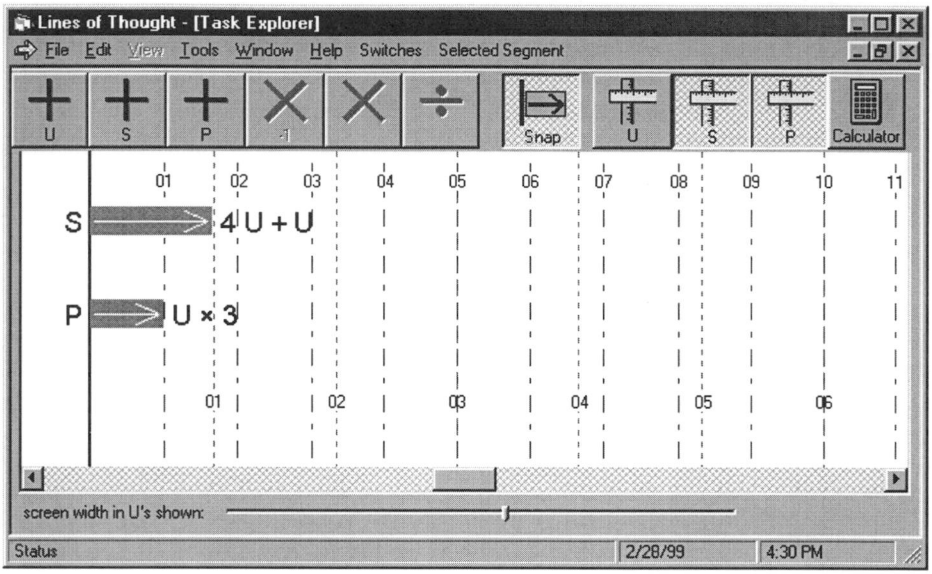

Figure 7.3.Units created and compared by Pilar (P) and Sharmin (S).

The students were struck by the fact that the numbers from one ruler occasionally aligned horizontally with numbers from the other ruler. This was a common reaction among 5th and 6th year students we observed. It was not immediately obvious to them what these patterns meant, but by thinking about and discussing what the lines stood for, they formulated a description of how the two units of measure were related. Sharmin wrote out her discovery as "P x 5 equals the same as S x 3". Pilar expressed the same relation, in writing, as "5P = 3S".

These descriptions were different from the notation they had been taught in school. Yet they seemed to flow forth naturally in this setting where units were given identifying names. It seems to us that these algebraic-like statements, once written, helped the students clarify for themselves (and for us, the researchers) the patterns they noticed among the grids. The transition from notation, as a means of registering operations and actions to be carried out, to a means for describing relations among objects is an important one. It evokes the important distinction between process and object that other authors have recently drawn attention to (Dubinsky, 1991; Sfard, 1991).

Determining an Unknown Ratio. We now summarize how a 5th year class solved a problem of determining an unknown ratio of two quantities. A 5th grade teacher asked us to show the Visual Calculator to her class one day, because not all of the students had been able to participate in our out-of-class interviews using the software. We showed how the basic operations were represented on screen. We talked about how to describe the relations among diverse units that the students had created. The teacher asked the students to determine whether three units of measure would eventually line up together. (The units were 2.5, 3.5, and 1, respectively.)

In the second half-hour, we set up a problem situation in which there were problem posers and solvers. We asked two students to select a pair of numbers between 1 and 10. They posed the problem, that is, chose an unknown ratio. The rest of the students attempted to discover the ratio chosen by exploring two quantities constructed from that ratio. The following screen captures display the visual information students had at their disposal as they discussed the problem.

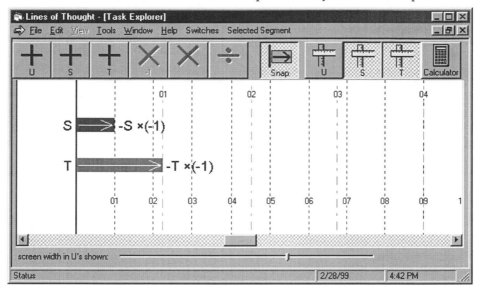

Figure 7.4. Illustration of the unknown ratio problem.

The first suggestion came from Ben, who stated that "the top [line] is two and I think the bottom is four and a half." When the teacher clarified that the numbers were whole numbers, he changed to, "The S is four and the T is nine, because I think this (the space between the dotted lines produced by the S ruler) is four, so there is four and then four and then a little bit to make nine."

The lines for the T ruler were then displayed. A few students took turns in attempting to prove that Ben was right. One explained that "Because in the beginning of the T one of those looks like one fourth of two Ss... Its one fourth past two. So that means it has to be either 4 or 8 or 16". Another says that "I said, 2 times 4 is 8, and it's right here, and I think this part is one more, so that's 9".

When the examiner counter-argued that the little bit that is left over could be one fifth and not one fourth, another student stated that she thought that "the top one is 3 and the bottom one is 7". The class was thus faced with two competing possibilities for the ratio.

After some discussion, Rachel volunteered to present her argument in support of Ben's proposal that one line is 4 and the other is 9. Our interpretations are bracketed.

> Rachel: This [the piece of T that projects beyond the second S-line] has to be one fourth, because, and then that would be one half [i.e., the second T-line falls halfway between the 4th and the 5th S-lines] and that would be three fourths [the third T-line falls _ of the way between the 6th and the 7th S-lines] and this would be... if there were one more [T-unit], this would be a whole. If you look at these lines, you see, this is one fourth and then this is in the middle between these two, and so that would be a half, and then this would be three fourths.
> D: Show me the middle again. Where is the middle?
> Rachel [pointing to the T-line falling at 4.5 S]: Here.
> D: ... So you're saying that second line is in the middle of two of the other ones?
> Rachel: Yes, well, no, in the middle of the Ss.
> D: In the middle of these two [pointing to the 4th and 5th S-Lines with the mouse]?
> Rachel: Yes, and then this one [at 6.75 S] is over a little, and this one is... they're both the same [i.e. the 4th T-line aligns with the 9th S-Line]. They both line up.
> Teacher: So you're thinking that this is a whole unit and you've got this much...
> Rachel: Yes, I'm saying...
> Teacher: Put your fingers like this, between the 2 and the 3 so people know what you're talking about. So, you're basically spanning the distance between 2 and 3, and then you're showing that two lines.
> Rachel: Yes, this line is in the middle of these two... and this is over to the right and this is three fourths.
> D: Look at that last one, let's go carefully on that one. What happened there?
> Rachel: They're both at the same.
> D: What are the numbers that are there?
> Rachel: It's a 4 and a 9.
> Several members of the class (with surprise, as they figure it out): Oh.....

This visual method of proof was convincing to the class, including the girl who had put forth the alternative idea that the segments were 3 and 7 units, respectively.

When the teacher asked them what number would serve as a multiplier to make the shorter segment, S, equal in length to the larger segment, T, a boy suggested that they use the number 2.25. When they carried out the multiplication they saw that the result (2.25S and T equal in length) was consistent with the prediction. Although technically not a proof of the relation, it provided fairly convincing evidence that the students were correct.

CONCLUDING REMARKS

This chapter only begins to scratch the surface of how technology can exploit pedagogical issues that have repeatedly emerged from research and teaching. Researchers are still at a beginning stage of investigating how children can make sense of traditionally difficult concepts in computer-supported learning environments.

The computer does not define a learning environment. Software does not work on its own but depends heavily on the spirit of inquiry that teachers or researchers are able to establish together with students (see also Chap. 5, this volume, this volume). Given the proper social climate, which should not be presumed to exist but must be achieved, software may nonetheless lend support for discussions among students and teachers about ideas and mathematical objects that are difficult to talk about in normal circumstances without the aid of such technology.

Some have argued that the key contribution of computers to mathematics education lies in immersing students in realistic situations. They look forward to improvements in virtual reality and increases in internet bandwidth so that students might experience simulated environments as if they were real. Then, vivid pictures of the mathematical objects discussed could presumably be delivered. Who knows, perhaps researchers could even find ways of allowing students to grasp with their very own hands the illusive mathematical objects.

Such expectations bear an uncanny resemblance to a certain view of everyday mathematics research. On occasion, people have taken the findings to suggest that educators need to instantiate in the classroom situations just like those out-of-school settings where people successfully use mathematics. These expectations fail on at least two counts. Classrooms are part of social reality, and the situations that take place in classrooms are no less real than those that occur outside of classrooms. Yes, it is true that many of the problems and circumstances in classrooms are contrived and imagined. Students reason about the sale of flocks of sheep or about the building of nuclear reactors, even though no one in the classroom is a shepherd, a meat packer, or a nuclear engineer. However, much of life entails reasoning and making decisions about entities individuals do not presently see, much less hold in their hands. Mortgages, insurance, and planning in general provide many cases in point.

Meaningfulness, not realism, has been the hallmark of everyday mathematics research. People are good at mathematics out of school in large part because they are comfortable with how quantities are represented and transformed. When they break up quantities into constituent parts they have a pretty clear notion about how the parts relate to each other. This contrasts with many situations that arise in the classroom, such as the division algorithm, where students are asked to operate on symbols, the quantity referents for which have been lost along the computational way.

Realism does not provide the answer many had hoped for. In fact, it focuses attention on the wrong issues altogether. Knowledge, particularly mathematical knowledge, does not seep into the brain via the sensory organs. No matter how vivid are the pictures, how palpable are the objects, mathematics will continue to present deep challenges to learners. Mathematics is about relations, and relations are not palpable objects like tables, knives, and forks.

Even as educators recognize the importance of understanding, they should be careful not to elevate it too high. If educators insist that students only face those situations and use those symbols they already fully comprehend, they will find themselves constantly putting off topics to later moments in the curriculum. Were the same logic to be used in teaching infants to speak their first language, individuals would be silent, because initially infants understand no words at all. Teaching mathematics involves the constant introduction of new situations and new symbols. There is no choice but to use new representations and symbols together with others students are fairly familiar with. Everyday mathematics research, as well as developmental research, can provide ideas about how to ground present learning in what students already know and understand. Historical developments can inspire researchers to find representations that become progressively schematized and increasingly closer to bona fide representations. New knowledge cannot be reduced to what students already know; otherwise nothing new would ever be learned. Yet if it is totally detached from present experience and understanding, it will not be understood. Striking the right balance between former and new knowledge involves a tension that can never be fully eliminated. Research on children's thinking before and out of school can provide some interesting leads for educators to follow, as they see students struggling to make sense of new topics. It cannot fully resolve the issues, because the outcome depends on the efforts of the students themselves as well as social processes that lie outside the purview of teaching as presently conceived.

REFERENCES

Acioly, N. (1994). *La juste mesure: Une étude des competences mathématiques des travailleurs de la canne a sucre du Nordeste du Brésil dans le domaine de la mesure.* Unpublished doctoral dissertation. Université René Descartes, Paris, France.

Bell, A., Fischbein, E., & Greer, B. (1984). Choice of operation in verbal arithmetic problems: The effects of number size, problem structure, and context. *Educational Studies in Mathematics, 15,* 129-147.

Beth, E. W. & Piaget, J. (1961). *Epistémologie Mathématique et Psychologie. Etudes d'Epistémologie Génétique* XIV. Paris, Presses Universitaires de Paris.

France.Bodanskii, F. G. (1991). The formation of an algebraic method of problem-solving in primary schoolchildren. In V.V. Davydov, (Ed.) *Soviet Studies in Mathematics Education: Vol. 6: Psychological Abilities of Primary School Children in Learning Mathematics* (pp. 275-338). Washington, DC: National Council for Teachers of Mathematics.

Booth, L. (1986). *Fractions.* NFER-Nelson.

Braunfeld, P. & Wolfe, M. (1966). Fractions for low achievers. *Arithmetic Teacher,* 647-655.

Carraher, D.W. (1990). Understanding the division algorithm from different perspectives. In *Proceedings of the International Group for the Psychology of Mathematics Education,* Oxtapec, Mexico.

Carraher, D. W. (1991). Mathematics in and out of school: A selective review of studies from Brazil. In M. Harris (Ed.), *Schools, mathematics and work* (pp. 169-201). London: The Falmer Press.

Carraher, D. W. (1993). Lines of thought: A ratio and operator model of rational number. *Educational Studies in Mathematics, 25,* 281-305.

Carraher, D. W. (1995, April). *Building upon students' understanding of ratio and proportion.* Paper presented at the annual meeting of the American Educational Research Association, San Francisco, CA.

Carraher, D. Nemirovsky, R., & Schliemann, A. (1995). *Situated generalization.* Paper presented at the XIX International Conference for the Psychology of Mathematics Education, Recife, Brazil.

Carraher, D. & Schliemann, A. (1993). Learning about relations between number and quantity in and out of school. *Dokkyo International Review,* (Tokyo), Vol. 6, 63-96.

Carraher, D.W. & Schliemann, A.D. (1991). Children's understandings of fractions as expressions of relative magnitude, in F. Furinghetti, (ed), *Proceedings of the XV PME Conference* (pp. 184-191), Vol II, Assisi, Italy.

Carraher, D.W. (1996). Learning about fractions, in L. Steffe, P. Nesher, G. Goldin, P. Cobb, & B. Greer (Eds.), *Theories of Mathematical Learning*, Hillsdale, NJ: Lawrence Erlbaum Associates.

Carraher, T. N. (1985). The decimal system: Understanding and notation. In L. Streefland (Ed.), *Proceedings of the Ninth International Conference for the Psychology of Mathematics Education* (pp. 288-303). Noordwijkerhout, The Netherlands.

Carraher, T. N. (1986). From drawings to buildings: Working with mathematical scales. *International Journal of Behavioural Development, 9*, 527-544.

Carraher, T. N., Carraher, D. W., & Schliemann, A. D. (1982). Na vida, dez; na escola, zero: Os contextos culturais da educação matemática. *Cadernos de Pesquisa, 42*, 79-86.

Carraher, T. N., Carraher, D. W., & Schliemann, A. D. (1985). Mathematics in the streets and in schools. *British Journal of Developmental Psychology, 3*, 21-29.

Cassirer, E. (1923). *Substance and Function*. New York: Douglas Publications.

deAbreu, G. de, & Carraher, D. W. (1989). The mathematics of Brazilian sugar cane farmers. In C. Keitel, P. Damerow, A. Bishop, & P. Gerdes (Eds.), *Mathematics, education and society* (pp. 68-70). Paris, France: UNESCO.

Dubinsky, E. (1991). Reflective abstraction in advanced mathematical thinking, in D. Tall, (Ed.). *Advanced Mathematical Thinking* (pp. 95-123). Dordrecht, Germany: Kluwer..

Freudenthal, H. (1983). *Didactical phenomenology of mathematical structures*, Dordrecht, Germany: Reidl.

Fridman, L.M. (1991/1969). Features of introducing the concept of concrete numbers in the primary grades, in V.V. Davydov (Ed.) *Soviet Studies in Mathematical Education, Vol 6: Psychological Abilities of Primary School Children in Learning Mathematics*, 148-180.

Gay, J., & Cole, M. (1967). *The new mathematics and an old culture*. New York: Holt, Rinehart & Winston.

Gerdes, P. (1986). How to recognize hidden geometrical thinking: A contribution to the development of anthropological mathematics. *For the Learning of Mathematics, 6*(2), 10-17.

Gerdes, P. (1988a). A widespread decorative motive and the Pythagorean theorem. *For the Learning of Mathematics, 8*(1), 35-39.

Gerdes, P. (1988b). On culture, geometrical thinking and mathematics education. *Educational Studies in Mathematics, 19*, 137-162.

Grando, N. (1988). *A matemática na agricultura e na escola.* Unpublished masters thesis, Universidade Federal de Pernambuco, Recife, Brazil.

Harris, M. (1987). An example of traditional women's work as a mathematics resource. *For the Learning of Mathematics, 7*(3), 26-28.

Harris, M. (1988). Common threads: Mathematics and textiles. *Mathematics in School, 17*(4), 24-28.

Kline, Morris (1990) *Mathematical thought from ancient to modern times*, vol. 1. Oxford: Oxford University Press.

Kobayashi, M. (1988). *New ideas of teaching mathematics in Japan*. Tokyo: Chuo University Press.

Lave, J. (1977). Cognitive consequences of traditional apprenticeship training in Africa. *Anthropology and Educational Quarterly, 7,* 177-180.

McMurchy-Pilkington, C. (1995). *Maori women engaging in mathematical activities in Marae kitchens.* Unpublished master's thesis, University of Auckland.

Millroy, W. L. (1992). An ethnographic study of the mathematical ideas of a group of carpenters. *Journal for Research in Mathematics Education* (Monograph no. 5). Reston, VA: The National Council of Teachers of Mathematics.

Nunes, T. (1992). Ethnomathematics and everyday cognition. In D. Grouws (Ed.), *Handbook of research in mathematics education* (pp. 557-574). New York: MacMillan.

Nunes, T. N., Schliemann, A. D., & Carraher, D. W. (1993). *Street mathematics and school mathematics.* New York: Cambridge University Press.

Piaget, J., Inhelder, B., & Szeminska, A. (1952). *The child's conception of number.* London: Routledge & Kogan Page.

Reed, H. J., & Lave, J. (1979). Arithmetic as a tool for investigating relations between culture and cognition. *American Anthropologist, 6,* 568-582

Saraswathi, L. S. (1989). Practices in linear measurements in rural Tamil-Nadu: Implications for adult education programs. *Journal of Education and Social Change, III*(1), 29-46.

Saxe, G. B., & Moylan, T. (1982). The development of measurement operations among the Oksapmin of Papua New Guinea. *Child Development, 53,* 1242-1248.

Schliemann, A. D. (1985). Mathematics among carpenters and carpenters apprentices: Implications for school teaching. In P. Damerow, M. Dunckley, B. Nebres & B. Werry (Eds.), *Mathematics for all,* Paris, Science and Technology Education Document Series, UNESCO, No. 20.

Schliemann, A. D. (1988). Understanding permutations: Development, school learning, and work experience. *The Quarterly Newsletter of the Laboratory of Comparative Human Cognition, 10*(1), 3-7.

Schliemann, A. D., & Acioly, N. M. (1989). Mathematical knowledge developed at work: The contribution of practice versus the contribution of schooling. *Cognition and Instruction, 6*(3), 185-221.

Schliemann, A. D., & Carraher, D. W. (1992). Proportional reasoning in and out of school. In P. Light & G. Butterworth (Eds.), *Context and cognition: Ways of learning and knowing* (pp. 47-73). New York: Harvester Wheatsheaf.

Schliemann, A.D., Carraher, D.W., Pendexter, W., & Brizuela, B. (1998) *Solving algebra problems before algebra instruction.* Paper presented at the Second Early Algebra Meeting. University of Massachusetts at Dartmouth/Tufts University, Medford, MA.

Schliemann, A. D., & Magalhães, V. P. (1990). Proportional reasoning: From shops, to kitchens, laboratories, and, hopefully, schools. *Proceedings of the Fourteenth International Conference for the Psychology of Mathematics Education* (Vol. 3, pp. 67-73). Oaxtepec, Mexico.

Schliemann, A. D., & Nunes, T. (1990). A situated schema of proportionality. *British Journal of Developmental Psychology, 8,* 259-268.

Schliemann, A. D., Araujo, C., Cassundé, M. A., Macedo, S., & Nicéas, L. (1994). School children versus street sellers' use of the commutative law for solving multiplication problems. *Proceedings of the Eighteenth International*

Conference for the Psychology of Mathematics Education (Vol. 4, pp. 209-216). Lisbon, Portugal.

Schliemann, A. D., Santos, C. M., & Canuto, S. F. (1993). Constructing written algorithms: A case study. *Journal of Mathematical Behavior, 12,* 155-172.

Schliemann, A.D. (1995). Some Concerns about Bringing Everyday Mathematics to Mathematics Education. In L. Meira & D. Carraher (Eds.), *Proceedings of the XIX International Conference for the Psychology of Mathematics Education* (Vol. 1, pp. 45-60). Recife, Brazil.

Schwartz, J. (1996). *Semantic Aspects of Quantity.* Unpublished paper, Harvard Graduate School of Education.

Scribner, S. (1984). Studying working intelligence. In B. Rogoff & J. Lave (Eds.), *Everyday cognition: Its development in social context* (pp. 9-40). Cambridge, MA: Harvard University Press.

Scribner, S. (1986). Thinking in action: Some characteristics of practical thought. In R. Sternberg & D. Wagner (Eds.), *Practical intelligence. Nature and origins of competence in the everyday world* (pp. 13-30). New York: Cambridge University Press.

Sfard, A. (1991). On the dual nature of mathematical conceptions: reflections on processes and objects as different sides of the same coin. *Educational Studies in Mathematics, 22,* 1-36.

Ueno, N., & Saito, S. (1994, June). *Historical transformations of mathematics as problem solving in a Nepali bazaar.* Paper presented at the Thirteenth Biennial Meetings of the ISSBD, Amsterdam.

Vergnaud, G. (1982) Additive structures, in T. P. Carpenter & J. M. Moser (Eds.), *Addition and subtraction: a cognitive perspective..* Hillsdale, N.J., Lawrence Erlbaum Associates.

Associates, c1982.

Weckesser, H. (1970). 'Die Einführung von Brüchen mit Hilfe von Modellen', *Mathematikunterricht 16,* 30-77.

Zaslavsky, C. (1973). *Africa counts.* Boston, MA: Prindle & Schmidt.

8

Socially Shared Cognition:
System Design and the Organization of
Collaborative Research

Katherine Brown
University of California - San Diego

Michael Cole
University of California - San Diego

INTRODUCTION

The concept of socially shared cognition plays an important role in our efforts to create and sustain model systems of educational activity. In this chapter, our discussion of socially shared cognition focuses on our ongoing attempts to design, implement, and sustain educational activities in community institutions during the after-school hours. We use the notion of socially shared cognition to discuss two aspects of our work: (a) the organization of learning within educational play worlds called Fifth Dimensions and (b) the organization of collaboration among a team of scholars conducting research on the Fifth Dimension.

Sharing is a Janus-headed concept (Cole, 1991). On the one hand it refers to receiving, using, and experiencing in common with others. On the other hand, sharing also means to divide or distribute something between oneself and others. Both of these aspects of sharing with respect to socially shared cognition are relevant to our research.

First, in the design of the system of activities themselves, we are acting from our assumption that cognition is distributed among such important elements as the participants, the artifacts they use, and the social institutions within which they are housed. Second, as a research collective we share some beliefs and practices, such as an intellectual affinity for the ideas of John Dewey, Lev Vygotsky, and George Herbert Mead, and an agreement to incorporate qualitative and quantitative methodologies into the work of the collective. At the same time we divide up the work between and among members who are on implementation or evaluation teams, or both, located at institutions of higher learning that have different populations, priorities, missions, and locations.

In the joint activities of the research team and in the education and play world of the Fifth Dimension, both senses of sharing are simultaneously relevant. No two people can ever entirely experience a situation or use a tool in exactly the same way, even as they are cognizant of the fact (which they may communicate to each other) that there are aspects of their experience that can be said to be shared in the sense of held in common.

Viewed in this way, there is an obvious affinity among the various terms used to designate the problematic of this book: To say that cognition is socially shared is to say that it is distributed (among artifacts as well as people) and that it is situated in time and space. Because it is distributed, and its assembly requires the active engagement of those involved, it is to some extent constructed (see also Chapters 3 and 5, this volume).

THEORETICAL FOUNDATIONS:
CULTURAL PSYCHOLOGY AND SOCIALLY SHARED COGNITION

The theoretical orientation of our research collective resonates with and encourages diverse research interests, analytic levels, and units of analysis. It also supports interdisciplinarity, regardless of the participant's departmental or institutional affiliation. The intellectual tradition informing our work is elaborated in Cole's (1996) book *Cultural Psychology* and can be summarized in the following list of characteristics he associated with the enterprise of a cultural psychology:

- It emphasizes mediated action in context.
- It insists on a genetic method understood broadly to include historical, ontogenetic, and microgenetic levels of analysis.
- It seeks to ground its analysis in everyday life events.
- It assumes that mind emerges in the joint mediated activity of people. Mind, then, is an important sense that is coconstructed and distributed.
- It assumes that individuals are active agents in their own development but do not act in settings entirely of their own choosing.
- It rejects cause and effect, stimulus-response, explanatory science in favor of a science that emphasizes the emergent nature of mind in activity and that acknowledges a central role for interpretation in its explanatory framework.
- It draws on methodologies from the humanities as well as from the social and biological sciences.

FIFTH DIMENSION: NORMATIVE DESCRIPTION OF THE MODEL SYSTEM

In this section, we provide a description of a generic Fifth Dimension model to show how the theoretical ideals above are embodied in the design of an after-school activity system.

In a prototype Fifth Dimension system (local names for them vary), a dozen or more 6 to 14-year-old children encounter a large variety of off-the-shelf computer games and game-like educational activities. As a rule, the Fifth Dimension area contains a variety of kinds of computers (Mac and IBM;

low end and high end) at a ratio of one computer for every two to three children. The computer games are a part of a make-believe activity system, which transforms the way individual games (or activities such as origami, chess, boggle) are experienced by the children. Task cards or adventure guides accompany each game or activity to help participants get started, to specify expected achievements, and to provide evidence necessary for obtaining credentials as an expert. The task cards also provide a variety of obligations to write to someone, to look up information in an encyclopedia, or teach someone else what he or she has learned.

A Wizard

There is a real make-believe Fifth Dimension Wizard, an anonymous electronic entity who lives in the Internet, writes to the children, chats with them via modem, and acts as their patron. The Wizard has a home page and helps the children gain access to the World Wide Web, where they may display their own creative work. The wizard also affords a locus for conflict resolution, helping to mediate typical power relations between children and adults and preserving the mobility of expert and novice roles. Each Fifth Dimension has special ceremonies, such as birthdays for their electronic entity or status passage parties for children when they become Young Wizard Assistants, designating their mastery of the local Fifth Dimension content. These parties often occasion interaction and exchanges with other Fifth Dimension sites in other locales around the country and the world.

The Children

Children typically visit a Fifth Dimension on a drop-in basis. Some children spend 4 to 6 hours per week of their after school time participating in the Fifth Dimension, whereas others may only come once a week for a few hours. Opportunities and constraints vary across locations, seasons, populations, and sites. Girls outnumber boys in some Fifth Dimensions even where larger club setting activities are dominated by boys.

At some locations, adults expect the children to participate regularly in the Fifth Dimension and arrange for them to do so, whereas at other sites children are free to choose if and for how long to participate, with homework, basketball, crafts, reading, or other activities as alternatives. Many children enter the Fifth Dimension directly after school or homework sessions and remain there until their parents or school transportation services take them home.

A Site Coordinator

In our model system, there is a site coordinator who greets the children and supervises the flow of activity in the room. This person is trained to recognize and support the pedagogical ideals and curricular materials that mark the Fifth Dimension as different — as a different way for kids to use computers, as a different way for adults to interact with children. The site coordinator monitors the balance of education and play in interactions between children and undergraduates. A site coordinator may be employed by the community institution and may have taken university courses that put undergraduates into the community settings, but this not the case everywhere. Arrangements for funding the site coordinator position vary — sometimes the partner university or college research or outreach funds cover the salary to help grow a Fifth Dimension in a setting with modest resources. In other cases, site coordinator salaries can be absorbed into the operating budget of a club.

The Undergraduates

In addition to the presence of a mysterious Wizard who writes to them and pays attention to their progress through the maze, the chief draw for the children is the presence of university and college students in the Fifth Dimension who are there to learn and play with them. In our model, an important feature of the Fifth Dimension is that the participating college students are enrolled in an intensive research methods course focused on fieldwork in the community.

At the University of California (UC), San Diego, the university course associated with student participation is an intensive laboratory class that emphasizes deep understanding of basic developmental principles, familiarity with the use of new information technologies for organizing learning, and methods for collecting and analyzing data on the processes that undergraduates help to put into play. Students are treated as, and act as, junior researchers engaged in participant observation. They write detailed clinical field notes after each session with the children. These notes are read and critiqued by the professor and his teaching assistants.

The class meets twice weekly to discuss assigned readings and to evaluate the scholarly articles students read at the University for their fit with their own field experiences with the children. Students also discuss their work with students in other Fifth Dimension-linked courses in the UC system through the UC system's Distance Learning network. Finally, the undergraduates write papers tracing the development of individual children, the relative effectiveness of different games, differences in the ways that boys and girls participate in the activities, or other developmental topics.

Why After School?

We focus on after-school time for several reasons. First, our research has revealed a broad desire to increase the number of hours per day that children are engaged in academic tasks. Second, the changing nature of adult work has brought about significant changes in the organization of family life that make it difficult for adults to be available for their children's needs for playful interaction or to help with homework until 6 or 7 o'clock in the evening. Third, after school institutions are generally funded at a low level because they depend heavily on philanthropic giving from the local community. This form of support works well for sports programs, where adults volunteer their time to supervise 25 or so youngsters a few days a week.

In the culture at large, several core after-school institutions, such as Boys and Girls Clubs, Y's, and church clubs, manage loosely supervised, low overhead efforts that provide a safe space, few supervised special activities, and a great deal of free play. The turnover of staff is rapid because only a few members of the institution are paid a full time, albeit low, wage. Often, teenagers who have coached in a sport league are hired to provide programming and supervise the children. These institutions do a great service to the community along many dimensions, and the term *education* is likely to appear in their publicity materials. But educational activity is only fitfully present, as it is expensive to maintain. The Fifth Dimension provides a way to increase the educational programming of such institutions without substantially increasing the costs of operation.

Introducing education into the after-school hours is not an easy achievement. After school is, traditionally, play time. It is the space between schoolwork and homework (which currently amount to about the same thing). But there is a great need to arrange for children, as a part of their playful, after school hours, to engage in the kind of educational activity that might boost their chances of attending college or university.

One obvious strategy, made more potent owing to the proliferation of computer-based games and telecommunications, is to arrange for them to learn while playing. Alongside learning fearlessness, strategic thinking, and social responsibility on the soccer field, we arrange for children to sign up for a form of play in which they learn perseverance, the basic content of many valued intellectual domains, and the ability to organize their problem-solving skills in collaboration with others.

In more general terms, we locate our mandate in the following contradiction: There is overwhelming evidence that U.S. children spend less time engaged in academic pursuits than the children of any other industrialized country, by many days a year, hundreds of hours a year. U.S. citizens seem perfectly content with that situation on the one hand, and on the other hand worry about kids learning new technologies, gaining the kinds of knowledge that they need to have to avoid being left behind as we enter the 21st century.

Researchers at the Lab of Comparative Human Cognition have spent more than a decade mediating the problems and situations in the organization of learning environments (whether high or low tech) that cause many children to be deeply alienated from school. The Fifth Dimension allows us, then, to give school-age children an experience of learning that is fun and different from their routines at school. Second, it allows us to do this while providing undergraduates — including those who are preparing for careers as teachers and lives as parents — with nonhierarchical, nonauthoritarian models for promoting learning, initiative, and responsibility. Third, the organizational structure supports sharing between university and community partners that allows each to do more with their resources in pursuit of their institutional mandates than they would by acting alone.

The possibilities for development for children, adults, and institutions participating in a Fifth Dimension are situated in a place that supports cooperative exploration of new tasks and new roles. These possibilities are constructed in joint mediated activity around special materials, traditions, technology, and objectives. Responsibilities, rewards, and goals directing participation in the Fifth Dimension are distributed between adults and children, novices and experts, and, of course, the local wizard or wizardess.

EVALUATING THE FIFTH DIMENSION PROJECTS

From 1994 to 1997, the Andrew W. Mellon Foundation extended its initial support for our efforts to fund a network of sites that is now a nationwide Distributed Literacy Consortium connected through the Internet. In order to grow, sustain, and propagate the system, we needed to know how the Fifth Dimension model worked in a variety of contexts, who was benefiting from participation, and what aspects of the model could be adapted to serve the needs of other populations of children, undergraduates, and scholars.

Over the years there has been an ongoing program of evaluation of the efficacy of the Fifth Dimension as an environment for the academic development of children and undergraduates (Blanton, Moorman, Hayes, & Warmer, 1997; Mayer et al., 1997; Schustack, Strauss, & Worden, 1997). In those cases where the social ecology permits, standard experimental-control group comparisons have shown that elementary school children who attend the Fifth Dimension for 15 or more sessions over the course of several months have improved scores on school-district tests of achievement in reading and math problem solving, increased ability to follow written directions, and increased familiarity and capability with using computers.

A Cognitive Evaluation team comprised of both implementers and external evaluators documented improvement in children's demonstrations of verbal, mathematical, and technical ability as well as gains in their abilities to follow written instructions as an effect of Fifth Dimension participation. This team also found evidence that children transfer their Fifth Dimension acquired experience to other problem-solving domains. They showed strong post-Fifth Dimension performance on school-like tasks and, in North Carolina, on the end of grade state-mandated test gain scores (Blanton et al, 1997).

Studies using qualitative methodologies (both case histories of individual children and analysis of teaching-learning interactions) show that children engage routinely in authentic problem solving mediated by basic literacy and numeracy skills in the context of their interactions with the undergraduates and the various computer and noncomputer-based games and associated activities. In addition, analyses of the undergraduate experience indicate that they become adept at guiding the children's learning while, gaining an increased appreciation of, and mastery over, basic theoretical concepts that are the core of the practicum class that places them at the sites. In cases where the population of children served speaks a language other than English in the home, data indicate that participation in the Fifth Dimension serves to both maintain the growth of competence in the home language and the acquisition of spoken and written English (Gallego, Moll, & Rueda, 1997).

In the analysis that follows, we focus on qualitative evidence of change in individual children over time. These data best illustrate how our use of cultural-historical activity theory incorporates the concept of socially shared cognition.

INDIVIDUAL CHANGE AND CULTURAL DEVELOPMENT IN SITU

The following case study is excerpted from a recently completed CD-ROM entitled An incomplete guide and starter kit for the Fifth Dimension. Ray McDermott, Jim Greeno, Mimi Ito, and Vanessa Gack (from the Institute for Research on Learning) gathered videotape and synchronized screen-capture data from several California sites in order to document the microgenesis of learning in the Fifth Dimension. They were especially interested in the way undergraduates and children supplement each others' knowledge base in order to solve problems in the Fifth Dimension.

Case Study: Remediating Number Sense

The undergraduates working with children in the Fifth Dimension are encouraged to stretch their partners' capabilities by providing opportune help and by suggesting tools and strategies for extending budding abilities to solve problems. Rather than provide the answer for children, adult partners are coached by research directors and lecturers on how to remediate a child's relationship to a given content area in a way that eventually helps the child to accomplish the task on his or her own. Remediation, in this sense, can be understood as a shift in the way that mediating devices regulate coordination with the environment.[1]

In the following interaction, an undergraduate newcomer to the project is working with a child on a game that involves identifying the multiples of certain numbers. A graduate student researcher, who has worked in the Fifth Dimension for many years, is observing and coaching the interaction, giving suggestions for the kinds of advice and interaction that would provide tools for the child to determine multiples of 2, 3, and 4.

This case illustrates how effective helping behavior is learned by the undergraduates (through one-on-one coaching with a more experienced adult in the system) and how this influences undergraduate interactions with kids. The game is Number Munchers, which involves "munching" all the numbers that are multiples of a given number. The player's character moves about the screen full of numbers while being pursued by a "troggle" which can destroy the character.

At the beginning of the interaction, the child, Lisa, has the problem of munching multiples of 2, and the undergraduate provides help in determining what numbers are multiples of 2.

UG = undergraduate, L = Lisa
1 UG: Multiples of two.
2 L: (Munches a two, moves two spaces right then munches another two, then moves one more space for a third two.)
3 UG: Yummy (laughs).
4 L: (inaudible)
 UG: Do you? Huh? (inaudible)
5 L: (Skips over an eight and a ten, then munches a two.)
6 UG: Ten, not three, uh oh.
8 L: (Skips over three. Keeps moving her character around the screen.)
 9 UG: OK what else does-- Is ten a factor of two, a multiple of two?
10 L: I don't know.
11 UG: If you multiply five times two, you get ten. So ten is a multiple of two. So you can eat all the tens.
12 L: (Passes over some tens.) Should I eat tens?
13 UG: Yes!
14 L: (Eats a ten.)
15 UG: Uh-oh. Great troggle man is coming!
16 L: (Moves her character away, passing over eights).
17 UG: Do you know how to count by two?
18 L: (Shakes her head from sides to side.)
19 UG: No? OK, well even numbers are multiples of two: so ten and six and eight also. They are all multiples of two.

Although she knows that she is supposed to munch 2s (line 2), Lisa is apparently not orienting to numbers that are multiples of 2, such as 8, 10, and 12 (lines 2, 6, 12, 16). The undergraduate provides help in identifying multiples of two, by first posing a direct question — "Is ten a factor of two, a multiple of two?" (line 9). When Lisa answers that she does not know (line 10), the undergraduate proceeds to provide her with an answer, telling her the numbers that are multiples of 2 (lines 11, 19).

Soon the graduate student intervenes, by suggesting that the undergraduate show her how to count the multiples on her fingers or on a number line, introducing mediating devices to help Lisa understand the concept of multiples rather than just be provided with the correct numbers.

GS = Graduate Student
1 GS: Maybe you can show her on her fingers?
2 UG: OK, that sounds good.
3 GS: Or another suggestion would be to write evens and odds on a piece of paper, like on a number line. But that's a hard one to explain.

With the help of the graduate student, the undergraduate picks up on this strategy, and works with the child on developing it, using the number line and her own fingers to count up to each subsequent multiple.

1 L: (Moves around and munches several threes.) Uhhh.

2 UG: And then, what's three plus three? Do you know what three plus three is?

3 L: No.

4 UG: No, OK. (Orienting to the number line and referencing her open hand) Now one, two, three, four, five, six. And then three more fingers, so three and three is six, right?

5 L: (Nods)

6 UG: So you can eat all the sixes too.

7 L: (Moves around the screen, eating sixes.)

8 UG: Uh-oh, red troggle man.

9 UG: OK now, so what's six plus three? So you have six. (Laying out six fingers.) What's three more? (Lays three more fingers out.) How many is that?

10 L: (Moves her hand and lips, but not counting out loud) Seven.

11 UG: No.

12 GS: Count them all.

13 UG: Eight.

14 GS: Go like this. (Leans across the keyboard toward UG and L and taps UG's fingers.) One, two, three, four, five, six, seven, eight, nine.

15 UG: So can you get all the nines?

The undergraduate breaks down the concept of multiples into an addition problem (line 2) and then starts to perform the additions on her fingers for Lisa (line 4). The undergraduate first tries simply laying out the additional fingers (line 9), but Lisa does not count them correctly (line 10). Then the graduate student intervenes again, suggesting that the undergraduate count up while pointing to her fingers (lines 12, 14).

As they proceed with the game, they start working smoothly with the finger counting strategy and effectively remediate their activity in a way that coordinates successfully with the game environment. They work between the undergraduate's fingers and the game, counting up to each multiple and then munching that number before proceeding to the next. A few moments later, the graduate student intervenes again to suggest that the undergraduate now encourage Lisa to count on her own fingers.

1 UG: OK, now you need to do eight plus four. Now you have eight. (Lays out eight fingers.) Then four more (Lays out one hand and taps her first finger). Nine.

2 L: Ten, eleven, twelve (L begins looking for twelves). Uhh?

3 UG: Hey! There are no twelves in there!

4 GS: Maybe you can gradually have it so that she does it on her own hands. Cause that's, well, closer to memory that way. Besides, her fingers are so cute.

5 UG: (Laughs.) Cute little fingers. OK what's twelve plus four?

6 L: (Puts her hands on her leg.)

7 UG: Now put down four fingers. Right. Yeah. Then count: twelve, thirteen, fourteen, fifteen, and sixteen. So sixteen, that's one six.

The undergraduate lays out her fingers for the next multiple (line 1), and Lisa counts up aloud (line 2). They look for the number in the game and find that there are none (lines 2 and 3). The graduate student then suggests that they take another step in their use of mediating devices and encourages the undergraduate to have Lisa count on her own fingers (line 4).

Through the course of this interaction, an undergraduate who is new to the club is coached by a more experienced adult in strategies for helping a child perform a task and take more and more responsibility for its accomplishment. It is also a nice example of changes in what is shared (both in terms of the common ground and how the work is divided) that affect what the three actors are able to achieve in the end.

At the outset, the graduate student understands the point of the game, the trouble the child is having, and the utility of a finger-counting strategy. The undergraduate starts with an understanding of the first two of these. Then the undergraduate grasps the graduate student's idea and introduced it into the activity using her own fingers. Finally, the undergraduate involves the child (as advised by the graduate student) in appropriating the strategy by shifting over to using the child's own fingers.

The aforementioned case demonstrates how helping strategies are developed and disseminated informally in Fifth Dimension interactions. It also underscores the role of guided appropriation of mediating devices in augmenting children's capabilities. Other case studies (included on the CD and in recent publications of the team) explore the following: (a) the dynamics of novice interaction in the Fifth Dimension (Gack, 1999; Ito, 1997), (b) the use of language and multiple forms of literacy in the club, (c) the compromises between entertainment, fantasy, and educational game content to support learning; and (d) peer interaction and expert-novice interaction.

In each case we analyzed, we looked for patterns in the division of labor in the learning and decision-making tasks and patterns in the joint appropriation of artifacts and problem space. We now turn to a discussion of the organization of the Fifth Dimension research collective as enabling socially shared cognition.

THE RESEARCH COLLECTIVE:
SHARING CORE PRINCIPLES WITHIN AND ACROSS SITES.

The first attempts to generate a list of core principles of the Fifth Dimension model came in Cole's 1986 proposal to the Spencer Foundation. The question driving this work was the well documented failure to thrive of ostensibly successful educational innovations (Cole, 1996). Cole and his colleagues in several states outlined a research program that would apply principles of cultural-historical theory to document and compare the reorganization of activity within context and reorganize relations between contexts in pursuit of a central goal: "creating a new kind of educational activity system which can be taken up and maintained by the community with its own resources. (Cole & Nicolopolou, 1990, p. 1).

The next set of principles appeared in Cole and Nicolopolous (1990) report to the Spencer Foundation summarizing the result of the research from 1986 to 1990. In this document, the researchers' linkages between the idea of sustainability and a pedagogy informed by cultural historical psychology were made clear:

1. To create sustainable systems of educational activity based on a culture of collaborative learning in which play and imagination have a major role;
2. To promote computer literacy and to use computer software to promote cognitive and social skills of 6 to 12-year-old elementary school kids;
3. To make workable models for developing certain forms of community-based, after-school educational activity and a framework for basic research into processes of learning and development;
4. To bring together undergraduates, a site coordinator, special physical space, levels of difficulty, conceptual or physical maze, wizard, and task cards, and to get children involved in their own development; and
5. To create a system of shared rules, undergraduates guiding and facilitating, not directing, a culture of collaborative learning: to feature choice and structure in an impersonal normative system not dependent on individual authority. (pp. 36-42)

Cole and Nicolopolou (1990) noted that the theoretical foundations underpinning this list were drawn from Durkheim, Vygotsky, and Piaget, centering on their shared view that thinking and cognitive development involve participating in forms of social activity constituted by systems of shared rules that have to be grasped and voluntarily accepted (Cole & Nicolopolou, 1990).

Research on Sustainability in Diverse Settings

After the Spencer funding cycle was complete, the Andrew W. Mellon Foundation began to fund a new national configuration of researchers working with the model. Between 1993 and 1996, this group was known as the Distributed Literacy Consortium. The proposal for their research was entitled, "Using new information technologies in the creation of sustainable after-school literacy activities: From invention to maximizing the potential."

We who study sustainability and dissemination hypothesized that differences across Fifth Dimension sites would reflect the mission of a researcher's home institution or departmental affiliation as well as the influence of local norms and values of the target population. Some variations on the model, we assumed, would be harder to sustain than others depending on the types of resources and goals of a particular community. Our assumptions are reflected in the fact that three types of educational institutions were included in the plan. Two large public, two small private, and two midsized state colleges and universities participated, each with researchers based in either departments of education, communication, or psychology. There was also diversity in the types of community settings where the sites were grown. The mix included Boys and Girls Clubs, a YMCA, a church center, and schools.

After several years, we found that success or failure of sites was not caused by the size or type of college, the discipline of the researcher, or the type of community setting per se. We also noted that the researchers' understandings of the model changed over time as they sought to develop their local systems. Each node developed in a unique way.

Through the shared experience of diversity in development, people within and across node partnerships have come to understand in a deeper way what is central to the enterprise they shared at the level of principle: ideal types in philosophy and pedagogy. This has shown up in everything from the researchers' stances on ingredients for sustainability, to their beliefs about what constitutes a successful activity, to how to measure success. All of these issues were partially held in common, acknowledged as salient categories, and expected to vary in conjunction with local constraints.

Barriers to Sustaining the Shared: Short-Term and Long-Term Strategies

Looking across sites, we see common sources of developmental crises: Short-term goals in daily life at the sites require spot decisions, improvisation, technical patches, and unilateral efforts. They typically require the presence of a source of invisible labor (both in the community and in the university) — invisible because this work is done beyond the call of job descriptions and regular duty by whoever happens to be free to help.[2] Examples of this patching abound: At one site, computers are frequently purchased and replaced with grant funds, yet no durable arrangements for repair and maintenance have been established. At another site, students and staff from the university frequently fill in when community centers have not arranged for staff back-up on sick days or in case of emergency.

Whose Ideas Was This Anyway? This patching and filling in demonstrates an ethic of care and teamwork on the part of the research and implementation team. It delays confrontation that would force problems into the open, while keeping alive the organism grafted onto a community setting. To the extent that the researchers and implementers operate the Fifth Dimension on a reactive, daily, crisis-oriented basis, in community settings that are often run the same way, the conversations are delayed that might bring out contradictions and imbalances in the shared ideas and responsibilities of university and community partners. Such conversations might yield a redistribution of investments and resources necessary to keep the activity going in the long haul.

It is often said that changing institutional norms, especially norms that keep institutions and groups from cooperating to share investments and ownership, is a slow process, like turning large ships. As long as grant funds are secured by the university partners and daily problems are solved by the university researchers, or the pedagogy (mixing play and education, artifact design, the role of the wizard) flows from researchers to the community, the long-term sustainability of these adaptations may be undermined. A goal worth striving for in seeking to design culturally diverse activity systems (see Chap. 4, this volume) from the perspective of socially shared cognition, is a consistent investment and sharing of knowledge, initiative, responsibility, and planning for the future.

An Example of Socially Shared Cognition as Research Practice

The following data excerpt illustrates how the assumption that the university partners are in charge of the activity can be challenged through reflective practice and dialogue within implementation teams and between researchers and community members. A community volunteer staffing La Clase Magica, a bilingual, bicultural adaptation of the model, reported a problem with site operation to the project director, via the project listserv:

> Date: Fri, 19 Feb 1999 17:46:51 -0800 (PST)
> From: karla andrade <karlaandrade@yahoo.com
> Subject: conecciones interrumpidas
> To: Mike Cole <mcole@weber.ucsd.edu>
> Cc: LCHC UCSD <xproject@weber.ucsd.edu>
>
> Mike, We had a little problem today at La Clase Magica. We went to the headstart classroom to connect with the "Maga" but the person who was cleaning told us that he was locking up in about thirty minutes and since he couldn't leave us in there by ourselves he didn't let us in. An hour and fifteen minutes later he still hadn't left. Basically, we weren't able to use the computer in there. Lourdes said that in the past the staff would wait until we left at 5:30pm to clean the room. I was wondering if you could please speak to Laurie or Fran because we don't know what's going on and we don't want any problems.
> Muchas Gracias,
> Karla, Lourdes, and Alejandra

Michael Cole replied quickly, inviting his colleague Olga Vasquez, the founding research director of La Clase Magica to respond:

> Date: Fri, 19 Feb 1999 17:52:40 -0800 (PST)
> From: Mike Cole <mcole@weber.ucsd.edu>
> To: karlaandrade@yahoo.com

Subject: Re: conecciones interrumpidas
Cc: xproject@weber.ucsd.edu

Dear LCM friends—

I believe it is really your task to speak to Fran and Laurie. I believe it is a strategic mistake to turn to me to do this task. What do you think, Olga? mike

> Honorine Nocon, a LCHC staff member and graduate student researcher, was reading the exchange and responded as well. Nocon worked for over two years to support the formation of a community coalition to address issues of long-term sustainability, including conflict resolution, funding, space use, and programming issues:

Date: Fri, 19 Feb 1999 21:51:06 -0800 (PST)
From: Honorine Nocon <hnocon@weber.ucsd.edu>
To: karlaandrade@yahoo.com, mcole@weber.ucsd.edu
Subject: Re: conecciones interrumpidas

Hi,
At the last Coalition meeting, when the issue of using the computer in the Head Start classroom was brought up, both Fran and Lori were very hesitant about disrupting the custodian's work. The issue in that discussion was that when the room was made available for use of the computer, kids would come in and be playing, etc. I got this from a tape and don't have details, but...it appears that there are some reasons why Fran and Lori are not supportive. It might be good to present the problem, not assuming that it has to be solved by using the big classroom, and asking their help in finding a solution. They have been, and continue to be, very generous to the program. Honorine

Olva Vasquez contributed to the conversation in Spanish:

Date: Mon, 22 Feb 1999 10:20:33 -0800
To: xproject@weber.ucsd.edu
From: ovasquez@weber.ucsd.edu (Olga Vasquez)
Subject: Re: conecciones interrumpidas
Status: RO

Lourdes, Alejandra y Karla,
    Yo creo que Mike Cole tiene razon, ?Porque le toca a el resolver problemas que le pertenecen al equipo de la clase magica? El tiene el dominio de la quinta dimension para que preocuparse. Mi estratejia como directora de la clase magica en este etapa de la evolucion del projecto hacido de entregar mas la direccion a ustedes. Tengo fe que ust-

edes tienen la capacidad y el poder de instituir los cambios necessarios para que la clase magica funcione de una manera favorable a sus preferencias. Me consultaron cuando la idea de que maga se comunicara desde del bano (bathroom)no dio resultado y hablamos de cambiar la conneccion a otro lado de la mission y la clase de head start fue la mas apropiada. Veo que no dio resultado tampoco que se mencionara en el mitin de la coalicion. Ok, tengo que pensarlo un poco mas pero les urjo que sigan independisandose, buscando remedio dentro los recursos y capacidades del grupo de padres de familia.
Olga

The gist of this message is that Vasquez agreed with Cole that the long-term strategy as she saw it was for site staff to initiate negotiations over the use of space and access. She wanted to think about the issue further but said that ultimately the solution needed to arise from the resources and the abilities of the parents affected by the conflict.

The use of this e-mail data helps illustrate how the parties to the conversation identified the problem as shared and distributed in the particular local history of La Clase Magica. The researchers and staffers tried to form a context-relevant solution in virtual space on the project listserv. Mike, Olga, and Honorine jointly constructed a solution that shifted the situation definition away from one requiring a top-down, individualistic response from the university people, Cole, Vasquez, or Nocon.

Their having a talk with Fran and Laurie, the Head Start staffers, might be an effective intervention but only in the short run. Using the e-mail list forum makes the suggested alternatives public for all members of the project to consider. A redistribution of roles and investments is invited and signaled here by all, especially in the use of Spanish, by Olga. This is the first language of many members of La Clase Magica, and her use of Spanish suggests that a long-term strategy requires the affected people to take up the challenge of institutional politics for themselves.

Developments like those hinted at in the e-mail exchange begin to move the parties involved into a strategy for long-term sustainability that must be negotiated by each node in the consortium. There are recent, promising developments. The formation of coalitions like the one mentioned previously — the Solana Beach Coalition for Community Education — provides a structure for reflective practice for the community members. These can be a resource for building toward a future, like the weekly meetings held by university team members who move between and discuss their university and community roles in running the activity.

The e-mail exchange created a space for questioning the long-standing default assumption that the reflective practice, crisis management, or improvement of La Clase Magica was to be initiated by people from the lab or by Olga. Collectively, the research group and the site staff were able to remember their long-term, shared goal of sustaining the project in an effective bit of socially shared, electronically mediated cognition.

CONCLUSION: SOCIALLY SHARED COGNITION AS A RESOURCE FOR CHANGING THE RELATIVE CONTEXT OF INTERPRETATION OF THE ACT

Similar to the findings from the aforementioned case, we notice in explicit, formalized, reflective statements about core Fifth Dimension principles that our collaborators have confronted and addressed the reality of multiple contexts for interpretations of their actions, interactions, and activities. In some cases, the implementer or the researcher deliberately contributed to the molding of a new context or the location of a new audience for our work by recasting or reordering descriptions of our priorities and principles.

In other cases, the components of a Fifth Dimension came into and out of prominence in a particular setting as it was transforming. These transformations appeared as changes in the context for interpreting the work at hand. Changes in the core principles or understandings about sustainability at one site influence the collective view that development is a change in the relative context.

Both the fact of a division of labor and of something held in common support the ability to shape the relative context in which actions are interpreted. We are able to move up and down in levels of analysis, invoke wider networks of significance, or focus on multiple aspects of the project (research, teaching, service, technology, literacy) because there is so much going on in the Fifth Dimension.

In one sense, then, no list of core principles guiding Fifth Dimension activity can exist independently of the knowledge that the list must change as the site lives, because living things change, and the contexts for their interpretation change even faster. Each researcher and implementation leader makes choices about research designs, funding structures, and the names (e.g., La Cláse Mágica, Club Proteo, Fifth Dimension, Magical Dimension) and contents of their efforts, reflecting the diversity of assumptions and goals they bring to the table.

We talk about family resemblances in comparing attributes of the Fifth Dimension adaptations over time rather than replication or franchising. Across the network of adaptations, members of this collective agree to the utility of certain components or goals in making the programs they run in various community centers recognizable adaptations of the Fifth Dimension. Members also agree to disagree about other aspects of the model or else find it awkward to insist on recommending ideas because of limited local resources or opposition to the ideas.

However, after several years, members of our research collective have clearly persisted in their sharing of several core assumptions about the model system that each has adapted, for example, the use of features such as computer technology, the internet as an organizing force, the mix of play and education, the presence of undergraduates as researchers and helpers at the site, and the use of maze and task cards; these features have endured across time and place.

The two kinds of sharing we discussed earlier in this chapter have a good deal to do with the embrace of difference approach we value for sustainability.   The diversity across the system both in terms of the content of the activity and the different priorities of implementers, researchers, children, parents, undergraduates, and community leaders is an important part of the experience of socially shared cognition.   The way any particular implementation team adapts the Fifth Dimension artifacts and metaphors is intimately bound with the director's teaching and research goals. Ultimately, the fate of the activity truly lies in the cumulative rewards or frustrations that the children, undergraduates, community site hosts, parents, and implementers experience in the Fifth Dimension as compared with other ways they might invest their time and energy for learning.

For the students of sustainability, where someone succeeds, we all are allowed to learn about what is possible and what a particular node has achieved. When a site fails to thrive, we know it could easily be our turn next if we cannot draw lessons from the failure.   This information can help us interpret the experiences of other nodes and reflect upon our own choices.

NOTES

1 The authors of the case study text are Ito, M. Gack, V. McDermott, R. and Greeno, J. Institute for Research on Learning..

2 Honorine Nocon is making a formal study of altruism in community settings and the importance of voluntarism in the dynamics of sustainability for her dissertation.

REFERENCES

Blanton, W., Moorman, G., Hayes, B., & Warner, M. (1997). Effects of Fifth Dimension participation on far transfer. *Journal of Educational Computing Research, 16*(4), 371-397.

Cole, M., & Nicolopolou, A. (1986). Creating sustainable new forms of educational activity in afterschool settings. *Proposal to the Spencer Foundation.*   Lab of Comparative Human Cognition, La Jolla, CA.

Cole, M., & Nicolopolou, A.   (1990) *Annual Report to the Spencer Foundation.* Lab of Comparative Human Cognition, La Jolla, CA.

Cole, M. (1991). Conclusion. In L. Resnick, J. Levine, & S. Teasley (Eds.), *Perspectives on Socially Shared Cognition*(pp. 398-417). Washington, DC: American Psychological Association.

Cole, M. (1996). *Cultural Psychology: A once and future discipline.* Cambridge, MA: Harvard University Press.

Gack, V. (1999). Fantasies of mastery or masteries of fantasy? In G. Smith (Ed.), *On a silver platter: CD-ROMS and the promises of a new technology.* New York: New York University Press.

Gallego, M., Moll, L., Rueda, R. (1997). Report of the language and culture evaluation team. *Annual Report to the Andrew W. Mellon Foundation.* Laboratory of Comparative Human Cognition, La Jolla, CA.

Ito, M. (1998). *An incomplete guide and starter kit for the Fifth Dimension: A CD-ROM.* [CD-ROM]. Produced by Case study by Ito, M. Gack, V. McDermott, R. and Greeno, J. Menlo Park, CA: Institute for Research on Learning.

Ito, M. (1997). *Interactive media for play: Kids, computer games and the production of everyday life.* Unpublished doctoral dissertation. Stanford University, Stanford, CA.

Mayer, R., Quilici, Moreno, R., Duran, R., Woodbridge, S., Simon, R., Sanchez, A., & Lavezzo, A. (1997). Cognitive consequences of participation in a Fifth Dimension after school computer club. *Journal of Educational Computing Research, 16*(4), 353-405.

Schustack, M., Strauss, R., Worden, P. (1997). Learning about technology in a non-instructive environment. *Journal of Educational Computing Research, 16*(4), 337-353.

9

Theory and Practice of Case-Based Learning Aids

Janet L. Kolodner
Georgia Institute of Technology

Mark Guzdial
Georgia Institute of Technology

INTRODUCTION

Case-based reasoning (CBR), inspired by people, was developed as a model for creating intelligent systems — systems that can reason by reference to previous experiences. Such systems, it was said, had the potential to behave more like real experts than did traditional expert systems. Reasoning based on experience would allow intelligent systems more flexibility and less brittleness than rule-based systems, and, with learning from experience built into the architectures, the systems would become more capable over time (Kolodner & Simpson, 1989). Many experimental automated case-based reasoners have been created (see the lists, e.g., in Kolodner, 1993) and, indeed, CBR has proven to be quite a useful technology. More interesting to us, however, are the implications CBR holds as a model of cognition — implications about what it means to be a learner and implications about learning and education.

CBR, as a cognitive model, values the concrete over the abstract (Kolodner, 1993). Whereas most traditional theories of cognition emphasize how general-purpose abstract operators are formed and applied, CBR makes concrete cases, representing experience, primary. CBR suggests that individuals think in terms of cases — interpretations of their experiences that are applied to new situations. To find the milk in a supermarket I have never been in, for example, I walk around the perimeter of the store until I reach the dairy section. Why? Because the dairy section of the supermarket I usually shop in is located in the perimeter. When I throw a ball in the air, I expect it to come down because that is what I have always seen before. When I do strategic planning for my organization, I recall previous situations strategies and tactics and pitfalls. When I plan a dinner party, I consult menus I have served before; I may even serve the same meal I served another time if it worked well and different guests are invited this time.

CBR also helps researchers understand how individuals develop expertise and how an expert uses his or her own experiences and those of others to reason and learn. Consider, for example, an architect designing an office building. He or she calls on his or her experiences and those of others who have designed buildings that address similar needs in order to make decisions about how to proceed. He or she knows that many modern office buildings have atriums. Should this new building have an atrium? To answer that, he or she first looks at the reasons for including atriums in those buildings. In some, it was to provide light to inside offices, in others, to provide a friendly informal space to meet. Are those goals in the new design? They are, but the architect wonders whether the noise of a central meeting space might be problematic. He or she examines those buildings again, looking at the effects of the atriums on use of the offices. Indeed, some did cause too much noise, but others were quite successful. Why did some succeed and some fail? The architect looks at the reasons for failures. Will they be present in the new building? If so, is there a way to avoid the failure by doing it another way (perhaps suggested by one of the successful atria), or should an atrium not be used?

As a theory of learning, CBR has much in common with constructivism: Both claim that an individual builds his/her knowledge for him/herself from experience. Both see learning as active; the learner plays an intentional role in deciding what to learn and in going about the activities of learning. CBR also has much in common with constructionism (an approach to education): both approaches value learning from concrete experiences and the interpretations of the individual. But case-based reasoning goes further than both constructivism and constructionism; it defines a model of cognition (including processes and knowledge structures) that can be turned to for advice and predictions and that can be simulated on a computer as a test of ideas. Like constructivism and constructionism, case-based reasoning has lessons for the teacher and for the designer of technological learning aids. CBR makes suggestions about how to orchestrate and facilitate students' experiences so that they can draw productive lessons from them and makes suggestions about how to encourage transfer so that lessons learned might be applied in more than one situation. It suggests help students might need so that they can turn their experiences into accessible and easily reusable cases in their memories.

In this chapter, we first review CBR as a model of cognition and describe its critical features. Then, we present its implications for supporting learning with and without technology. Finally, we review some examples from the research community of applying the lessons of CBR to promote learning.

CASE-BASED REASONING AS A MODEL OF COGNITION

CBR explicitly integrates memory, learning, and reasoning. A reasoner, it says, is a being in the world that has goals. The being seeks to navigate its world in such a way that its goals are successfully achieved. It has experiences, some of them successful and some not as successful, some pleasant and some not so pleasant, that allow it to learn about its environment and ways of using that environment to achieve its goals. As it has experiences, it seeks to learn the skills and concepts that allow it to achieve its goals more productively in the future. It is engaged, therefore, in recording its experiences, interpreting its experiences to derive lessons useful to its future, anticipating when those lessons might be useful, and labeling its experiences appropriately so that it will be able to recognize the applicability of an experience in a later situation. A case-based reasoner is also engaged in noticing the similarities and differences between similar situations and experiences so that it can draw conclusions about its world and notice the subtle differences that suggest when each of the lessons it has learned is most appropriately applicable. Essential to its learning is failure — it needs to attempt to apply what it thinks is relevant and fail at that in order to know to focus its attentions on subtleties of which it had not previously been aware.

CBR suggests three components of cognition that we focus on: cases, case indexes, and the case processor.

Cases

Cases are interpretations of experiences. Cases have several subcomponents just as stories do: the setting, the actors and their goals, a sequence of events, results, and explanations linking results to goals and the means of achieving them. The better the interpretations of each of these pieces, and the better the explanations linking them to each other, the more useful a case will be when it is remembered later. For example, if it is known that a plan carried out in a case failed, an individual can wonder whether it might fail again in a similar situation, but he or she cannot make predictions. If, on the other hand, what caused the failure is known, he or she can check to see if the conditions that led to failure are present in the new situation. If they are, failure can be predicted; if not, the old plan might be reused.

The explanations that tie pieces of a case together allow individuals to derive lessons that can be learned from the case — its lessons learned. For example, if I unknowingly served fish to vegetarians, and they did not eat, I might explain the failure as due to my not having inquired about whether any of my guests were vegetarians or had special eating requirements. The lesson learned is that I should make those inquiries whenever I invite guests for dinner. On recall of a case, the lessons an individual has derived from it are available for application to the new situation, as are the explanations from which those lessons were derived.

Cases reside in an individual's memory, and the set of cases in any individual's memory is referred to as his or her case library or library of cases. Cases in an individual's case library might be derived from his or her own experiences or from the experiences of others. For example, one might read about someone else's experience and remember its lessons to apply in the future. In general, his or her own cases will be more embellished, but the cases of others play a very important role in learning and reasoning, filling in where his or her own experience is deficient.

Case Indexes

A library is as good as the indexes and indexing scheme available for locating something in the library. So too with an individual's case library. People can find the right cases in their memories if they "indexed" them well when they entered the cases into the library and if the indexing scheme is well enough defined that they can recreate an index for an appropriate case when trying to locate something in memory. If the reasoner cannot recognize a past experience as being applicable in a new situation, he or she will have no case to apply.

A good indexing scheme for a case-based reasoner allows the reasoner to see a past situation as relevant to the current one. Thus, a case's indexes should allow individuals to find it at times when it might be productive to apply. Good indexes are critical for transfer, the ability to apply knowledge or skills derived in one kind of situation to a situation that might be quite a bit different.

The best indexing results from anticipating the circumstances when a lesson learned from a case might be useful and marking the case so that it will be recalled in such circumstances. For example, if I index the case where vegetarians did not eat the fish I served under serving fish as the main course of a dinner party, I will be reminded of that case each time I plan to serve fish at a dinner party. Remembering the case reminds me to apply the lesson it teaches: Ask guests if they have any special eating requirements. Or, I might index the case more specifically under having a dinner party, allowing me to be reminded that I ought to ask guests for their eating requirements even before I begin planning dinner.

It is important to keep in mind, though, that it is almost always impossible to identify every lesson an experience might teach and every situation in which it might be applicable. It is common to have an experience that an individual does not completely understand or appreciate until much later — sometimes because he or she is lacking the knowledge necessary to interpret it, sometimes because one is lacking the experience to know whether a result is positive or negative, sometimes for other reasons. An individual might recognize that his or her understanding is incomplete at the time of experience or may only come to realize that his or her understanding was incomplete when attempting to use the case later and finding that its application led to poor results. Either way, indexing is incomplete.

But incomplete indexing does not have to mean that cases are inaccessible if the reasoner engages in situation assessment at the time he or she or it is trying to address a new situation. Situation assessment is a process of analyzing a new situation so as to understand it better. An individual attempts to infer unknown details of a new situation or to look at the situation from several different perspectives. This interpretation process allows the reasoner to construct a better description of the new situation than he or she has available. Though the description is hypothetical, it plays a critical role in reasoning: The hypothetical interpretation of the new situation serves as an index that allows old cases to be recalled. One way to look at situation assessment is as a process of imagining, "If I had encountered a situation like this in the past, what would it have looked like, and how would it have been described?"

Neither does a poor index at the time an individual encounters or experiences a situation mean that the situation can never be well described as a case or well indexed. Situation assessment allows a reasoner to remember a case that was not well indexed. If, after a case is recalled and used, the reasoner is better able to interpret it, he or she or it might extract new lessons from the case or identify something critical about it, reinterpret the case, and update the indexes associated with it at that time.

The Case Processor

The case processor has a variety of responsibilities. It carries out the processing that results in understanding and indexing an individual's experiences, finding appropriate cases in memory, applying them in a new situation, and learning for example,

- interpreting a new situation in such a way that relevant cases can be located in the case library;

- deciding which of the old cases that are remembered is most applicable;
- applying the lessons learned from an old case to the new situation: for example, decomposing and recomposing pieces of old cases to create a new solution, adapting an old solution to fit a new situation, or choosing a strategy for moving forward;
- noticing results and explaining the reasons some scheme did or did not work;
- structuring an experience as a case and choosing ways of indexing it; and, when necessary,
- reinterpreting and reindexing an old case in light of new findings (e.g., derived by applying its lessons learned and finding that they did not work as expected).

Each of these is important to productive use of cases for reasoning and learning.

CBR has been explored for many years in artificial intelligence as a way of creating more intelligent computer software. A variety of the experimental case-based reasoners that the community has designed serve as the basis for CBR's cognitive model. The earliest case-based reasoner was CYRUS (Kolodner, 1983a, 1983b), a case library that knew about the life of statesman Cyrus Vance[1]. When CYRUS was asked a question, it would answer by constructing a model of what the answer was likely to look like and then searching its memory for a matching case (a process of reconstructing the stories it held in its memory). Sometimes it did not find a case but rather answered questions by using this construction process to construct plausible stories. It was the first attempt to deal with indexing and management of a case library. Early CBR systems, such as MEDIATOR (Kolodner & Simpson, 1989), CHEF, and JULIA (Kolodner, 1993), showed researchers many of the processes involved in reasoning with cases. CHEF, which created recipes (plans for cooking), taught much about the role of failure in learning and the role cases can play in helping individuals anticipate pitfalls as they are reasoning. A later system, called CELIA (Redmond, 1992), modeled the troubleshooting and learning of an apprentice mechanic. From CELIA, researchers learned about the powerful role cases can play before an individual has a full understanding of a domain and how important it is for a reasoner to have a variety of similar experiences so as to be able to extract the subtleties and nuances of the lessons and when each applies. Still later reasoners, such as Creative-JULIA and ALEX, showed the role of CBR in creativity. The lesson from those models is that the quality of an individual's explorations before giving up on an idea, anticipation of the circumstances in which he or she might go back to it, immersing him or herself in an environment where he or she is likely to come on such circumstances, and willingness to try, fail, and explain, are essential to reasoning that goes beyond the obvious.

Those schooled in traditional models of cognition will notice that CBR puts little explicit emphasis on abstract operators in the mind. There is no hierarchy of production rules, nor do we discuss networks of neuron-like components. Rather, we emphasize concrete experience in the form of stories that can be manipulated directly. CBR in many ways corresponds to our own introspection on how individuals think — in terms of stories and experiences. However, CBR does not exclude abstractions altogether. Rather, it places abstraction in roles that promote productive use of concrete experience: for organizing similar cases in the case library so that individuals can choose one or a small number from the category from which to reason, for creation of an indexing vocabulary, and for managing partial matching — to allow the reasoner to recognize that two things that are similar but not identical are a close enough match. Abstractions are extracted from concrete experience and formed as needed.

More detail about CBR and early case-based reasoners can be found in Kolodner (1993), more detail about CBR as a cognitive model from Kolodner (1993, 1997), and more detail about CBR's implications for learning and education from Kolodner (1997), Kolodner Crismond, Gray, Holbrook, & Puntambecker (1998), and Schank (in press).

CBR'S IMPLICATIONS FOR SUPPORTING LEARNING

CBR shares much with constructivism and constructionism. Both claim that what individuals learn is consciously constructed from their own concrete experiences. Constructionism goes on to say that experiences of actively constructing an artifact are particularly good for learning. Thus, CBR shares much with constructivism and constructionism in terms of its approach to supporting learning. Like both of those, it begins by suggesting that instructors create environments that promote the kinds of hands-on experiences and active construction that lead to good learning.

But CBR goes farther. It looks to its cognitive model to provide explanations for how learning happens and, from there, begins to make suggestions about how to ensure that active construction has the results it affords. CBR suggests a form for what individuals store in memory about their experiences and the kinds of reflection that are effective for being able to reuse those experiences, suggesting several critical processes that promote good transfer.

In particular, CBR suggests five important facilitators for learning effectively from hands-on activities: having the kinds of experiences that afford learning what needs to be learned; interpreting those experiences so as to recognize what can be learned from them, drawing connections between their parts so as to transform them into useful cases, and extracting lessons that might be applied elsewhere; anticipating their usefulness so as to be able to develop indices for these cases that will allow their applicability to be recognized in the future; experiencing failure of an individual's conceptions to work as expected, explaining those failures, and trying again (iteration); and learning to use cases effectively to reason.

With respect to what the right kinds of experiences are, CBR suggests that they be experiences that afford concrete, authentic, and timely feedback so that learners have the opportunity to confront their conceptions and identify what they still need to learn and that learners have the opportunity to iteratively move toward better and better development of the skills and concepts they are learning so as to experience them in a range of situations and under a variety of conditions.

CBR's suggestions about promoting learning have informed two forms of learning supports:

- Supports for reflection. Prompts and other guidance for learners aimed at promoting productive reflection.
- Case libraries as a resource. Collections of cases and experiences that can act as external memory for a reasoner.

CBR-Informed Supports for Reflection

It has been since the late 1980s that Collins and Brown (1988) first suggested that the computer could be used to support reflection. In that first conceptualization, the emphasis was on skills and process learning. Collins and Brown talked about capturing an expert's process, then allowing the student to compare his or her process to that of the expert. The computer's role was to record the expert's reasoning, making it available whenever it could be useful and to whoever needed it. In this way, the computer was supporting a kind of reflection that was difficult to do without a computer.

More recent supports for reflection have emphasized the use of design journals as a way of getting students to reflect on their plans and past experiences. In Harel's (1991) Instructional Software Design Project (ISDP), the only daily requirement for students was that they had to write down what they did each day and what they planned to do the next. The hope was that they would articulate how they did things and what they were learning.

Collins and Brown's work has also been used as the basis for supporting reflection during reasoning or during project activity. KIE (Bell, Davis, & Linn, 1995) prompts students to think about evidence and its uses as they are creating a scientific argument. Reciprocal teaching helps students recognize the questions they need to ask themselves as they are trying to understand something they are reading. CSILE (Scardamalia, Bereiter, & Lamon, 1994) prompts students to think about actions and their discussion as they are having knowledge-building conversations.

Reflection is an important component of learning, and each of these approaches looks to some difficult-to-learn skill and helps students reflect in a way that helps them learn the skill or looks to some important time for reflection and prompts students to reflect at that time.

CBR allows individuals to go the next steps. Because it makes explicit the role of reflection in learning, it allows individuals to understand the kinds of reflection that are productive at different times and to understand what the results of those reflections should be. In particular, CBR emphasizes that reflection is critical for (a) interpreting an experience to connect its pieces together and extract what might be learned from it, (b) creating indexes, and (c) creating and evaluating solutions. In other words, CBR tells us that (as researchers) we should help learners understand their experiences in ways that help them describe and index the experiences well so as to be able to use them well later (Kolodner, Hmelo, & Narayanan, 1996). We should also help students reuse their experiences productively and in ways that help them gain better understanding of the experiences they are using.

CBR-inspired support for reflection encourages students to think about the kinds of difficulties they have faced in solving a problem or developing a skill or achieving a design challenge, the kinds of solutions they constructed, and the future situations in which the solutions might be used again, focusing particularly on how the lessons learned from an experience might be utilized in new ways. For example,

Turns' "reflective learner" (Turns, Newstetter, Allen, & Mistree, 1997) helps students write learning essays about their design experiences. Puntambekar described good results with paper-based, CBR-informed design journals (Puntambekar, Nagel, Hübscher, Guzdial, & Kolodner, 1997) in which students keep records of their design experiences.

Motivating students to reflect is a critical issue in learning, and the computer provides a motivation that children find compelling. For example, Shabo's JavaCAP (Shabo, Nagel, Guzdial, & Kolodner, 1997) and its successor, Kolodner and Nagel's Storyboard Author (1999), help students summarize hands-on learning-from-design experiences and write them up as stories for publication in a permanently accessible case library for use by other students. The networked computer creates motivation for the students' reflection: Students enhance their own learning as they are trying to write summaries that can act as guides and supports to future students.

Nagel and Kolodner's Design Discussion(1999) uses the computer similarly to encourage reflection during hands-on activities. It provides a forum for students to share their ideas with others, to get advice and criticism from others, and to provide advice and criticism to others. Students write up the results of experiments they have done, ideas about achieving design challenges or solving problems they are working on, or what happened when they constructed and tested a design idea. They publish it for others to see. The computer prompts students to include relevant information in their write-ups. Publishing their materials makes it available to others to incorporate into their solutions. Reading the ideas of others gives them ideas. Commenting on others' ideas requires consideration of how the ideas of others work. Comments from others encourage deeper thought about the implications of their own ideas.

There are several challenges to creating good CBR-informed supports for reflection:

- **Motivating reflection:** Reflection is hard to do and offers few extrinsic rewards. Motivating good reflection is a real challenge.
- **Generating feedback:** Computer-based supports for reflection can rarely respond intelligently to a students' reflection. In work such as Shabo's, collaborative discussion areas can generate feedback on the students' reflections, but this kind of feedback will necessarily occur after the reflection is complete and is dependent on the quality of the discussants.
- **Encouraging quality reflection:** Reflection is hard to do, but easy to fake, that is, generate text that sounds reflective but really is not (Ng & Bereiter, 1995). Encouraging students to reflect about things that can lead to better learning is hard to prompt and structure.
- **Not overdoing it:** Periodic reflection while attempting to solve a problem or understand a situation is productive, as is summative reflection when one is finished. It is easy to identify times when reflection would be productive, but it is also easy to overdo it — to try to force reflection at times when it interferes with other reasoning or so often that it becomes a hated activity. Instructors need to find that happy medium — a way of promoting reflection at productive times and without damaging a train of thought.

Supporting Learning With Case Libraries

The most common place where CBR has influenced learning tools is in the creation of case libraries. A case library offers the opportunity for students to learn from others' experiences. And, as implied previously, a case library offers students the opportunity to learn by sharing their own experiences with others.

Case libraries can offer a variety of different kinds of information of value to learners:

- *Advice in the form of stories:* When individuals first think about case libraries, they normally think of stories — from experts, from peers, from people in unusual situations. Stories about success are valuable for the advice they give about how to proceed or what strategies to use. Stories about failure provide advice about what to avoid or issues to focus on. Stories can also provide the basis for predicting what might happen if an individual tries out his or her solution. Valuable stories are those that help a student understand a situation, the solution that was derived and why it was derived, and what happened as a result, as well as the explanations that tie those pieces together. Stories might be presented in a variety of media; the important thing is to present them in ways that make their points, or lessons that can be learned from them, most clear. Also important is that stories be indexed in ways that anticipate their use. That is, the indexer needs to think about the ways the case library will be used and the questions with which a user might come to the case library. He or she indexes stories so that it will be easy to find those that address the rele's J questions (Kolodner, 1993).

- *Vicarious experience using a concept or skill:* We know that it takes several encounters with a concept or skill to learn it well (Redmond, 1992) — encounters that cover the range of applicability of the concept or skill allow the learner to see its varied uses, the other concepts or skills it is related to, and to debug its applicability and refine its definition. aKolodner Storyboard Authorot time in school for students to actively experience the full range of applicability of a concept. Sharing experiences with other students or looking at the ways experts applied concepts and skills can fill those gaps. In Learning by Design (Kolodner et al., 1998), such sharing is built into the system of activities students do in class in three ways — students engage in "gallery walks," sharing their design experiences with each other several times in the course of every design challenge they engage in; students use DDA (Kolodner & Nagel, 1999) to write up their design experiences after in-class gallery walks to share across classes; and students write up what they have learned at the end of a unit (using StoryBoard Author), and the best are put it in an archive (Peer Publications) for students in following years. In all of these instances, students have the opportunity both to present their work and to engage in discussion with other students about it — they clarify for others, answer questions about why they did things a certain way, and then entertain suggestions about how to improve their designs.

- *The lay of the domain and guidance on what to focus on*: An on-line case library's indexing system, if it is available for examination, can serve as an advanced organizer for the student or even scaffolding for how the student might think about his or her own cases (Spiro, Feltovich, Jacobson, & Coulson,

1991). For example, the system of indexes in ARCHIE, which helped architectural students design libraries, helped students develop an understanding of the issues that need to be addressed in designing libraries, the kinds of spaces libraries have, and the perspectives different kinds of library users might take on how well it functions. In this role, the case library's indexing system provides a view of the domain's major concepts and their relationships and guidance on what to focus on when designing or solving problems.

- *Strategies and procedures:* Sometimes what is most valuable about a story is not the solution itself but the strategies employed or even just the starting point. For novices in a domain, the biggest problem is sometimes how to start (Guzdial, 1991) — what is the first thing to do or to try or to explore? In many models of design, simply the definition of the problem is the most challenging aspect (Schon, 1982). Cases that describe someone's problem-solving or design process can show how others have defined problems and proceeded through to a solution.

- *How to use cases:* Learning about others' experiences in such a way that learners can reuse the lessons learned in novel situations is a complex meta-cognitive activity (Silver, Branca, & Adams, 1980). Cases that are about applying someone else's case can help students understand how experts reuse cases. Case libraries that prompt for the kinds of analysis that is necessary in deciding whether a case is relevant and how to adapt it for reuse can help learners develop case-based reasoning skills.

The context in which case libraries are used is critical to their effectiveness. Case libraries have proven most useful as a resource that provides information as needed while students are engaged in constructive learning activities. In a project-based learning situation, a case library may provide guidance for getting started, for moving forward, and so on — if its cases answer the project-related issues that arise as students are working on a project. In a problem-based learning (Barrows, 1986) situation or in a learning-from-design situation (Kolodner, 1997), cases can provide those same benefits. But in a more traditional lecture-based or fact-based classroom, cases may not be useful or may even be ignored by the students.

For cases to be a useful resource to students, the students must be engaged in an activity where their impasses might be answered by cases in the case library. If the students are simply memorizing facts, then the challenges that the students face (e.g., learning to memorize a particularly complicated fact) will not lead them to utilize a case library. However, if students are facing challenges that arise naturally in problem-solving (e.g., "How do I model a situation like this?" or "What is a good starting point for this kind of problem?"), then a case library of relevant situations and problems can help them address those impasses.

Building case libraries can be as valuable educationally as using case libraries, as suggested previously, and sometimes even more valuable than simple use. A finding from one of the earliest case libraries explicitly designed for learning was that the graduate students who were building the case library seemed to be learning as much or more than the students who were using the case library in their design work (Zimring, Do, Domeshek, & Kolodner, 1995). Students building a case library explicitly have to deal with issues of identifying appropriate indices, identifying strategies and process elements, and decomposing the case for others to use. By making these activities explicit, instructors help induce learning goals for the student that are appropriate for generating transferable knowledge (Ram & Leake, 1995). The activity of building a case library is frequently motivating for students because it is creating a public artifact with the purpose of helping future students. This is the same kind of motivating activity that Harel and other constructionists have been building on (Harel & Papert, 1990; Papert, 1991). Cognitively, the need to explain to others in a way that allow them to understand requires reflecting on a situation, sorting out its complexities, making connections between its parts, and organizing what an individual has to say into coherent and memorable chunks. Story telling aids sense making and remembering (Schank, 1982).

Case libraries can be a particularly rich source for educational content and process. As a content, case libraries offer resources for students to study and to use in actual problem-solving activity. As a process, case libraries offer opportunities for students to articulate knowledge and reflect on their experiences in a way that other hands-on activities do not usually provide.

EXAMPLES OF CBR-INFORMED LEARNING SUPPORTS

Case-based reasoning and case libraries have a rich research history, but educational applications of CBR are relatively new and still relatively few. We select a few projects and describe them in the following to provide concrete examples of how CBR can inform the creation of learning supports.

Reflective Learner

Students in project-based design courses face a huge number of challenges as part of their learning. They have to design while they are learning about design, using theory and engineering principles that they may have just learned a term before (Turns, Guzdial, Mistree, Allen, & Rosen, 1995). Often, they are working in groups, so they also have to deal with issues of collaborative work (Turns, Mistree et al., 1995b).

What Turns discovered in her ethnographic studies of students in engineering design courses was that students often did not even know what they were supposed to be learning, why they were engaging in the activities they were being asked to engage in, and worse yet, how to reflect upon their activities in order to learn from them (Turns et al., 1997). She decided to build a support for learning that directly addressed the issue of reflection.

Her tool, the Reflective Learner, supports students in producing learning essays about their experiences. The requirement for the students to write learning essays already existed in the engineering design class that she chose to study. However, the unsupported learning essays were not particularly satisfying to the teacher or students. Students still seemed confused about why they were doing what they were being asked to do.

The Reflective Learner provided scaffolding in the form of prompts to help students write learning essays in a more effective manner. Her prompts were informed by CBR. She explicitly asked students

- to identify and describe a problem that they had encountered when undertaking the current phase of their design project
- to describe their solution to the problem
- to state what they had learned from the experience, and
- to anticipate the kinds of situations where a similar solution might be useful.

Her interviews and discussions with students suggest that they found this activity useful and that it helped them to understand why they were doing what they were doing.

Archie and Descendants

Archie-2 (Zimring et al., 1995) was originally created as a case-based design aid for professional architects. Its cases describe public buildings, focusing on libraries and courthouses. The intent was that as an architect was working on the design of a public building, he or she could consult Archie periodically for advice. To get started, the architect would use Archie-2 much as architects now use file cabinets, architectural journals, and the library — to find projects similar in intent to the new one and to see how others had handled the issues. We thought an architect would browse Archie's library, looking briefly to see what issues other architects had addressed and how they had addressed them. An architect designing courthouses would browse the courthouses; one designing libraries would browse the libraries. Later, while addressing a particular issue (e.g., placement of the children's section in a library, lighting reading areas, access to management), the architect, we thought, would go back to Archie-2 again, this time focusing on that particular issue.

To insure that such access could happen easily, we needed to structure cases for easy usability and accessibility. Usability was an issue because the cases we were dealing with were very large (whole public buildings). We could not simply present to users a case in all of its complexity and expect them to be able to easily use it. Rather, we needed users to be able to examine the case in parts. The big issues, then, became how to divide a large complex case into easily usable parts, how to provide a map of a case that would provide a big picture of the case and a map to its parts, and how to provide access to a case's parts. We divided cases into parts, called snippets or stories, based on a physical and functional breakdown of the artifact coupled with an issue that was addressed with respect to that component and for which there was an interesting solution. One of our library cases, for example, had stories associated with it about placement of the children's space, lighting in the check-out area, way-finding, placement of bathrooms, and so on. Cases had tens of stories associated with them, each indexed by a relevant component of the artifact and the issue it addressed. We found we had to provide several different maps of each case, as there were many different ways of thinking about a case.

Easy accessibility had several parts to it: We wanted users to be able to ask for and then browse all cases of a kind (e.g., library, courthouse); We wanted users to be able to ask for and then browse all snippets of cases that addressed the same issues (e.g., way-finding, placement of children's area); From a case, we wanted users to be able to examine stories that were all about how a particular physical area or functional system was being handled.

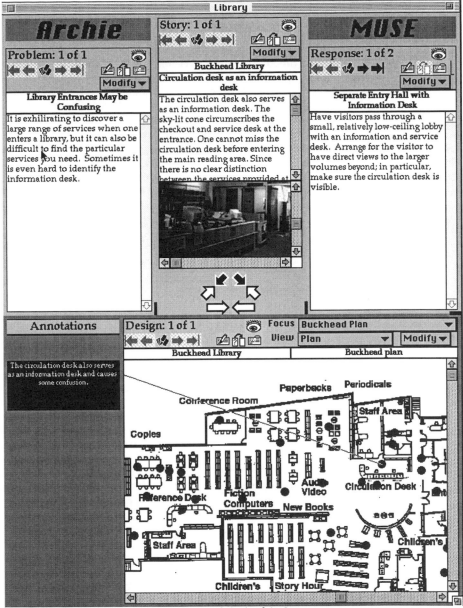

Figure 9.1 Archie 2.

It was hard to gather enough cases to make Archie-2 useful to practicing architects, but architecture faculty told us that its cases would be useful to students working on design projects. We completed the case library of public libraries and made Archie-2 available to students in an architectural design studio who had the assignment of designing public libraries. Indeed, once they learned how to navigate Archie-2's case library, they found it quite useful. It provided issues to focus on as well as suggestions. But, Archie-2's case library, as we had created it, was really only useful for assignments of library design or courthouse design (later prison design), and it was quite time consuming to collect and format all the data necessary to build additional case libraries.

Luckily, another faculty member in the College of Architecture had an idea about how to build case libraries easily. A teacher of industrial design, he wanted to create a case library for learning about industrial design — in particular, the design of simple mechanical appliances. He was teaching two classes — a lower-level (freshman) one where students were examining and evaluating such devices and a higher level (junior) one where students were doing design. He had the students in the lower level class record their descriptions and evaluations in a case library, using ARCHIE-2's case-authoring tool, called Design Muse. He was quite happy with the depth of what students in the lower-level course learned and also quite happy with the way students in the design course used the case library.

Since then, Design Muse has been used to create libraries of skyscrapers, and Archie-2 has been rewritten to be far simpler to use. It has been used extensively in architecture studios at Georgia Tech (Zimring et al., 1995).

Goal-Based Scenarios

One of the originators of CBR is Schank. In his work on learning supports, he has been applying the lessons of CBR to creating a new kind of learning environment called a *goal-based scenario* (Schank, Fano, Bell, & Jona, 1994).

Key to Schank's vision of learning is that motivation is a critical aspect of learning. Basing his claims on the cognitive model implied by CBR, he claims that unless students have a reason for wanting to learn or do something, nothing that anyone wants them to learn will make sense to them. Further, until a student fails (reaches an impasse) at something, Schank (1982) believed that they have no reason to question what they are doing and therefore no reason to want to learn anything new. For example, case libraries play a significant role in a goal-based scenario, but setting up the context of use so that students have a reason to want to use the case library and a context for understanding what it is offering is as important as creating the content of the case library itself.

A goal-based scenario is a learning environment that places students in a situation where they have to achieve some interesting goal that requires them to learn whatever is in the curriculum goals. In one goal-based scenario, for example, students play the role of advisors to the President in dealing with a hostage situation in a foreign land (Bareiss & Beckwith, 1993), in the process learning about several hostage-taking events that have happened in history and also learning some foreign policy. In another, students advise couples about their risk of having children with sickle-cell anemia (Schank, Fano, Bell, & Jona, 1994), in the process learning about genetics in the context of sickle-cell disease. Using Broadcast News, students put together a news story, in the process learning both history and writing skills. Students learn about history or genetics or writing because they need to learn those things to successfully achieve the challenge set for them. The trick, of course, is to design challenges that both engage the students and focus them on the content and skills instructors want them to learn.

The student engaged in a goal-based scenario is provided with a case library of videos of experts telling their stories, strategies, and perspectives that might help him or her with the task. When the student reaches an impasse in achieving the goal, he or she asks a question of the case library, and an appropriate video is retrieved and shown. Sometimes a story suggests a topic he or she should learn more about or a skill he or she needs to learn; other times it will tell how that expert dealt with some difficult issue the student is addressing. Students are in a situation where the case library is relevant for their impasses. The goal-based scenario inculcates in the students the goals that lead them to want and know how to use the recorded experiences of others.

Based on suggestions made by the case library, students move forward with their task — choosing a policy to recommend to the President, choosing a blood test, making a recommendation to a couple about whether they should have children, or deciding how to refer to a leader. In all goal-based scenarios, there are clear right answers to each small task they are working on, and the software can detect when the students have selected the wrong answer. The software takes on as an additional role clearly informing students when they have failed at their task.

This provides a second context for a case use: recognizing, explaining, and recovering from failure. A goal-based scenario indexes stories not only by content, but on the ability to explain why a student's action failed and how to recover. A story told to the student after a failure can successfully lead to learning because the student is in a context where he or she needs the story.

Case libraries used in a goal-based scenario have indexing focused very tightly on the context in which a retrieved case will be used — what task is the student working on? What is his or her solution in progress? What difficulty is the student having? What poor answer has the student settled on? Indexes are chosen for cases in the case library by anticipating the situations in which a student will want to hear a story. By focusing indexing on the learner's goals, these case libraries are more than simple case libraries; they can act as true supports for learning.

Research papers by Schank and his students reported more details of how the cases in a goal-based scenario should be organized and accessed (Bareiss & Osgood, 1993; Ferguson, Bareiss, Birnbaum, & Osgood, 1992). Most critical to keep in mind is that the design of a goal-based scenario requires anticipating learner's goals when working on a challenge. This, in turn, requires anticipating the tasks students will carry out, the avenues of thought and strategies they will pursue, and the kinds of choices they will make. By using a student's tasks to promote goals students will pursue, the designer of a goal-based scenario can anticipate the kinds of impasses students will encounter and therefore the kinds of stories the case library needs to include and the ways those stories ought to be indexed for easy access.

STABLE

Goal-based scenarios are more difficult to build if the learning goal for the student is a design challenge. There is no single correct solution to a design challenge, and even defining a space of correct solutions is very difficult in most design fields. The goal-based scenario approach of presenting a story at the point of failure becomes nearly impossible because it is impossible to anticipate all failures and because failure is often nearly impossible to determine.

One way around this is to build more general case libraries that are indexed by the kinds of issues that arise in design tasks of some type and by the kinds of failures and judgment errors that are known to occur with frequency. This is essentially what we did with Archie-2 — we designed a case library about courthouses and public libraries that was indexed by the kinds of architectural issues that arise in designing courthouses and libraries and the kinds of failures experts in the field have encountered. The case library cannot anticipate all errors that students might make, but it can provide reasonable guidance for design.

THE SmallTalk Apprenticeship-Based Learning Environment (STABLE) is a descendent of Archie-2 that was designed to help students learn the skills involved in performing object-oriented design and programming (see Fig. 9.2). Whereas Archie-2 focused on helping students make design decisions, STABLE went the next steps in helping students learn design and programming skills. STABLE uses a Web-based (hypermedia) collection of cases made from previous students' work. Students using STABLE were learning object-oriented design and programming in a required computer science course. The problems that the students were asked to solve were related to the cases in STABLE at varying levels. For example, students were asked to create a spreadsheet that accepted functions for cell entries, and a spreadsheet that did not accept generic functions was already in STABLE. Students were asked to create a discrete event simulation of a subway system with multiple possible routes, and STABLE contained several solutions to a simulation problem involving a bus system on a single basic route.

Because STABLE's intent was to support skill learning, its was based on theories of apprenticeship learning (Collins, Brown, & Newman, 1989). In apprenticeship learning, a student attempts problems under the supervision and coaching of a master in the domain. The master uses a variety of methods to help the student learn. These methods are often referred to as scaffolding. For example, the master might model the process for the student but be cautious in telling the student too much. Later, the master might ask leading questions to help the student focus. In successful apprenticeship learning, the master answers questions but does not explicitly volunteer rationale for his or her actions, in order to encourage the student to generate rationale him or herself (Redmond, 1992). In this way, the master scaffolds or structures the student's learning, encouraging him or her to think for him or herself and solve problems on his or her own.

STABLE was designed to provide a large amount of information but scaffolded in such a way that students were encouraged to think for themselves and only request the information that they needed.

- Each step of a design process was provided at three or more levels of detail. The initial visit to a step was at the least amount of detail (see Figure 9.3).
- Strategy information ("Why was this step done now or in this way?") was available but not initially presented.
- Potential problems and solutions were presented but mostly as links to previous steps. For example, a given step might say, "A problem like this might occur," and "If it does, the cause probably occurred during this step," with a hyperlink provided to the previous step.
- Each step was linked to experts' observations on the case (e.g., "This is an example of a part-whole object relationship"), and the observations were also

linked to other steps in order to provide more concrete examples of an abstract observation.

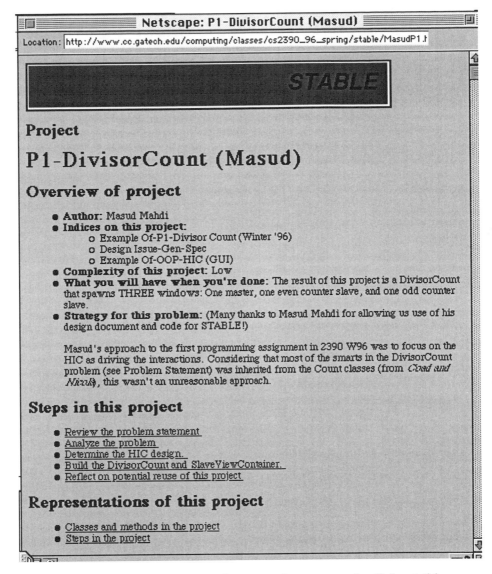

FIG. 9.2 A STABLE project page with steps and representation links visible.

Evaluation of STABLE suggested that it was successful in improving student performance and learning.
- Students were able to solve more complicated problems earlier in the term. We gave students a more complicated version of a problem that had been

attempted in a previous term. Students did solve the problem (explicitly using STABLE), and a coding of the STABLE-using students' problems showed that they were higher quality than the earlier problems.

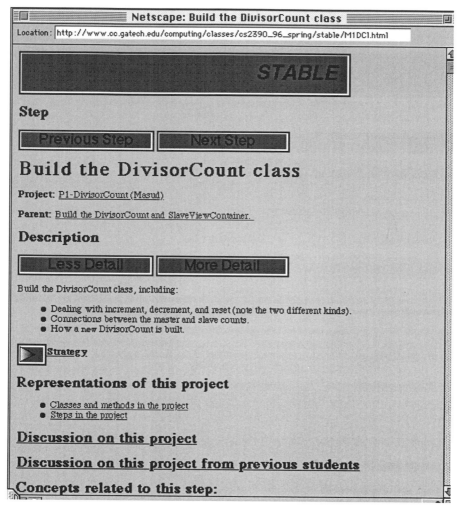

FIG. 9.3 A STABLE step page. Note the ability to increase or decrease the amount of detail on the step, as well as the link to Strategy information.

- Students were able to solve isomorphic design problems on a final exam better than previous students. STABLE-using students were asked to repair a faulty design. The STABLE-using students did better on the repair task than previous students. We believe that these students demonstrated improved design repair skill due to seeing more varied designs (e.g., multiple design solutions for the same problem) than previous students had.

Surprisingly, though, students expressed several complaints about STABLE. From interviews and observation of use, we found that students were identifying cases that they wanted to compare and contrast to each other that were not already connected to each other by hyperlinks, and such comparisons were hard to do. For example, students might become interested in how objects are created and want to look at several examples where objects were created. Or, students might be interested in how a user interface is created in an object-oriented program and thus want to compare how multiple cases implemented user interfaces. STABLE was designed to offer various levels of details about a case. It was not designed to offer much in the way of support for comparing cases, except through experts' observations.

The lesson learned from STABLE was that a case library to support students engaged in design activities can facilitate student learning, be successful in supporting design, and be placed in a curricular setting that creates the relevant context that Schank identified as critical for successful learning from cases. However, STABLE also showed that what students see as relevant is important to determine and may not be always evident. Several iterations of a tool are needed to ensure that all the capabilities that need to be in it for productive use are indeed included. There are open and interesting research questions on what relevance means in a case library context and how to best support it.

Learning by Design and Its Supports for Learning

Like goal-based scenarios, learning by design (LBD; Kolodner, 1997, Kolodner et al., 1998) takes CBR's cognitive model seriously in the design of learning environments. LBD curriculum units give students the opportunity to encounter design challenges as compelling contexts for learning science concepts and skills. Design challenges provide opportunities for engaging in and learning complex cognitive, social, practical, and communication skills. For example, students design parachutes made from coffee filters to learn about air resistance and gravity and their relationship, miniature vehicles and their propulsion systems to learn about forces, motion, and Newton's laws, and ways of managing the erosion on barrier islands to learn about erosion, water currents, and the relationship between people and the environment. Construction and trial of real devices give students the motivation to want to learn, the opportunity to discover what they need to learn, the opportunity to experience uses of science, and the opportunity to test their conceptions and discover the bugs and holes in their knowledge. The teacher helps students reflect on their experiences in ways that help them extract and articulate and keep track of both the content and skills they are learning.

Using guidelines from CBR, we provide libraries of cases to students to use as resources; the kinds of paper-and-pencil and software tools that allow students to keep track of their design experiences so that they can remember what they did and draw lessons from their experiences; a system of classroom activities that help students make contact with their own previous experience and bring it to bear (messing about), help them anticipate what they need to learn more about (whiteboarding), and help them share their ideas with each other ("gallery walks" and pinups); software tools that prompt students to explain their design decisions and design experiences to each other and get feedback from their peers; software tools that prompt students to extract and articulate the content and skills they are learning from their experiences and write them up as stories to share with other students; tools that help students read the cases written by experts and extract from them the science and advice that can help them with their design challenge; and teacher guidelines for facilitating reflective discussions and other activities in ways that help students to turn their experiences into cases — stored in their memories in ways that allow them to remember and apply them in later situations (e.g., helping them identify what they learned, how they learned it, under what conditions it might be applicable, and when such conditions might come up in the future). The tools we provide act as resources, help students create cases for others to use help students keep track of what they have been doing and help students reflect on their experiences and turn them into cases in their own memories. Each tool is used in the context of other classroom activities and discussions that support their use.

Design Challenges as an Approach to Learning. CBR tells instructors that learning requires impasses and expectation failures — to show what individuals do not know, to focus us on what they need to learn, and to motivate individuals to want to learn. This suggests an iterative approach to learning from experience — try to solve a problem or achieve a challenge, use the impasses and failures of expectation to show what needs to be learned, investigate to learn more, and try again. But how to orchestrate failures of expectation? If an individual simply plans solutions, he or she gets no feedback to enable recognition of failures. CBR suggests that the best learning experiences will be those that afford real feedback in a timely way. Designing, building, and testing working devices provides that kind of feedback. LBD's curriculum units are centered on the design and construction of working devices or working models that illustrate physical phenomena or that measure phenomena (e.g., to get feedback about biological function).

Classroom Rituals That Promote Learning. CBR tells us that learning from experience requires reflecting on an individual's experiences in ways that will allow learners to derive well articulated cases from their experiences and insert them into their own memories. We also know that learning is most effective when learners have been able to identify what they need to learn — when they have had a chance to think about what they do know and how to apply that and then identify where the gaps are. LBD includes in its activities a system of classroom rituals that promotes such derivations. Messing about is guided play done in small groups that promotes making connections between a design challenge and what students already know. Playing with toy cars, for example, seeing which can go over hills and which cannot, gets students thinking about what it takes to get a vehicle over a hill and the different ways they have made things move. Whiteboarding, borrowed from problem-based learning (Barrows, 1985), follows messing about and is a whole-class activity in which learners articulate together what they discovered during messing about and generate ideas about how to proceed and learning issues to pursue. Pin-ups, borrowed from the architecture design studio, give small groups the opportunity to share their plans with the whole class and hear other students' ideas. Gallery walks, adapted from pin-ups, provide a venue for presenting an individual's designs in progress to the rest of the class. Pin-ups and gallery walks require students to articulate what they are doing well enough for others to understand; they also provide students with ideas to build on in moving forward, a venue for getting feedback on their articulations (are they communicating well), for asking for advice and getting suggestions, and for vicarious experience applying the concepts and skills they are learning.

Design Discussion Area (DDA). An important lesson learned from exploration of apprenticeship and case-based learning (Redmond, 1992) was that it takes several encounters with a concept or skill to learn it well. The first encounter allows the learner to build an impoverished picture of the concept or skill. Later encounters, in which that impoverished picture is applied and fails to work as expected, let a learner know that his/her knowledge base is incomplete or incorrect, prompting the engaged learner to want to revise his or her knowledge, cases, or indexing so that it works better. But school does not provide the time for students to have the full range of experiences that allows them to build up a complete understanding. The gallery walk and pin-up, and their electronic extension, the Design Discussion Area (DDA; Kolodner & Nagel, 1999), are designed to help students share their experiences with each other so that they can vicariously learn from each other's experiences.

For such learning to happen, students need to be able to present their design ideas coherently, and in order for students to learn science from their own experiences and those of others, students need to talk of science as they are presenting their ideas and conversing with others. DDA is designed with two learning goals in mind: It helps small groups of students present their design ideas and results to others coherently and using the right kinds of vocabulary, and it guides students in other workgroups through conversations about those design ideas. Figure 9.4 shows a design idea and short discussion along with the simple prompts provided to aid discussion. We help students articulate their design ideas by providing three kinds of scaffolding — a structuring of the writing area into well organized chunks (our solution idea, functions it satisfies, and how it will work can be seen in the figure), hints for what belongs in each of those structured paragraphs, and examples to examine. The intention is that for each design idea or design experience students report on, they tell about the design decisions they made, why they made those decisions, the evidence they used to come to those decisions, and, if they applied it, what happened, their explanation of why, and anything new they feel they need to learn. DDA does not currently allow pictures to be added easily; we are working on that. Diagrams are certainly an important tool in articulating an individual's ideas.

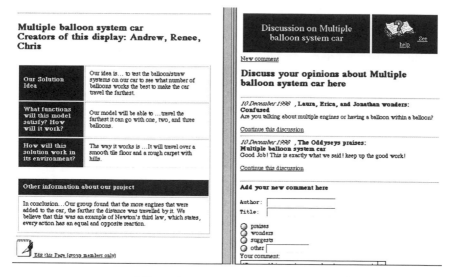

FIG. 9.4 Design idea with discussion.

Case-Authoring Tool (CAT). Some design challenges do not lend themselves to messing about with real materials. It is hard, for example, to mess about with erosion in any way that gets across the complexities of managing erosion when winds and currents and tides are all interacting with each other. For these kinds of situations, we have a different way for students to gain perspective on the challenge they are addressing — by looking at real-world cases that address those same sets of issues. For example, students working on the erosion problem read about the ravages of erosion on islands up and down the East Coast of the United States and around the world and the ways engineers have tried to control erosion and the problems that come with it. Those working on a tunneling problem read about cases where interesting tunnels have been built and what went into building them — for example, the Chunnel, railroad tunnels through the Rockies, the sewer system in New York. But reading expert cases is difficult, and knowing what might be learned from such a case can be difficult as well. The Case Authoring Tool (CAT; Nagel and Kolodner, 1999) provides that guidance. It helps students divide their challenging task into manageable chunks and provides hints and examples for each. Figure 5 shows some of the help we give students in articulating the solution the experts came up with. We actually provide three kinds of help (as in DDA): structuring of what they need to articulate into manageable chunks, hints for each of those chunks, and examples. We provide similar prompting to help students record the challenges the experts were up against and the issues they had to address and to record the results and how they effected the people and environment.

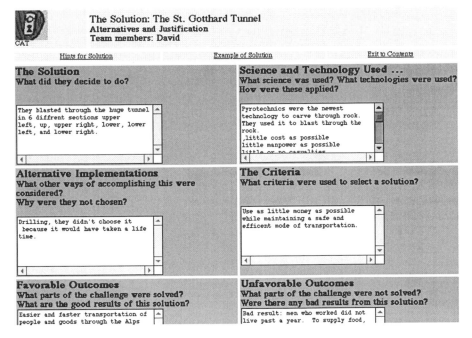

FIG. 9.5 Case authoring tool.

Our intention is that students use CAT in small groups to read an article, extract what it says, and write that up for the rest of the class. We suggest they first use CAT's prompts to skim the article they are reading and extract some of its important parts, then use the prompts to see where they should pay special attention in reading the article, and next read those parts of it and write down what they have read. We suggest that they then do another iteration of rewriting their notes to compose a presentation of the case that others can use as a reference. They present the case to the class, and their write-up becomes a resource to the class as they all continue working on their design challenge. The CAT might also be used by the teacher to provide a set of cases to the students to use as they address challenges.

JavaCAP and its Descendent: StoryBoard Author. JavaCap (Shabo et al., 1997) and StoryBoard Author (Nagel & Kolodner, 1999) are designed to help students reflect on an entire project experience, summarize it and put it into perspective, extract from it what they have learned, and write that up in ways that other students can learn from. We ask students to articulate the challenge they have been addressing, their solution to it and how they came to that solution, the science they applied in getting to the solution, and how well their solution works. Figure 6 shows a description of a project challenge.

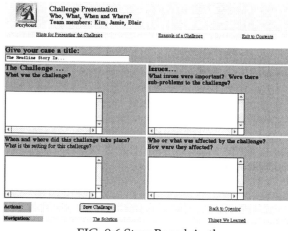

FIG. 9.6 StoryBoard Author.

To help students identify what they have learned, we ask them to think back on the things that used to confuse them but do not anymore, the things that still confuse them, surprises they encountered, things that made them angry, and things that made them happy. We ask them to jot down short notes to themselves on the computer about these things. We help them sort each of those into one of three categories: science or technology concepts (e.g., gravity, inertia), science or technology skills (e.g., choosing variables, measuring), and project skills (e.g., collaboration, communication, planning). For each category, we provide prompts and examples to help them tell the story of what they learned and how they learned it. Figure 7 shows our first attempts at helping students write stories regarding what they learned about science concepts. This tool is in development and we are working on the other categories.

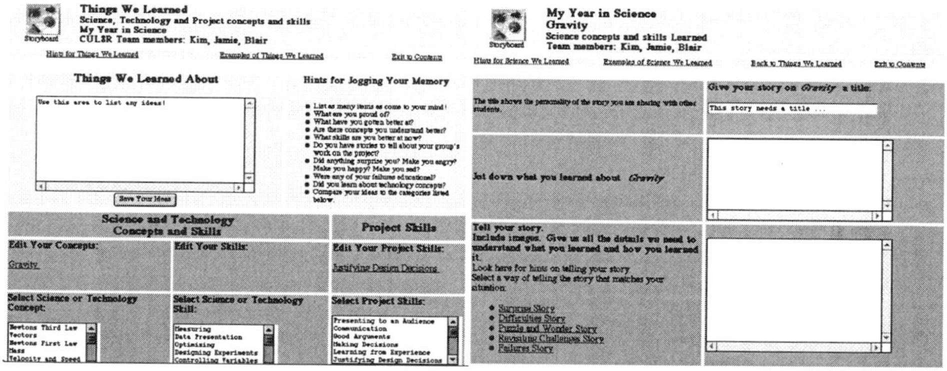

FIG. 9.7 Encouraging students to write stories about science concepts.

The intention is that students use StoryBoard Author to prepare presentations about their projects for their classmates. As with DDA, the tool prompts them for the kinds of things they should include in their presentations. After presentation to the class and discussion that helps them better articulate what they meant, they go back to StoryBoard Author and revise their presentations. Reports made using StoryBoard Author are available to others in the class and across classes for comment, ideas, and suggestions, as in DDA. At the completion of the project, the best reports and their lessons learned will be published in Peer Publications (Nagel & Kolodner, 1999) for classes in later years to learn from.

CONCLUDING THOUGHTS

CBR suggests a variety of ways to promote better learning.
- CBR suggests ways of making lea hands-on learning activities more effective: Make sure students have the opportunity to iteratively apply what they are learning — getting real feedback about what they have done so far, being helped to explain what happened if it was not what was expected, and having an opportunity to try again and again until they are successful and come to a full understanding of what they are learning; make sure to include in the classroom rituals the kinds of discussions and activities that ask students to reflect on their experiences, extract what they are doing and learning, and articulate it for themselves or others, and make sure students anticipate the kinds of future situations in which they will be able to apply what they are learning.
- CBR suggests resources that might be useful during learning —well-indexed libraries of expert cases and well indexed libraries that hold the ideas and lessons learned by their peers.
- CBR suggests activities that can enhance learning in any setting — writing cases to share with others, reading the cases of experts and preparing them for other students to learn from.
- CBR suggests ways of managing a student-centered problem-based, project-based, or design-based classroom so that students help each other move forward at about the same pace – gallery walks for sharing ideas keeps everyone at about the same pace; archives of on-line cases allow those who can move forward at a faster pace to gain from the experiences of those who came before.
- CBR suggests ways of creating useful case libraries without an undue amount of up-front work by the teacher — seed a case library with several cases that model what is expected, and then have students each year add to that case library for students in the years to come.

This is a simple list. But we do not want readers to walk away thinking CBR has all the answers and if an individual simply does these things, learning will be enhanced. We hope the discussions of the different systems and what makes them effective will help readers understand that a great deal of planning and thought is needed to integrate these kinds of activities into a classroom in ways that work. We hope too that these discussions provide some guidelines on how to get started.

NOTES

[1] Interestingly, CYRUS was created before we used the term "case-based reasoning." It was created as a way of exploring how to create a memory that a language understanding program could use well. It was only later that we came to the realization that such a memory had the broad implications suggested by work in CBR.

2 However, after he left Georgia Tech, no one continued with the experiment, and we were unable to continue it further using the DesignMuse tools. We did continue the experiment, however, in the context of STABLE, described previously in the chapter.

REFERENCES

Bareiss, R., & Beckwith, R. (1993, April). *Advise the President: A hypermedia system for teaching contemporary American history*. Paper presented at the annual meeting of the American Educational Research Association.

Bareiss, R., & Osgood, R. (1993). Applying AI models to the design of exploratory hypermedia systems, *Proceedings of the ACM Conference on Hypertext* (94-105).

Barrows, H.S. (1985). How to design a problem-based curriculum for the preclinical years. New York: Springer.

Barrows, H. S. (1986). A taxonomy of problem-based learning methods. *Medical Education, 20,* 481-486.

Bell, P., Davis, E., & Linn, M. C. (1995). The Knowledge Integration Environment: Theory and design. In T. Koschmann (Ed.), *Proceedings of the Computer Support for Collaborative Learning 1995 Conference (CSCL'95)* . Bloomington, IN.

Collins, A., & Brown, J. S. (1988). The computer as a tool for learning through reflection. In H. Mandl & A. Lesgold (Eds.), *Learning Issues for intelligent tutoring systems* (pp. 1-18). New York: Springer.

Collins, A., Brown, J. S., & Newman, S. E. (1989). Cognitive apprenticeship: Teaching the craft of reading, writing, and mathematics. In L. B. Resnick (Ed.), *Knowing, learning, and instruction: Essays in honor of Robert Glaser* (pp. 453-494). Hillsdale, NJ: Lawrence Erlbaum Associates.

Ferguson, W., Bareiss, R., Birnbaum, L., & Osgood, R. (1992). ASK Systems: An approach to the realization of story-based teachers. *The Journal of the Learning Sciences, 2*(1), 95-134.

Guzdial, M. J. (1991). The need for education and technology: Examples from the GPCeditor. *Proceedings of the National Educational Computing Conference* (pp. 16-23). Phoenix, AZ.

Harel, I. (1991). *Children designers: Interdisciplinary constructions for learning and knowing mathematics in a computer-rich school* . Norwood, NJ: Ablex.

Harel, I., & Papert, S. (1990). Software design as a learning environment. *Interactive Learning Environments, 1*(1), 1-32.

Kolodner, J. L. (1983a). Reconstructive memory: A computer model. *Cognitive Science, 7*(4), 281 - 328.

Kolodner, J. L. (1983b). Maintaining organization in a long term dynamic memory. *Cognitive Science, 7*(4), 243 - 280.

Kolodner, J. (1993). *Case based reasoning* . San Mateo, CA: Morgan Kaufmann Publishers.

Kolodner, J. L., Hmelo, C. E., & Narayanan, N. H. (1996, July). *Problem-based learning meets case-based reasoning.* Paper presented at the International Conference on the Learning Sciences, Evanston, IL: Northwestern University.

Kolodner, J. L. (1997). Educational implications of analogy: A view from case-based reasoning. *American Psychologist.*

Kolodner, J. L., Crismond, D., Gray, J., Holbrook, J., Puntambekar, S. (1998). Learning by design from theory to practice. In A. Bruckman, M. Guzdial, J. Kolodner, & A. Ram (eds.), *Proceedings of International Conference of the Learning Sciences* (pp. 16-22). Atlanta, Georgia.

Kolodner, J. L., Nagel, K. (1999, December). *The design discussion area: A collaborative learning tool in support of learning from problem-solving and design activities.* Paper presented at the Computer Support for Collaborative learning Conference, Stanford, CA.

Kolodner, J. L. & Simpson, R. L. (1989). The MEDIATOR: Analysis of an early case-based reasoner. *Cognitive Science, 13*(4), 507 - 549.

Nagel, K., Kolodner, J. L. (1999). *SMILE: Supportive multi-user interactive learning environment.* Paper presented at the Computer Support for Collaborative learning Conference, Stanford, CA.

Ng, E., & Bereiter, C. (1995). Three levels of goal orientation in learning. In A. Ram & D. B. Leake (Eds.), *Goal-Driven Learning* (pp. 354-370). Cambridge, MA: MIT Press.

Papert, S. (1991). Situating constructionism. In I. Harel & S. Papert (Eds.), *Constructionism* (pp. 1-11). Norwood, NJ: Ablex Publishing Company.

Puntambekar, S., Nagel, K., Hübscher, R., Guzdial, M., & Kolodner, J. L. (1997). Intra-group and interrgroup: An exploration of learning with complementary collaboration tools. In R. Hall, N. Miyake, & N. Enyedy (Eds.), *Proceedings of Computer-Supported Collaborative Learning'97* (pp. 207-214). Toronto, Canada.

Ram, A., & Leake, D. B. (1995). Learning, goals, and learning goals. In A. Ram & D. B. Leake (Eds.), *Goal-Driven Learning* (pp. 1-37). Cambridge, MA: MIT Press.

Redmond, M. (1992). *Learning by Observing and Understanding Expert Problem Solving.* Unpublished Ph.D. Thesis, College of Computing, Georgia Institute of Technology.

Scardamalia, M., Bereiter, C., & Lamon, M. (1994). The CSILE Project: Trying to bring the classroom into World 3. In K. McGilly (Ed.), *Classroom Lessons: Integrating Cognitive Theory and Classroom Practice* (pp. 201-228). Cambridge, MA: MIT Press.

Schank, R. C. (1982). *Dynamic memory* . Cambridge, England: Cambridge University Press.

Schank, R. C., Fano, A., Bell, B., & Jona, M. (1994). The design of goal-based scenarios. *Journal of the Learning Sciences, 3* (4), 305-346.

Schon, D. A. (1982). *The reflective practitioner: How professionals think in action* . New York: Basic Books.

Shabo, A., Nagel, K., Guzdial, M., & Kolodner, J. (1997). JavaCAP: A collaborative case authoring program on the WWW. In R. Hall, N. Miyake, & N. Enyedy (Eds.), *Proceedings of Computer-Supported Collaborative Learning '97* (pp. 241-249). Toronto, Canada.

Silver, E. A., Branca, N. A., & Adams, V. M. (1980). Metacognition: The missing link in problem solving? In R. Karplus (Ed.), *Proceedings of the Fourth International Conference for the Psychology of Mathematics Education* (pp. 213-222): University of California: Berkeley, CA.

Spiro, R. J., Feltovich, P. J., Jacobson, M. J., & Coulson, R. L. (1991). Cognitive flexibility, constructivism, and hypertext: Random access instruction for advanced knowledge acquisition in ill-structured domains. *Educational Technology, 31* (5), 24-33.

Turns, J., Guzdial, M., Mistree, F., Allen, J. K., & Rosen, D. (1995a). I wish I had understood this at the beginning: Dilemmas in research, teaching, and the introduction of technology in engineering design courses, *Proceedings of the Frontiers in Education Conference* . Atlanta, GA.

Turns, J., Mistree, F., Rosen, D., Allen, J., Guzdial, M., & Carlson, D. (1995b). *A collaborative multimedia design learning simulator.* Paper presented at the ED-Media 95: World Conference on Educational Multimedia and Hypermedia, Graz, Austria, June 17-21.

Turns, J. A., Newstetter, W., Allen, J. K., & Mistree, F. (1997, June). The reflective learner: Supporting the writing of learning essays that support the learning of engineering design through experience, *Proceedings of the 1997 American Society of Engineering Educators Conference* , Milwaukee, WI.

Zimring, C.M., Do, E., Domeshek, E., & Kolodner, J. (1995) Supporting case-study use in design education: A computational case-based design aid for architecture. In J.P. Mohsen (Ed.), *Computing in Engineering: Proceedings of the Second Congress*. New York: American Society of Civil Engineers.

Author Index

Subject Index